Also by Charles Shere

The Expressive Sculpture of Alvin Light
Thinking Sound Music: the Life and Music of Robert Erickson
, even recent cultural history: place, art, and poetry
    in everyday life
Why I Read Stein
How I Saw Duchamp
The Company of Strangers: letters from Europe, October 2006
Getting There: the first thirty years (memoir)
Roman Letters

with Virgil Thomson and Margery Tede:
Everbest Ever: correspondence with Bay Area friends

with Charles Strong and Gerald Nordlund:
Uncompromising Vision: the art of Jack Jefferson

translation:
Francis Ponge: Douze petits écrits

Mostly Spain

for la Eva, who finally got us there

Mostly Spain

Travels, 2002 and 2005

Charles Shere

℄

por lindsey siempre

cover : north of Antequera : facing page: fort in Tarifa (*p. 138*)
all photographs by the author
© 2007 : ear : press : healdsburg : california
printed by lulu.com
ISBN 978-0-6151-6583-7

CONTENTS

Introduction

Introduction

IN THE LAST FEW YEARS, outside of ongoing reminiscences, I seem to have been writing in three styles: Travel Dispatches; Blog; and E-mail. (Well, there's always another book in the works too, but let's not talk about that.) When not writing, I may be composing a little music, or reading, or dithering at the computer, or walking, or occasionally — very occasionally, some might say — doing a little something useful about the house and grounds.

Or revising, or re-thinking: which is what you will not find here. Here instead you will find travel dispatches, as they were sent to a number of friends from Spain, and Italy, and Paris, and the Netherlands.

The ambitious determination to make a book of these things raises problems, of course. One wants to revise, and that for a number of reasons. Some references are mistaken. Others, especially those to things read on the Internet, are now obscure. Days and even weeks go by unrecorded: this is particularly the case when we walked in Friesland and Drenthe with friends, for it's well known that conversation trumps writing.

One day if there's time I'll get around to doing justice by that walk, and walking in the Netherlands in general, for that has been an ongoing enthusiasm; it's no exaggeration to say it's changed my life, my way of responding to Society and Nature. But this is not the place for that. This is simply a repository of much of the writing from two European tours, hasty as the writing was, and very lightly edited for publication in this medium.

Charles Shere
February 2007

Finding Spain
2002

Decollage

17 Oct 2002—

AFTER THE REQUISITE NUMBER of undone errands and tasks we are en route, and after two hours or so we are between Fort Collins and Omaha, and decently fed.

The location is a little alarming. We should be over Canada, in my experience. Somewhere around Edmonton. But we are taking a much more southerly route according to the screen hanging over the aisle, the one that told us how to escape the airplane, then gave us a little news, and now entertains us with various speeds and temperatures and updates on our location,, waiting until we want to sleep to begin the movie.

"Decently fed," I say, meaning for an airplane, after all. We're flying Air France: it seemed the cheapest alternative. I flew this way in June, with Paolo, and found the food remarkably not disgusting. Much of it is not eaten, but drunk: a quarter-bottle of white for the aperitif; another quarter-bottle, red this time (from the borders of the Tarn) with the sauté of beef (braise, I'd have called it) and its rice and its boring Camembert and, before, its refreshing melon with Bayonne-style ham.

And now, while Lindsey drinks a cup of freezedried decaf, I manage a Pear Williams (the *alcool*, not the fruit), which nicely recalls the *très caracteristique* apple pastry that came for dessert.

The newspaper so preoccupied me that I forgot my usual ritual. As my friend Kendall counts the plaster medallions in the Opera House proscenium, first thing after taking his seat a couple of rows back from the pit (and center, by the way), to reassure himself that nothing has changed and all is as it should be, so I count, when taxiing away from the airport, just which trip this will be across the Atlantic.

Of course this task becomes more difficult over time. By now it eludes me almost completely. The first trip, in '73, a press junket to Holland; '74, our first real tour; '76, '77 in Paris for our 20th anniversary, and then the others, up to '83 to Russia and all...

We've been pretty lucky, Lindsey and I, with these trips over the years. Of course they were all exercises i tax evasion. There's a story about that, but it will wait for another time. And now I suspect they're another kind of evasion. In fact, getting ready for this one, I thought often of my mother's many trips during her retirement.

They were much more enterprising than ours are. She went to Egypt, to China (several times), to Machu Picchu. She rode the Trans-Siberian, and ate shashlik in Mongolia. And here we are, flying to Paris, then going on to Amsterdam, Nice, Turin, Barcelona, Seville. Nothing very courageous there.

But I read the news tonight, oh boy, the French news in *Le Figaro*, my first fix in some time on the European view of news. This is going to be a very interesting time to be in Europe. France, of course, is resisting what *Le Figaro* calls the U.S. "obsession" with Iraq.

The night-club bombing in Bali has put terrorism very much on page 1, and *Le Figaro* finds plenty of authorities who warn of likely implications in Europe. France and Germany have already been warned, apparently, of future events. And the European nations, or rather their administrations, or more probably their leaders and the apparatuses they gather around themselves, are cautiously stepping around one another in search of a working relationship to Al Qaeda, to Islam, to oil, to the United States.

It's fascinating to an American to see this somber European dance of diplomacy. One thinks of the European Union as one big meganation, very like the U.S.; but the individual nations are finding their individual voices in the debate: France takes seriously its responsibility as a sovereign member of the Security Council, for example.

One begins to envy the possibility of a national expression of this sort, a stance, concerning international affairs, that expresses the historically evolved voice of a nation, informed by its literature, its soil, its temperament, as they have all resulted from the response of generations to an intricate and eventful series of relationships, negotiations really, between her people, her soil and climate, and her geographic and economic position within her neighborhood.

Well, time enough for such musings. For five weeks we'll be reading these papers, having these discussions with friends and acquaintances.

It's suddenly morning, to paraphrase the poet; the second movie is over — an unsettling one for its thrust of London voices into a cabin full of passengers speaking American, French, and German. It feels like two in the morning, but it's nearly noon. We'll be landing soon, and dealing with the trains. Time to end this.

Back on the bicycles
18 Oct 2002—

A BUMPY APPROACH through thunderheads and a routine arrival at CDG Paris, a quick metro ride to the Gare du Nord, a noisy hour in the café of the station, and then our first high-speed train ever to Rotterdam.

That beautiful and inimitable light of the Northern Europe autumn, often raking in below clouds, making luminous the green and golden Flanders fields, picking out an occasional manor house.

The train — the "Thalys" — is eerily fast. It's so quiet and smooth you assume you're hardly moving, but now and then you're parallel the highway, and notice the businessmen in their Mercedeses (and the occasional Porsche), who are driving well over 100 miles an hour, are being left behind easily.

After Brussels, though, the train no longer has its own right-of-way, and pokes along like any other. We changed in Rotterdam, taking the wrong train to Utrecht and then catching the right one, then changing again in Amersfoort, for the Dutch rail system is a linear series of branching routes, and Apeldoorn is off in its own little direction.

So by then it was ten pm, and exactly twenty-four hours had elapsed since we'd left home. A few bits of that delicious cheese with cloves — *nagelkaas*, nailcheese — and a glass of elderberry liqueur, and a cup of tea, and get and send the e-mail, and a good night's sleep in the cozy loft on the wooded Wildernislaan.

Today we went after breakfast to the palace Het Loo. This had been the summer palace of the Dutch monarchy until the 1980s, when the government bought it — it always surprises me that the property of the monarch is not automatically the property of the people — and began to turn it into a national museum.

I've written about it before; it's a favorite place of ours. Partly for the interior and the collections. A bit more for the architecture — this is the Dutch Versailles after all, but it is a Republic as well as a Monarchy, and the modest brick palace is far from ostentatious.

Even more, though, for the park and gardens. You approach the palace from some little distance, parking your bicycle (or your car, if you're from out of town) maybe 200 yards away, then walking along an allée of beeches, tall, dark, and noble especially in this October light.

A couple of middle-aged people were at work sweeping the lawns with home-made whiskbrooms, bundles of twigs bound together. They were gathering the beech nuts, which they separated from twigs and bits of bark by shaking them back and forth in screen-bottomed trays.

Turks, Hans and Anneke explained, harvesting the nuts for their oil. "We used to do that, during the war," Anneke went on, not quite agreeing with me that it seemed a pleasant way to spend the day.

We stopped and talked to them a bit. The woman kept working silently, but her husband seemed happy for a momentary distraction. His Dutch was unaccented to my ear, though our hosts might not agree.

The oil is used for cooking — I'd like to try some. Anneke shelled a nut for me: it tasted somewhere between a hazelnut and a pine nut, complex and interesting.

We spent an hour or so in the elaborate garden full of knotted box and elegantly trimmed yews and spruces. Fifteen paid gardeners look after this huge park, and two of them trim the scores of topiaries, perfect cones of spruce, each say seven feet high and perfectly bullet-shaped. At the corners of the beds they are not cones but four-sided obelisks, for variety; otherwise they are all exactly alike, though trimmed by hand and eye, with neither machines nor templates.

Like the beech *allées* striking their diagonals across the lawns in front of the palace, these formal gardens behind it have an important function. They are not simply decorative. They instill and exemplify order, balance, and repose, important qualities in a monarchy, qualities I wish were more pervasive in today's world.

This was ironic, for the Dutch government fell yesterday. The much beloved Prince Claus was buried Tuesday, and the prime minister resigned the next day, having waited for the period of mourning to be completed.

The coalition had collapsed, we understand, because of the lack of professionalism of one of its major constituents, the "List Fortuijn," the "party" formed by the unlikely but charismatic Pim Fortuijn. I won't describe him here; there was a very good piece about him a few weeks ago in *The New Yorker*.

It's enough to say that he represented many otherwise disagreeing voices who all realized that the country was losing its character for various reasons mostly having to do with globalism, and that they all for different reasons didn't like that, and needed to do something about it.

Well. Fortuijn was assassinated, most inexplicably by an animal-rights activist, just before the election that would have made him prime minister. The party he'd quickly put together won a big share of the coalition — the biggest, in fact — but apparently couldn't turn into professional administrators quickly enough to deal with national politics — especially as they are complicated by the politics of the European Union, not to mention the "war on terrorism." So things are put on hold until January.

Meanwhile we eat our fine raw herring for lunch, and take a nap, and drive downtown for a bit of shopping and a cappuccino. Like so many European cities, Apeldoorn has made its retail center a pedestrian zone filled with shops full of leisure clothing, mobile

telephones, CDs, inexpensive jewelry, kitchen appliances, computers, shoes, books — all the detritus of modern civilization, most of
which is probably made of material from exploited undeveloped
countries, manufactured by urban peasants in the third world, and
advertised and marketed by international cartels.

On this Hoofstraat amble mostly young and young-middle-
aged citydwellers: black and white, muslim Christian and faithless,
prosperous and just getting by. Many have tattoos, facial jewelry,
and moussed hair. All seem, somehow, perfectly Dutch; none seem
tense or stressed; most flock in groups.

And this is a small city, say 150,000, in a largely open country,
a province of forest, heather, and a few farms. Thanks to its forests
and abundant water it was a paper-making center for a few hundred years, and this may have left its mark on the literacy of the
populace: there are lots of newsstands and bookstores, and television hasn't displaced print journalism.

A new concert hall is being built; there's theater and cabaret;
and always the surrounding parks of heath and forest. The town
center is busy and (to my taste) a little commodity-driven: but the
setting promises a degree of serenity and constancy, like the curious
bourgeois Dutch monarchy. It will be interesting to see how this
plays out in the next few decades.

Elfring weekend
Apeldoorn, Gelderland, Netherlands, 20 October—

THREE HOUSEHOLDS; A WALK in the woods; two *pannekoeken*; two
fine restaurant meals; visits to two previously unvisited provinces;
sailing on the Ijsselmeer; and still we slept to ten-thirty this morning, later than ever in our lives.

Walking in the Dutch woods is a favorite occupation of ours. We did this in the Speuldse Bos, at the very heart of the Veluwe, the great system of forest and heath that lies at the heart of the Netherlands.

The biggest forest in Europe, Hans says; and certainly the biggest in this country. And, Irma said today, a few years ago a discovery here that surprised all the scientists, a tree still living found with its root-system — or was it a number of trees, all interconfused — hundreds of years old, and underneath layers of soil deposit that had been put down in the intervening centuries.

Anneke, on the other hand, has said that the Veluwe is entirely planted, the work of man, and indeed much of it has that appearance.

Here there are foxes, deer, and wild pigs, not to mention the many birds; and an improbable mixture of trees — conifer and deciduous, crinkled and straight, trees whose leaves bounce back soft greenish light and trees whose twigs soak up every bit of light to give the appearance of black impenetrable and really quite spooky forests.

We drove through increasing rain to Speuld, then Drie, parked, and ran through the rainstorm into the Boshuils, a fine old tavern-café in an ancient barn. After a cup of tea the rain had stopped; we drove a mile or so to the White Peacock mansion, parked again, and set out.

I've written about these forest paths before. The trail is soft underfoot, usually wide enough to drive a car on though that is not to do, as the Dutch say.

Here the forest was straight trees on one side, crinkled on the other. They were nearly all straight to begin with, Hans explained, but over the years in one forest only the straight ones were harvested, leaving only the crooked ones to reproduce, and Selective Evolution took over, and now there were few straight ones to be found.

There were hundreds of mushrooms, perfectly spherical ones, honey-gold and studded with regularly spaced dimples, about the size of tennis balls, some past prime and breaking open in sections, like tangerines peeled back in quarters from the stem.

Then there were poisonous-looking red ones, some with comic-book white spots on them, growing like the others out of the carpet of fallen leaves.

We glanced at the white peacocks in their pen, and I thought of D.H. Lawrence and how much I detest the peacock's cry, and we walked on, past the manor-house, and its pond, and its mostly underground ice-house, and stopped to inspect a small water-driven electrical generator, taken out of service, a sign said, because of repeated vandalism.

We got back to the Boshuis just as the rain began again and had a pannekoek — that plate-size Dutch crepe, a little thicker than a crêpe and thinner than a pancake, mine with slices of ham and candied ginger inside, and then drove home for a rest and a change for dinner.

That was in Amsterdam at Kees's new restaurant, Marius — one dining room seating perhaps twenty-five, half at a single big table, the rest in variously conformable tables.

Kees and Yolanda have both cooked at Chez Panisse (as well as many other fine restaurants), and they form the entire staff of Marius. The format is inventive and daring: "staff dinner" at six or so, when you sit down and eat with the cooks, who serve a single main dish with a couple of those inevitable Dutch side dishes, then cheese and fruit, then coffee, €17 wine included, and you have to be out by 7:30.

Then comes the late seating, €50 I think, which is a more elaborate three- or four-course dinner with more wines. We had the late dinner: grilled pepper salad, mussel and clam soup, roast and braised lamb, potatoes and artichokes, a tossed roquette salad, quince tart. It was delicious, like eating at Chez Panisse.

Then we drove to Tom and Judith's home, a row house in Voorburg, the Hague suburb next to the Queen's park, hard by both the railroad and the main freeway between Amsterdam in the north and Rotterdam, then Belgium and France to the south.

We went to the Saturday market in Voorburg, trucks and stalls selling fruit and vegetables, fish, cheese, and household items. (At this last stand I asked for a charger for my ancient mobile phone, not expecting to find it. I was correct in this, but the proprietor smiled ruefully when he showed me that he carried exactly the same tiny Motorola.)

Fresh raw herring for lunch again, this time with a glass of milk — curiously exactly the right combination — and then to a second Elfring household, Tanja's, in a very different setting.

Tom's house is perhaps eighty years old, with steep stairs, an afterthought toilet-room, a fine back garden (Judith's work: like many Elfring women, she is a gifted and disciplined gardener), on a street in a suburb filled with trees, whose main commercial street is a couple of centuries old, with a brick church whose lawns are grazed by sheep, and set among cafés and restaurants and ice-cream shops and bookstores and the like.

Tanja and Joost bought a brand-new row house a year and a half ago in a brand-new suburb of identical houses. There are no trees, no shops, no cafés. A bus prowls the quarter regularly, but clearly most of the population drives to shop at a nearby mall.

Inside the living is clean, efficient, and pleasant. The apartment is filled with light, the ceilings are high, the windows at one end look out onto a canal that runs behind the back garden. Willows will grow up in time; in the meantime there are the ubiquitous lively gardens and the stately swans to admire.

Last night's dinner at Marius was she early one: a bowl of spaghetti in a smooth but pungent tomato sauce; sauteed peppers; a classic green salad in the house-oil vinaigrette (which couldn't be better), and a first-rate tarte Tatin that Lindsey complimented.

We talked to a journalist, there to meet Lindsey and ask about Chez Panisse, and we admired Tanja's daughters who put on aprons and helped in the kitchen, though they are only six and nine years old.

(Their father had had to stay home, alas, with their little brother, who was indisposed and unwilling to join the fun.)

It was this morning that we slept until ten-thirty, in Kees and Irma's Utrecht apartment, again very different, set on the ground floor of a block in a workingman's s quarter, with a big livingroom crowded with books, a narrow Pullman kitchen on the way to the tiny bathroom and the bedroom.

We drove today up past Amsterdam, surviving the third traffic jam of the trip, to an area we have never before visited — Noord Holland, famous for Edam's cheese and Alkmar's flower market and Hoorn's port.

We didn't visit any of these. We drove straight to the tiny port of Andijk where Kees keeps his five-meter sailboat, raised the sails, and put out for Medenblik.

This didn't work out, because there was most unconventionally no wind at all. So we fired up the outboard and steamed ahead, pulling into a fine old harbor full of sailboats, some boasting three masts.

We walked the sandy footpath along the harbor to its end, across the inevitable drawbridge, and into De Tijd, *sfeervol* (atmospheric) in the leaning-front brick building that's stood here these three centuries, and there had another *pannekoek*, apple-bacon this time, aged gin this time, and then motored back, and drove through Flevoland, the new polder drained only since World War II, and back through the Veluwe again to Apeldoorn to the old-generation Elfring house, where Hans had made his own fine dinner: pumpkin soup, macaroni in tomatosauce, and poached salmon, with not one but two green salads, and a smooth amaretto *vla* — a sort of soft pudding — for dessert.

At the table my Motorola rang for the first time on the trip. It was the first "instant message" I've ever received — Eve messaging from Seville to ask where and how we were.

Funny, I observed, that we're sitting at dinner among the Elfrings, who were father and mother to Thérèse when she went off to Europe at sixteen, and I get a message from her daughter Eve, nineteen and just off on her own for the first time.

Where R U, she'd asked; R N Apeldoorn, I answered, eating and having fun. And so, my friends, to bed.

Schepen en auto's
21 Oct 2002—

THE PENALTY FOR SLEEPING until 10:30 yesterday was, of course, waking this morning at 5:30, dozens of things crashing around in the mind.

Without a minute to spare Tanja drove me into town, that is, the nearest shoppingplaza to her new glass brick and asphalt apartmentcomplex suburb. To the left, more buildings rising among orderly grids of streets and sidewalks; to the right, sheep grazing peacefully — do they ever graze otherwise? — on green pastures dotted with oldfashioned windmills.

The first telephone store was closing as we approached it, and the fellow said they didn't have the charger anyway, go to the Bell Store. There, fortunately, they did have the charger my Motorola needs, so we got it and drove home more sensibly and then went on to dinner.

Next day Kees drove us, Irma Lindsey and me all sitting on the one seat of his delivery truck, up the *snelweg*, the superhighway, from Utrecht toward Amsterdam and his sailboat.

To the left the rising manystoreyed apartments and offices, to the right the sheep. Ahead of us, slowing clots of autos.

Bucolic, Lindsey said; What?, Kees answered, happy to be finding a new English word. Bucolic, she said, it means, well, rustic. It's amazing, she said, how rustic it is on one side, how urban on the other.

That's it, I said excitedly, that's why Holland is so important, and why it's too bad that its own government should be failing just when the world needs it most. Holland has its own lamentable history of exploitive colonialism and has paid terrible prices for it; it also knows very well how to be a global trader, to find its way among factions.

We have to find a way for Christians and Muslims to live together as the sheep and the autos do.

Hold on, Charles, Kees said, What are you saying, who are the autos and who the sheep? I think maybe you are making too far an analogy here!

I look back at the sheep and think how placidly they go about their business, each somehow finding just the right place in the pasture, following in orderly lines when on the move, spreading apart purposefully at mealtime.

Overhead the clouds moved along exactly so, great heaping sheep in the sky. Faced with closing lanes, the cars merge and change lanes with grudging courtesy.

The sheep are pagans. They know that it is the grass and water, not the autos and asphalt, that contains everything of significance. They are not interested in the hereafter.

In ancient Greece, I think, the relatively few who shared that relatively benign climate were able to live by their sheep and their olives, their grapes and their figs; and they knew it was Nature that was important, the clouds and the forests, pastures and springs; and they honored these determining forces with divinity, even if only minor or demidivinity.

Even in the cities, later, in the time of Pericles, when life was urban and complex enough to need manufactured items — jewels, musical instruments, fancy vases, weapons and armor — a certain few could take up poetry and music and even philosophy, sorting out the immediately significant and determinant from the transitional and the trivial.

Where life was harsher, or when civilization and its wars grew so complex as to need more repressive administration, monotheism began to prove its usefulness. The promise of a hereafter compensates, in some minds, for a present discomfort. Present injustices are easier to bear when you reflect that after death will prevail eternal justice.

But I could be wrong about this, and the sheep may be deluded. I'll look more carefully than usual at the Italian view of these matters.

* * *

Meanwhile Hans and Anneke. They are our age; they were our daughter Thérèse's parents while she lived a year in Holland in 1975, I think it was.

They have four children, three of whom we know. We have watched them grow to adulthood, go to school, marry, have children, develop their careers. Counting their spouses they are chef, lawyer, economist, investment banker, language teacher, judge-omboudsman,.

They move easily from Dutch to English, as I move easily from the manual-shift Camry to the automatic-transmission El Camino; and to these they add, variously, French, Spanish, Italian and German.

They are athletic: they ski, cycle, hike, play soccer. (Hans's father was on an Olympic team.) They are playful, often hilarious, and they are enthusiastic.

Teachers and economists are by definition intellectual, but the Elfrings are not mandarins as I suspect they suspect am I. When I speculate on an etymology or ask a question about terrain or ask for help about a historical complexity Hans says, with a glint and a grin, Typical Shere Question, and "TSQ" has become a watchword among all Sheres and Elfrings; it is a question about a needless piece of information with no immediate purpose.

(It separates me from the sheep, anyway. At least I like to think so.)

When I asked what lay at the bottom of the IJsselmeer, though, and Kees got that TSQ look in his eye, Irma told me it was clay, but not the same clay as lay under the older polders of Noord- and Zuid-Holland, where the clay was harder and thinner.

And I have already reported the different Elfring views on the nature of the Veluwe forest. In congeniality there is not necessarily unanimity.

Elfrings will read this, and will I hope realize my intent: I introduce them to you because we love them and respect them; they are fun and they are interesting; they are in short family, and if you want to know us you will gain by knowing them, at least a little, as much as I can give in a short account here.

We speak English with them, of course, and they go on among themselves in English, or fall back into Dutch. My own Dutch is nonexistent, though I pretend to try from time to time, and Lindsey I suspect begins to comprehend.

It is our usual pattern: I blunder toward speech, Lindsey finesses her way to comprehension. And tomorrow we slide into French, which will be easier, and then in a day switch to Italian.

* * *
*

the old "Salt Road" from Ventimiglia north to Cuneo (p. 18)

On to Italy

Colors and catchup

Savigliano, Piemonte, Italy, 23 October—

THE COLORS ARE THOSE of Fall. In Apeldoorn they were blazing in the sun on our first day, moody in the Monday rain, though with details thrown into sudden relief — a single leaf, for example, hanging from an invisible spiderweb, improbably catching a ray of sunlight and glowing copper against the muted background.

Yesterday we flew to Nice — an hour an a half, $55 apiece from Amsterdam: why drive? We left in near-rain, climbed through fog, then flew south through mostly cloudy sky, the clouds suddenly parting as we flew over the Maritime Alps, falling away abruptly on the left side to the sunny Po plain, but filling miles of landscape on the right across the Provençal Alps.

The plane banks to the right, flies over the blue Mediterranean south of Monaco and Nice, then does a U-turn to land, and we are definitely no longer in the Netherlands.

Dominique lives in a roomy double apartment in Cimiez, the uphill suburb of Nice just out of town — a sort of Piedmont to Nice's Oakland, for those of you who know California's East Bay.

Out her living-room balcony doors you look south to the sea. A big palm below; that characteristic Nice ironwork on the balcony, the double doors: you can't help think of Matisse.

We went out to an uncharacteristic restaurant for dinner, though: Bruno's, one of a series of five or six upscale places that chef has thrown across Provence.

This one specializes in truffles, and that's what we had. Ham and poached egg on shredded lettuce, covered with sliced truffles. A roll softened with Savoy fontina and covered with sliced truffles.

Brandade, for Lindsey, cooked under the salamander, and covered with sliced truffles. A tournedos beefsteak for me, accompanied by a good-sized round of scalloped potatoes, each under a thick slice of *paté de fois gras*, and covered with sliced truffles.

For dessert a nice fig tart with meringue flavored with truffles, of course, and a glass of *marc* suffering a similar disease. We went to bed stinking of truffles.

Today we drove one of our favorite roads, the old "Salt Road" from Ventimiglia north to Cuneo. It's my third drive up that road this year. In April it was snowing; in June the slopes were covered with various greens. This time the slopes were alive with color, and not all of it from the foliage. The road goes through a dramatic rocky gorge, the Royat tumbling through it, its water mostly white but granite-grey-green where it is stiller.

The riverbed is littered with enormous boulders, most of them white as chalk; but the rock exposed on the sides of the gorge shows much darker, nearing black, with occasional veins of lilac, or lavender, or salmon-rose. The rock is sedimentary, its layers twisted most alarmingly — vertical here, diagonal there; often in whorls like enormous thumbprints.

On the south side of the pass the mixed forest was green, dark green, and all sorts of red and russet; Vermont couldn't do much better. The gorse, or whatever it is, had that rich red of Persian carpets, like the wild huckleberry fields in Maine.

We dawdled and stopped and lost our way and still got to Savigliano in four hours, finding a comfortable hotel for $57, and I went out for a tonsorial operation: I can be a paesano in Amsterdam, but in Torino I must show a *bella figura*.

* * *

Catchup: I've meant to tell you about Lindsey backing carelessly into an oncoming bicycle in the woods; about the good *cuisine bourgeoise* at the Elfring table in Apeldoorn; about the continuing restoration of the park and gardens at Het Loo, where a *zichtlaan*, or view-allée, is being restored in the forest to continue the perspective of the formal gardens I've written about — a return to balance, a return to the Age of Reason after the excesses of Romanticism.

No doubt I'll have to explain this later.

I've meant also to write about birds: storks, herons, swans, and the garden birds in Apeldoorn. I've meant to write about the oddness of grown and middle-aged women, carefully dressed and coiffed, sitting on the floor in the crowded trains.

I've meant to mention the amazing amount of steel one sees when traveling by train, and driving past construction projects. Where does it all come from? And all those cars, which grow more numerous and bigger, a new species going forth and dominating the world. How will they be subdued?

But let's go out for a walk and find a nice *trattoria* for dinner. It's way too early by Italian standards, but we skipped lunch today.

And this was the dinner
Savligliana, 24 October —

WE GENERALLY USE the Slow Food guide these days when in Italy. When we first came to Italy we just took pot-luck, but before long, sometime in the 1980s, we discovered the guidebooks put out by Luigi Veronelli. These were slim pocket-size (well, inside jacket breast-pocket sized) volumes bound in a delicious green, and they had notes on retail operations near the recommended restaurants — where to get good ice cream, or salami, or whatever.

Veronelli liked cigars and spirits and meat, and annotated his guide to reflect these tastes, which were (and are) all right with me. So for several years we happily followed him; it was through him for example that we found one of The Great Restaurants Of The World, which no longer exists, but that's another story.

I don't know why or when or how we switched from Veronelli. I'd say it's one of those decisions made by someone else in the family, probably for political reasons; but I'd likely run into opposition on this.

In any case shortly after we discovered Slow Food, shortly after it burst on the scene, we switched to their guide. The first thing we noticed was that it is

ENORMOUS

and you can't slip it into
your pocket, inside or outside. Still it is useful. In Venice last year,
for example — a town where we'd never eaten well at all — well,
that's not quite true, there was that wonderful liver and onions at
Montin — we ate at something like a dozen Slow Food recommended places, and only one was disappointing, and that one only
a little.

But there is no Slow Food Recommendation anywhere near
Savigliano. This is strange, as Savigliano is just about in the center
of Piemonte, certainly centered between Cuneo and Torino, and
Piemonte is the home of Slow Food, and has more restaurant recommendations per capita and per superificie (I'm only guessing at
this) than any other region of Italy.

What, then, to do; where, then, to eat.

I asked the lady who cut my hair, of course, and I asked the
man who cut my beard. (One specializes in these things, apparently, though it doesn't make one rich: the haircut was seven euros,
the beardcut two.)

Neither could help. So I fell back on the usual technique: we
stepped into a place that sold promising sweets and such and asked
for a recommendation. Trattoria, across the piazza, came the quick
answer.

The homeopathic medicine and organic produce shop had another idea, though, so we walked down the arcades in the gathering
twilight in the opposite direction. I found a pizzeria upstairs that
hardly seemed what she'd had in mind; then a Chinese restaurant
that certainly wasn't what I had in mind.

Down another street was a wine store that was selling also
fresh white truffles. He recommended a place beyond the Chinese
Blue Heaven. It was closed on Wednesdays.

We went back to the Trattoria and discovered it wasn't a trattoria at all, it was a restaurant that hadn't bothered (or been allowed) to take down the Trattoria neon sign. It looked good; we
left a reservation and continued our slow perambulation, as we had
an hour to kill before the first (8 pm) seating.

A very pleasant woman in a kitchen-goods shop made small talk with me while Lindsey did pressure cooker research, for what reason I'm not quite sure. Where are you from, she wanted to know; California, I said, *Parbleu*, she said. No one has ever said *Parbleu* to me before.

Here in Piemonte of course everyone speaks Italian but the older people seem to have a good deal of French, the French of a long time ago, lurking in those secret recesses which are only tapped in moments of stress or surprise.

Parbleu, she said, *California, e lontano*, It's a long way off; I have a cousin whose father went to Argentina, I bet he's sorry he did that, it's not very good over there just now, but they won't come back, they say they like it there, it's easy and everyone's so excited all the time here in Italy, in the cities I mean, no, not the country-side, Monferrato and Valsusa and down around Dronero are very nice, but *ohime* the Torinese, not to mention the Milanese.

I agreed as best I could, which was better than last time. I asked about the restaurant, of course, and she said Oh that's very nice; there's another but I think it may be closed on Wednesdays.

No no that one is very nice her husband said, and above all clean, it's very clean, and anyway it's Wednesday and the other is closed. So we went back to the restaurant where we'd reserved, "l' Osto 'd na Volta," Piemontese for The once-upon-a-time osteria.

And there we found a clean brightly-lit dining room big enough for perhaps thirty, with wine bottles on shelves around the walls, some actually lying down on their sides.

We were poured a glass of Prosecco which I dearly love, a good one whose label alas I did not note.

We ordered a dish of cardoons in Raschera (cheese) cream sauce which we split; a dish of pasta in tomato sauce with radicchio for Lindsey, a plate of gnocchi in Castelmagno for me, and then we each had a big duck breast cooked in red wine and juniper berries.

With this we had a bottle of Grignolino from Monferrato, one of the best Grignolinos I've ever had, light and light-colored but fruity and not at all thin or sour.

Then we had, almost automatically, *bonet*, the Piemontese specialty, a sort of eggy chocolate pudding. But then the dessert cart rolled by and I ordered some pears cooked in red wine, and a grappa to adjust anything that might have been excessive.

The check added up to 65 euros. The grappa wasn't on it. I mentioned this to the waitress and she said Oh the grappa is an *ommaggio*, a salute to the customer. I argued by keeping silent and leaving a five-euro note on the table, and we walked through the chilly but luminous night, full moon overhead, back to the Hotel Eden. Eden indeed.

Another redistribution
Torino, 25 October—

WE GOT A CAB and rode away from this wonderful food show, the Salone del Gusto, Lindsey and Deb and Pat and I, and the ride was hilarious, in those high spirits you always have when you meet friends from home in a foreign country.

Four in a cab. They sat in back; I sat up front with the driver. He and I talked and joked in bad Italian. Well, I did; his was okay. You know the dalla Sale? I asked. Well, don't go there; it's full; take us to another similar restaurant, simple and quiet where we can talk.

But he didn't know the dalla Sale, so he took us to the nearby Urbino or Urbano, I keep getting it wrong. As we got out I warned the others to check the cab carefully; God knows how many times I've left something behind in a cab; once even my wallet, in New York, but that's another story.

Inside Urbone or Urbana or whatever it is we were seated at a round table set for six in a small dining room with maybe ten other tables, walls completely covered in mirrors, and perhaps five television sets, huge screens fully preoccupied with Popeye cartoons.

There were a few plates of food already on the table: octopus salad, artichokes and olives, *bresaola*, mortadella, tuna, Russian salad, ricotta with pepper, the sweet soft raw chopped Piemontese veal, mozzarella, bread sticks, maybe five or six other things. There was a bottle of wine, but I asked for a bottle of Arneis, that wonderful white Piemontese wine, because I was thirsty.

Before long there was a pizza, and then plates of mixed pasta: macaroni, risotto, ravioli; with the bottle of house red that had originally been there.

We were offered more, but we were full. I had just been to a raw-beef workshop where I'd had maybe 200 grams of sliced, ground, and chopped beef; and before that another workshop with three salames, two mortadellas, and a marvelous *coppacolla*.

A word about that last item. It came from a small area on the Italian heel, where a unique mix of oaks stands between perpetual winds from two seas,the Ionian and the Adriatic. Here range unique pigs, not the biggest; and here the peasants grow also a unique grape that makes a not exceptional white wine.

They put the pork into pig casings, rub them with the wine, and then introduce a mold that grows nowhere else. They hang the results in the wind to dry them, and then smoke them using the bark of the oak trees.

The result, as Deb said, is a sense of place folded back on itself many times, like layers of pastry folded and refolded to make croissants. This *copacolla* could come from nowhere else. It can't be duplicated, and it is immensely evolved, having honed and focussed the bloodlines of its ingredients over hundreds of years.

We paid the bill for dinner — $35 apiece, with their coffees and my grappa, and the three desserts and the biscotti and *vin santo*. Then, though Deb and Pat had only arrived today from Santa Fe via Cincinatti and Paris, and she had presided over one of the workshops at the Salone, we went for a nice walk over toward the magnificent avenue leading up from the railroad station, admiring the fashions and furnishings and silks and leathers in he windows, and the great piazzas and façades lining the avenues, and the glittering Christmas decorations already festooning the streets.

And then we stopped into one of the grand cafés in the Piazza San Carlo. There three of us had decaf espressos and one had a Fernet Branca, and then we struck up a conversation with three women at the next table who had yellow sacks with the word Britain on them.

I've always wondered when it's England, I said, not altogether truthfully, and when it's Britain, and when Great Britain. Oh well I'm the wrong person to ask, the alpha woman at the table quickly volunteered, I'm Irish, and so is she, pointing at a younger woman.

But I'm English, the third said, and then we began to talk about other things because it turned out Deb and Pat had met the woman, Daria Allen, at some food excursion in Turkey; she runs a famous organic garden restaurant in Bally Mullough, and is a great friend of our friend Alice.

So we had a nice talk, and then I announced it was time to go, getting on to midnight, and we walked out onto the piazza to flag a cab to take Deb and Pat back to the Plaza; we would walk on home to our nearby Victoria Hotel.

No cab came, and none answered when I telephoned, so we finally walked back to he railroad station where we could be sure to find one.

En route I discovered my wallet was missing, and announced the news to the others. None of us could believe it. Back to the café, of course; no wallet, of course. Back to the piazza, ditto. I called the Urbane or whatever it is, ditto; and by then we'd walked nearly to it, and dropped in, ditto; but just before reaching it we ran into a clutch of policemen and asked what we might be expected to do next.

What we were expected to do next of course was to go to the police station and file a form, name address numbers numbers numbers, all in quintuplicate with many signatures and two copies for me. And then back to the hotel at midnight to call the credit-card people who cancelled all the cards and promised to send new ones by Saturday, and we won't worry about the drivers' license, the passport, the medicare, etc., etc. until tomorrow, which will be a busy day.

Well there was money in it too, of course, but not a lot; Lindsey had insisted I give her most of it before we set out this afternoon, leaving me only forty or fifty bucks.

But then, just as I finished typing all the foregoing, the concierge called: someone was coming in a few minutes with my wallet.

I dressed and went downstairs. Two men appeared and handed me the wallet. Everything was there except the cash.

I found it on the sidewalk in front of our restaurant, the one who spoke English said. I'm the chef, I was getting off work, and there it was. I telephoned a few nearby hotels, and found you here.

There was no doubting this guy, he was and is an honest man. I offered him and his friend a twenty each, but they refused any reward. I guess we'll just have to drop into Al Garamond, via G. Pomba 1, for a meal one of these days, and overtip, making sure the kitchen gets a share.

The cash is gone, of course, but I figure it's just another little redistribution of wealth. I talk so often about the justice of redistribution, I can hardly complain about this.

But tomorrow I get a smaller wallet, one harder to dislodge from my pocket. Only thing is, I won't be able to charge it.

Meat
Torino, Oct. 27—

THE FACT REMAINS, it really isn't easy. I'm not complaining, of course, partly because after all it was my idea in the first place, partly because in fact we're having a lot of fun.

But it isn't all beer and skittles (or more accurately wine and sausage). It's also waking up at 7:30 (after getting to bed at 2:00) to buy parking, driving through twenty acres of parking-lot several times before squeezing between two badly parked cars, walking several blocks in crowds to get to the entrance lines, keeping an eye out for pickpockets while in those lines; and then, once finally in, spending several hours standing or wriggling through crowds, on concrete floors, in noisy spaces.

The sit-down times are the workshops, and that's what we're really here for. The three huge exhibition halls full of food exhibits would be worth it without the workshops, I suppose. And the restaurant dinners, specially prepared to showcase traditional or updated adaptations of traditional regional cuisine, are equally laudable.

But the workshops are the center of this Salone del Gusto (for which Taste Parlor is the best translation that comes quickly to mind). And they too are fatiguing, partly for he focussed attention one gives the tasting; partly for the complex nuanced intellectual content of the commentaries (heard on headphones in simultaneous translation); and much because of the overwhelming richness and lingering persistance of the food itself.

Yesterday for example it was three parmesan cheeses with three white wines at noon, then three sausages followed by three blood-sausages with three more wines at 3 p.m.

That was folllowed by a 40-mile drive to a small country restaurant — though quite an elegant one — for a seven-course dinner with four wines.

Day before yesterday, as I've already written, was several salamis at three o'clock, three versions of raw beef at six, and then dinner at eight.

Today has been the best so far, ending with a truly memorable workshop. The afternoon was already pretty good, devoted to three products of a single artisan. I've already told you about his coppacolla; this afternoon I revisited that, and had also his *lardo* and his salame.

Lardo is a concept that, um, alarms many Americans. It's essentially raw unsmoked bacon, with very little pink meat. In fact it is simply sowbelly-fat. Yesterday we tasted one we thought couldn't be bettered, at a floor exhibit.

The pork had been cut into flat rectangles say twelve by eighteen inches and two inches thick; probably seasoned with something I don't know what; and then put in brine for a time, after which it was slightly dried.

You eat it cut into very thin slices. You just pick it up with your fingers and pop it in your mouth. It melts there, giving up a burst of flavors that linger, subtly changing in the mouth. It is sweet, a little spicy, soft, warming, persistent. A glass of fairly sharp white wine completes it.

As was pointed out by a taste expert, a good *lardo* will also taste of the food the animal ate, and of the environment in which the food and the animal grew. You taste pork, but also grass and oak and fruit; and beyond that it may not be entirely poetic to say that you taste the forest and the soil and, perhaps, the sea.

The workshop *lardo* in fact didn't better it, but it was as good, and quite different. It is washed in white wine, then dried, then very lightly smoked. The expert described its taste: sweet, melting, meat, oak, fruit. There was a light scent of smoke when you held it under your nose, but that scent was completely absent when you tasted it.

This astonished me, and I asked the producer about it after the workshop. He smiled at my interest and explained: I smoke it only when the tramontana is blowing, never when the scirocco blows. So the smoke is blown off the meat, not into it, because the tramontana is cooler; and the smoke does not enter the meat, it only rests on its surface.

Fascinating as this afternoon workshop was, tonight's was more — in fact, moving; I could only go up afterward and press the producer's hand between my two and look into his eyes with complete admiration.

This was a tasting of cured meats from wild game — pheasant, boar, venison, and mouflon.

He told about himself:

I started thirty years ago when I realized my son might never milk a cow. My father had a butcher shop but we never slaughtered an animal; we weren't strong enough. When I decided to go back into meat I felt it was wrong to kill an animal by injection; it is cruel.

I liked the idea of using animals that would otherwise be wasted — wild animals that have to be culled because the parks are growing overcrowded. The wild pig I use is hunted by the gamekeeper. It has a relaxed flesh because it has been killed by surprise; it hasn't been anxious. And the wild pigs are small and thin-skinned, giving a complex finish.

He grew more and more excited as he spoke, telling us more about his methods, revealing more about his values.

I tell you everything because I am happy, he said. It is very strange to be sitting here with so many important people and seeing all of you so serious with your plates of salame and ham.

I am a very honest man and I want you to know how I feel about my work. It is wrong to be cruel to animals. I love the animals I work with. I love the colors most of all, the color of the hairs of the boars, of the plumage of the pheasants; farmyard pigs and cows have a very litte range of color.

The elegant woman who spoke for the excellent Rocca del Maccie wines was entranced; the Slow Food wine expert was riveted; the moderator, who knew who he would be dealing with, was amused and very much in agreement with this fellow.

Here is what I had: pheasant ham served on fresh cheese with a few leaves of wild marjoram; wild pig sausage; two crositini — thin rounds of bread spread generously with a spread the man makes of the left-over meat after ham or sausage is made; venison ham served with arugula and pine nuts and a tiny bit of olive oil; wild-pig ham served with redcurrants; mouflon ham served with a rum-soaked chestnut.

With this three Tuscan wines, one quite good, one very good indeed, one memorable.

It's the meat-spread that pays this fellow's bills; the hams are not cost effective, as he said. Ten wild pigs give him eight or nine hams, as the hams have to be perfect to accept the salting and drying. The mouflon is rare; he's lucky to get a hndred in a year.

This is how he makes that spread, which is similar to a good French rillette:

You cook onion sage and rosemary in oil; you add the chopped meat and continue cooking it for half an hour at least, maybe for an hour. This is ragù: there's no tomato sauce in it, no preservatives.

I'm a man who knows what he wants; I want to get better and better, when you're young you work because you need the money, but when you're old you work because you love it, and you want to do your best and learn to do better.

I don't want tomato sauce in my ragu; no; tomatos have nothing to do with this food; it is noble, becaue it is made of the most noble parts of the animal.

I nibbled some more of my crostini, a little meditatively, and thought of my vegetarian friend who would have been revolted with much of the last few days, and thought of the ancient Greeks whose poetry means so much to him, and of Homer's descriptions of the surprising deaths of warring heros at Troy, and how their lives went out from their livers and their hearts; and I thought of my cousin Hazel's urging that it is Generosity and Gratitude that make the world work, to the extent that it still does; and I was once again, as I so often am, grateful for the generosity of the creatures whose lives nourish mine.

Technology
28 Oct 2002

SOME OF YOU HAVE ASKED about sharing these dispatches with others. Fine with me, but please remember that I type them fast, late at night usually, after considerable food and drink usually, without looking them over for errors.

I type on a folding keyboard, into a Palm handheld computer — well, not a Palm, a Handspring Visor, but nearly the same thing. That's why I ask that you not send me attachments, not write me HTML messages full of " " and that sort of thing, and not quote my own messages back to me. A handheld computer only has so much memory, and when it's full I'm cooked — I have to begin deleting things, and I'd hate you to be one of them!

Here in Italy the technology is impressive, especially the computer and electronic tech. Much of daily life remains the same, little misleading signs, things perpetually being cleaned or rebuilt.

The very center of Torino — I can never bring myself to call it "Turin"— is torn up by subway construction. I heard the other day that they plan to remove the Porta Nuova entirely, moving the railroad station quite far south, to Lingotto, the huge former Fiat factory now become exhibition center and shopping mall.

This would be too bad, I think; the station is a fine anchor to the magnificent axis-boulevard leading by way of Piazza San Carlo, lined with cafés and shops, to the brooding two-faced Savoy Palace to the north.

(That's a real palace of the royal house of Savoy, not a disco or hotel. I've often wondered why the name Savoy got attached to luxury, then trendiness. Savoy is simply the country straddling the present French-Italian border, comprising French Savoy and Isere and Italy's Piedmont, an excellent mountainous country of cows, vines, rushing rivers, stone houses, spruce forests and pastures.)

But people no longer arrive by rail; at least high spenders and travelers at leisure rarely do, so I suppose this is a logical evolution. Arrival and departure used to be momentous, separated by a period of recovery and rest; now they are transitory annoyances, bumps on tarmac and tips to taxi-drivers. Cities must find another monument to replace their rail stations, as the stations themselves replaced the city gates.

Driving here is simple enough, barring traffic congestion and overlooking the subway construction. Last night we drove to Verduno, near Bra, about fifty miles south, for the dinner Chez Panisse cooked in a rather posh restaurant participating in the Slow Food week. It took about an hour.

Russ had built a little bonfire outside to grill the pigeons; Chris was presiding over a fish-and-shellfish stew; Amy was handling the dessert chores; others prepared salad greens, and so on. I helped Samin clean white truffles, while Lindsey helped Cristina wrapping candies.

Most of these dinners are served to fifty guests or so; this one had attracted 75. Baryshnikov was there, and the mayor of Torino, and the consul who had driven over from Milan. Arriving police escorts and men I took to be bodyguards eyed the bonfire quickly, then dismissed it probably as some typical country phenomenon.

The dinner was of course delicious, served in three dining rooms, one of which — thankfully not ours — had a single long table set for thirty-four. And afterward the drive home, arriving at two am; and up this morning at 8 to put money in the parking meter, and then back for an hour's nap.

And now I plug this little pocket marvel into the phone line, send this and get your messages, and then it's off to the Salone for its last day.

Monferrato interlude
Savigliano , Nov. 1—

I WROTE TO MOST OF YOU a few months ago about our friends the Rampis, who operate a bed & breakfast on their farmstead in Monferrato, just fifteen minutes north of Asti.

We'd met them two years ago a the first Salone del Gusto we attended, and stayed with them immediately afterward. A year later we were there again, with friends from Verona. We'd hoped to stay there again last summer, after a month in Venice, but Franco had had a terrible accident and was in the hospital.

Paolo and I were there in June and glad to see Franco much mended; and Lindsey and I and the Veronese just spent another three days there.

Gabriela and Franco are two of the nicest people we've met, enthusiastic and sympathetic and kind and loyal friends. They have made a marvelous country place for themselves, tending a few acres of almond trees and grapevines, making wine and conserves, and installing a comfortable, clean, tranquil lodging in their bucolic setting.

The only thing it lacks, for me, is a telephone that will send out these e-mails. And that's my fault, not theirs; if I could just remember how to tell this little handheld computer to ignore the dial tone I'd be in like Flynn.

So look at this as a three-day vacation from travel dispaches. In any case there was nothing of moment to report, apart from three excellent dinners (one in the Rampis' dining room) and a nice walk in the country and a curious collection of tableaux-vivantes chapels and some impressive frescos and a wonderful lunch and a dreadful cold that has my eyelids itching and my nose in lamentable condition.

Monferrato has become a favorite region. It's a sort of elliptical island of hilly country bounded on the north by the Po and the south by the Tánaro rivers, anchored by Torino on the west and Alessandria on the east.

The region is not at all touristy. No one goes there. There are dozens of villages, some fairly good-sized; some perched on hilltops, others strewn about valley floors. Among them all, farmland for the most part, usually in small parcels: corn, grapes, woodlots, potatoes, sunflowers, each installed where the soil and setting are most appropriate for that use.

The woods are full of truffles. Most of the grainland is bare now, and has recently been ploughed leaving huge grey-black or tobacco-brown clods. The towns are linked by two-lane roads, barely wide enough for two small Italian cars to pass at sixty miles an hour; they curve (the roads, and therefor the cars) sharply and climb steeply and careen through towns between close-set stone buildings.

Some of the hilltops towns retain their medieval castles, for this was fiercely contended real estate. The architecture of castles and churchs is baroque — Piedmont Brick Baroque, I call it. Rarely did anyone seem to feel the need of stucco over these handsome buildings.

We talked to strangers on the street — an aging lady walking her dog, weeping as she recalled her husband's recent death. A proud workman who replasters and paints the interior of churches. A young woman who waits on us at lunch, bringing excellent food she'd prepared a bit before.

And we talked and talked to the Rampis, and to one another, our Veronese friends and we. Richard took their dog Teo on walks, counting his errands at doorways and fenceposts; Lindsey kept up her journal; Marta read; I nursed this wretched cold.

And today we left this idyll, driving to Chiomonte, where Lindsey's father was born nearly a century ago, to visit with his cousin's widow Rosa, and to leave some of Gabriela's chrysanthemums on his father's grave, for it's All Souls Day, and the cemeteries are at their best.

Family night out
Savigliana, Nov. 1 —

SMALL COUNTRY CITY, non-touristy, agricultural base. At center good-sized oval piazza. A little off center a much bigger one, once a martial parade-ground; at one end, brick covered market, built mid-19th c. for silkworm-raising industry, now being re-fitted as community cultural center.

We ate at the Osteria del Orsa (why a she-bear, here?). This is evening 1 of a three-day weekend (All Souls'), and the restaurant was full of families with kids. At the next table, a couple dressed à la 1970, she in microskirt that failed to come between her and her chair, fishnet stockings, huge dangly earrings; he in lengthy sideburns and bell-bottoms. With them two kids: boy say twelve, bored, playing with his telephone; girl say eight, more lively, flirting with her dad.

Behind us, another young couple with a girl say ten who slept at the table, head cradled in arms.

In the next room, a large family or multifamily. Four kids two or three years old alternated between table and floor, often crawling or toddling into our room; younger children made noises in their parents' arms — half the time one parent, half the other.

At the back of our room an electric-powered dumbwaiter brought food up from basement kitchen. One waitress; one older man who left halfway through dinner (the owner?); another woman who alternated between eating, tending bar, answering phone, helping clear tables.

Many of the "osterias" of two years ago seem to me to have elevated themselves into the restaurant category, with fancier glassware and such. This one, which is not listed in the Slow Food

"Osteria d'Italia," which we have used as a guide for two years, is authentic, everything we look for. And we had:

Four cold appetizers: Robiola (fresh) cheese, turkeybreast with cumin mayonnaise, a slice of tomato, a delicious piquant green sauce of oil, capers, parsley, garlic, and I know not what else.

Two warm appetizers: cauliflower soufflée, light and delicate; and pumpkin mousse baked into a form, pungent and lingering.

With these, a glass or two of sparkling Prosecco.

Tajarin — that delicate Piedmontese hand-made version of tagliarini — with butter and oil and sage and sliced white truffles.

Stroccotto: slices of roast beef covered with a clove-scented brown gravy, with the little diced potatoes fried in olive oil we've been getting everywhere.

With these, a bottle of Barbera d'Alba Bartolo Mascarello 2000, too young but rich, dark, deep, already maturing, mysterious, hints of blackcurrant, overripe blackberry, and tobacco — the best wine we've had yet, and that's saying a lot.

It wasn't cheap: €76. But it was worth it. The kids finally cleared out; we finally got the check; we walked back to the hotel in a very cold starry night, forgetting to look for meteors.

* * *
*

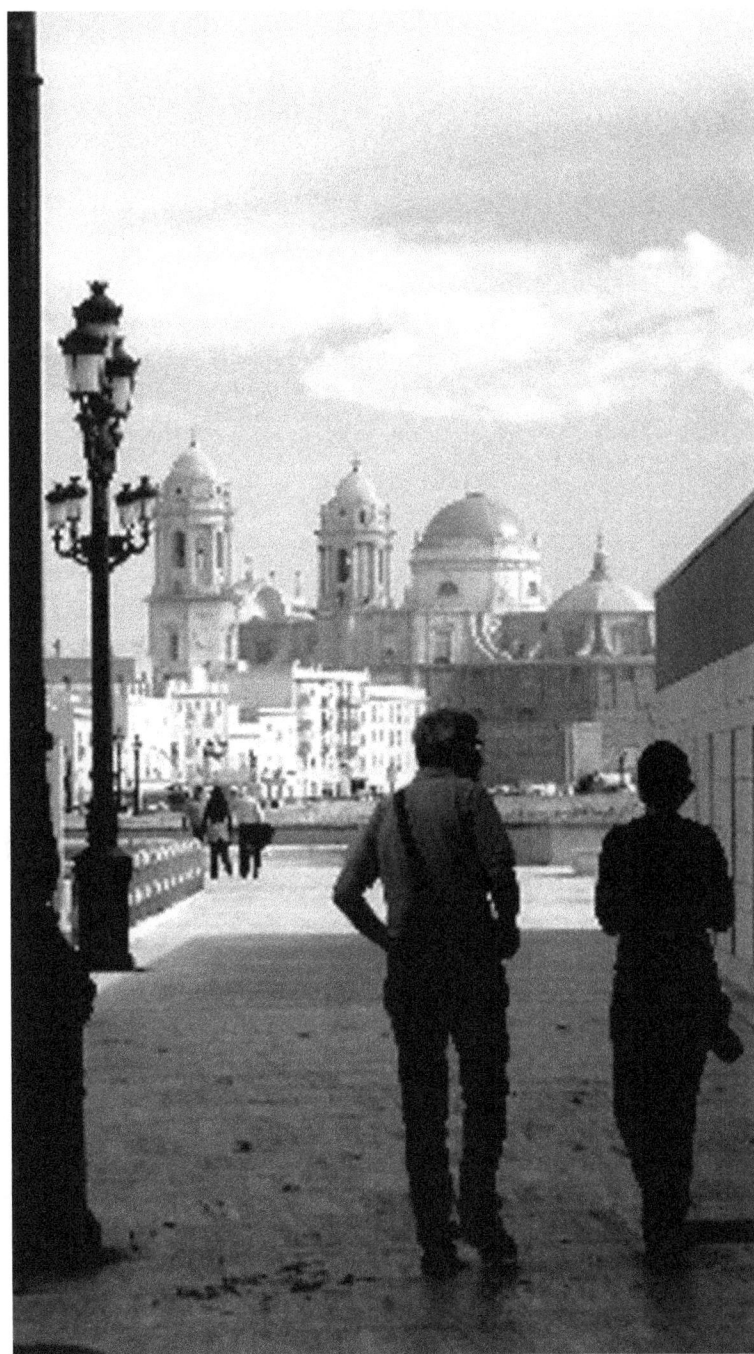

And Finally Spain

And finally Spain
4 Nov 2002—

THE CAMPANILE HOTEL in Montpelier, I mean the one we stayed in last night, there are four of them, was just like any Motel 6 in the States, except that it had a restaurant, and the restaurant served me guinea hen, Lindsey organic chicken, and 46 cl of red wine. I don't know why 46 cl: it seemed like a good quantity.

Then this morning at breakfast it provided not *USA Today* but a local rag. When we first began coming to France, nearly thirty years ago, I quickly noticed that every regional newspaper was required to run a story, preferably on page 1, about a kid falling off the balcony of a fire escape and miraculously escaping unhurt.

We read that story many times: in Besançon, Grenoble, Nice, Narbonne, Tours, and a little island off Vannes. The kid was never hurt; everyone was always quite amazed.

Things have changed, and today's paper told me about grandfathers, of all people, being accused of all sorts of nasty things, even though their grandchildren don't seem really to corroborate on direct cross-examination. No matter: off they go, the geezers I mean, to jail.

There was also a report on the results of the Turkish election, of course, and some speculation on what the effect might be on the American one tomorrow.

And there was a nice background story comparing this mid-term election (tomorrow's) with the one ten years ago that cost Bush Senior his seat. It was no good his boasting of winning the Gulf War, said the newspaper.

C'est l'économie, stupide, qui gagne l'élection, the newspaper quoted the Democrats. And it speculates that Bush may not do so well tomorrow.

Tomorrow as I write this, that is, Monday night, in the Spanish coast resort of Peñiscola, hold the obvious joke, Kendall. The Campanile's telephone was a little flaky, allowing me to send one e-mail but not a half-dozen others, and I don't know what the Hotel Prado telephones will manage.

There's been a lot of landscape since the last dispatch: that magnificent Tende road, not quite as good as ten days before because southbound, into the sun; but better, because the foliage was more advanced, the colors truly memorable.

There was the achingly familiar countryside around Barjols, where we visited George's neighbors, and reminisced about him, and wondered what would happen next.

There was the flat flat mysterious Camargue, from the autoroute apparently a huge pine forest, but we know there are cowboys and mustangs, salt flats and villages tucked away somewhere, and always mean to explore a little further.

There was Collioure beckoning us east from the highway, and Ceret calling us west, and we resolutely ignored both calls and continued into morose and cluttered Spain, whose landscape, from the border all the way down to this town, is jammed with suburbs, warehouses, light industry, truckstops, and all the other detritus of successful contemporary European society.

I managed in quite a limited way to converse simultaneously in English, French, and Italian at Alice's dinner last week, but here I must speak pidgin Spanglish and use my hands and be content with whatever turns up. There are three busloads of German tourists in this hotel and us. The deskclerk speaks good English, but the bartender does not. You can imagine how little that matters.

The truth is I am programmed to dislike Spain. I mentioned that to Lindsey today, and she suggested that I might just very well deprogram myself. This came up in Tarragona, where we meant to explore the old city, but contented ourselves with driving around in circles happy with the one real tourist item of value on view, the town's one and only street-sign. Of course its lettering was far too small to make out, but there it was, in its helpful way; you can't accuse the Tarragonese, or whatever they are, of not trying.

There was a magnificent Roman acqueduct — about two thirds of the Pont du Gard, but in better condition and not visibly being replaced stone by stone. There is said to be an even more impressive arena, but it will have to wait until I have changed my program.

It is nearly eight o'clock and we are growing a little hungry. There's a buffet here which will perhaps have something left after those three busloads walk past it. I don't know what the alternatives are, as the season is over and most things are closed for the winter.

But oh my friends this is a beautiful spot, at least if you look only at the old city. It's a sort of Collioure, but more vertical. The stone castle, church, lighthouse and old city stand watch over a double harbor, two beaches on either side of an elegant sandspit.

When we got here the sea and sky were lewdly exchanging phenomenal blues, mostly teal, with Prussian and midnight and cobalt thrown in as quickly changing nuances, and there were big flat rounded Wayne Thiebaud clouds in the sky, dove grey with apricot-coral undersides, then suddenly flaming into a proud flamingo color retained for several minutes.

Time to eat. Do the right thing in the polling-place tomorrow, if you get this in time, please. You'd never guess the extent to which all Europe is watching to see how unanimous American imperialism and bellicosity can be.

Dinner and politics
5 Nov 2002—

DINNER AT THE HOTEL PRADO, Peñiscola, was better than I expected. From a buffet laid out on what might otherwise have been five billiard-tables I chose potato salad, all the green Picholine olives I wanted, and a tasty lamb chop, lamb in the thin gamy Provencal style that I prefer.

We continued driving down the boring east coast, a few orange groves now appearing amont the suburbs, and then, skirting Valencia, turned west to cross into central Spain. For a little while the landscape grew more interesting, climbing into pine forests on red soil reminding me of northern Arizona.

But soon we were in La Mancha, and it felt like crossing Texas. Flat, seedy, uneventful, long straight roads broken by occasional listless towns.

Spain is like Arizona, like Texas, like Baja California. In short, so far, Spain is like Mexico. I suppose there's a geographical reason for this. (I've been thinking about Gertrude Stein, and her belief that in geography is cultural destiny.)

The Iberian peninsula, like Mexico, has a warm sea on the east, a cold one on the west, heat to the south, a long frontier on the north. Much of it is a vast open central mesa — it seems to lack Mexico's central north-south mountainous axis. So the Spaniards have something in common with Germans, Russians, and Americans, a huge flat center; and they are ready to leave these unconfined spaces for somewhere else. And so thay have been, for centuries.

But there are many countries in Spain, and we finally left La Mancha, driving through the dramatic Desfiladero de Despeñaperros in the Sierra Morena, to glide slowly down into Andalusia — more specifically, into the province of Córdoba.

Administratively speaking, Spain is complicated. It's as if the United States were to interpose seventeen regional groups of states between the present state governments and the Federal government. (Come to think of it, that might be a good idea.)

Of course there are two or three thousand years of political and military and cultural history behind this. But to a casual tourist it's the geography that tells much of the story. This corner of Córdoba, like the Monferrato corner of Piedmont, presents the possibility of a self-sustainable region: climate, soil, water, and minerals are in the right balance, and over the years the native intelligence and industry seem to have done well by these resources.

But on the way down we shared the road with more trucks than seemed necessary, and I began to wonder how many might be carrying Dutch shrimp. We'd heard about this from a Dutch journalist who interviewed Lindsey in Amsterdam a couple of weeks ago.

A particularly tasty brine shrimp (I'm told: unfortunately, I can't eat arthropods) grows in the gulf separating Dutch from German Friesland. They used to be even better, but in the last few years the Dutch have learned to prefer not to shell them for themselves.

Instead, after catching them, they freeze them, truck them through Belgium, France, and Spain, and send them to Morocco, where cheap labaor does the shelling for them.

Then, of course, they're frozen again and trucked back up the highway to Holland. They've gained a bit in expense to make up for what they've lost in taste.

This is emblematic of much of the problem facing the world, it seems to me. Technology — in this case, freezers and trucks — enables multinational exploitation of the differences in local standards of living. The profit system finds a third area of interest: adding to its traditional improvement in inherent value, and to the more historically recent manipulation of cash and credit operations, now to making a profit on the differences of cultural (and social, and economic) differences among the peoples of the world.

Add to this another technology-enhanced development: monoculture, with its sacrifice of local environmental and sustainable values to global profit-taking.

During this trip I've seen local resistance to all this. A Montpellier newspaper mentioned heated objecions to proposed new wind-generators: They will ruin our land, endanger our fauna, and for what? profits to investors in the electric company, not to us.

Can there be solutions to these problems? I hope so: but they will take a long time, and will present their own inconsistencies. There is head-shaking, for examaple, about the commercial interests that go to bed, excuse the figure of speech, with Slow Food.

The big issue in the news boils down, it seems to me, to Sovereignty. The amazing American attack in Yemen on Sunday is only the current most dramatic example. Spain has brooded over the problem for centuries, and continues to today.

We are staying in a splendid hotel in the city that produced Seneca, Averroes, Maimonides, and Gonzago, among others. Most of them wound up banished, but Andalusia is still bragging about them.

Córdoba
Hotel Maimonides, Córdoba, Nov. 6—

EVEN INCLUDING THE VICTORIA in Torino, which will always be a favorite hotel, this Maimonides is superb. We chose it from the Michelin Green Guide, largely because it is across the street from Córdoba's principal site; but we were quite unprepared for its beautiful lobby (though lacking in the Victoria's comfortable seating), or the amazing view from our bedroom, the baroque tower of the Mesquita just across the street.

Córdoba was in its day the most important city in Europe, they tell us; and its day was a long one, from say the fourth century to the twelfth or so. It was Moorish in that period, of course; but its citizenry was Muslim, Jewish, and Christian; and I bet there was still a sizeable number of decline-to-state, if not in fact out-and-out pagan.

We are sitting outside having lunch: three or four tapas, all based on salt cod, at the Bacala. The white doves are cooing; water flows softly into a nearby fountain; someone—probably a street vendor— plays an ocarina nearby. Tourists at nearby tables speak English and Spanish.

(Yesterday, in Peñiscola, I heard an American girl ask an Australian boy, in Italian, what the Australian word was for "automobile." "Car," he answered, in Australian Engish. Languages drift in and out.)

We visited the Archaeology Museum this morning, casually housed in a 19th c. house open to the soft local skies. It has marvelous Roman sculpture, Roman and medieval architectural details, glass, ceramics, and bronzes. (The prehistoric rooms were closed this week for restoration: too bad.)

Then to the Alcázar gardens. The Alcázar itself is interesting architecturally, and has some fine items — a wonderful 3d century Roman sarcophagus, for example. But it was the gardens drew us, and they are superb.

The intricate carving of the Moorish-period disturbs me, as such fastidious makework usually does. The labels at the Archaeology Museum referred to the "taste for luxury" of these caliphs, I guess they were, who paid for this work.

They were known for that taste in their own time, apparently. And I suppose some would say the gardens express a similar proclivity: for detail, symmetry, geometry, endlessness.

But walking from the museum to the Alcázar we passed a house under repair, and I heard that familiar sound of plastering — the quiet, repetitive, methodical *gritch, gritch, gritch* of small hard grains being passed and re-passed between trowel and surface.

(*Repasser*, I suddenly recall, is French for "iron," in the sense of ironing clothes; the gesture is similar).

In the gardens I spoke to workers: a man clearing the *acequias*, those brick-lined canals, only a hoe's-blade wide, that convey water from one orange tree to the next; and another man wheeling away barrowloads of clippings as the hedges were being trimmed.

How many gardeners here, I asked, Ten, he said, Not very many, I said, A lot of work, he said, But pleasant work, I said, You're right about that, he said.

Outside the museum there was a huge acacia tree, probably two hundred years old, that reminded me of a tree I particularly like in Paris, outside St. Medard. And at the Mesquita (about which more another time) an olive tree, its trunk apparently quite dead and hollowed, its improbable head bursting into foliage and proudly furnished with big green Seville olives.

I thought about the relativity of permanence. In our hotel at Peñiscola yesterday I leaned out the window, looking at the swifts flying about in the twilight, considering the old stone castle-city on its promontory, where it had been since long before an antipope lived out his ninety-plus years there centuries ago, and considering also the new ghastly hotels and condos sprouting up all around, all the same height and footprint.

They are distroying the place. But then, in the 16th century King Charles V complained to his architects, when they installed a Gothic cathedral inside the great Moorish mosque here at the Mesquita, You have destroyed something unique in order to build something commonplace. *Sic semper* urban redevelopment.

The gardener showed me how the little sluice-gates worked in the *acequias*, the ditches around the orange trees. It's an old technique, I said. Very old, he said. The old techniques are the best, I said. You're right, he said.

Well as I told Lindsey you can have gardens or you can have wars, and on the whole the gardens seem preferable to me. Her expression revealed no great enlightenment.

It's a question of contemplation and action. These articulating moments come — I'm thinking of today's election results, which disturb me, and Sunday's attack on that car in Yemen, which disturbs me even more — chiefly, I think, because someone's patience suddenly comes to an end.

The ditch grows gradually full, and then it abruptly overflows. You need gardeners standing by, ready to make the decisive action, the one that's been rehearsed for centuries, that is the right size and speed for its moment, that applies just enough technology to the task and no more.

The slow continental drift of languages is another example: French is poorly articulated Italian; Spanish is slurred Latin; and so on. But that's a subject for another day. The tapas are eaten, the rosé finished: time to head back to the mosque, and then on to Seville.

Cities and Seville

Calle Jamerdan, Seville, Friday, Nov. 8—

I WRITE, THOUGH THERE IS no guarantee the result will be sent any time soon. We checked into our Seville *pied-à-terre* Wednesday evening, after an easy hour's drive southwest from Córdoba. And I immediately went into City Mode.

There are cities, Great Cities, and provincial cities. The Great Cities are easy to name: New York, London, Paris, Berlin, Rome. I've been to some, but don't know them well. I'm not fond of them.

I like the Provincial Cities — San Francisco is an example. These offer all the cultural and intellectual and economic necessities but lack the international arrogance that so often disfigures the Great Cities.

The liner notes to a recording I used to have, of Respighi's *Roman Festivals,* quoted a Roman saying: Out of our way; we are Romans. Similarly, a New Yorker cartoon showed a pedestrian peevishly lecturing a couple of people walking ahead of him on a crowded sidewalk: Would you step it up a little? This is New York, you know.

The tempo of Provincial Cities is a little slacker, and that suits me. It may be partly a matter of scale: you have to go faster to cover more ground.

The lines blur, because Paris is a city I like, and so is Portland (Oregon); whereas there may be Provincial Cities I dislike. I suppose we have to modify the original classification: Great Cities; Great Provincial Cities; Provincial Cities.

It's too early for me to categorize Seville, but I can sure give you some immediate impressions. Physically its center, which is all I know yet, is like a dry Venice: the streets are too narrow for four-wheeled traffic, and they turn corners, stop abruptly, and change names unpredictably.

Acoustically it is a nightmare: hard surfaces set close together, barking dogs, motorscooters (thank God absent from Venice).

Culturally it reminds me of San Francisco — flattened-out, for the hills of central Seville are no more than gentle rises. Shops both elegant and plain, little cafés and bars, eating-places, and residences suddenly give way, at important plazas, to municipal or regional administrative buildings, museums, theaters.

Our apartment is on a short narrow street, directly across from one of the mapped landmarks, the Hospital of the Venerables — fitting, I though, on our arrival — which is being turned into a cultural center.

We are virtually next door the Alcázar and its gardens. The University is a few blocks away. There are several internet cafés, but none allow me to plug in my handheld computer, because they all have high-speed lines, not telephone lines.

And Seville, like so many cities we've seen, seems no longer to be hard-wired for telephones. Everyone has a cell phone, even us. So there are no sockets into which to plug this thing: but perhaps tonight, in a hotel in Granada, I will be able to send a few things out.

Before I go further with Seville I want to describe Córdoba's Mezquita, as if it were possible. This is the centerpiece of Córdoba where we spent Wednesday: an enormous building, rectangular, fairly low for its spread, entirely confined by walls: from the outside you'd think it was an open space within those walls.

Entering one of the huge double-leaf brass-sheeted doors — how those doors gleam at night! — you're in the forecourt, a huge orchard of orange trees watered by the *acequias* I mentioned the other day. This is pleasant enough in November; I can only imagine how essential it must be in July.

The orange grove is perhaps as big as a football field, and beyond it, end zones to your left and right, is the Mezquite proper. It is twice the size of the garden, and consists of what the guidebook calls a forest of about 850 columns, all perfectly set out on a grid, each supporting one end of a double arched vault of brick (I suppose).

The columns recall the orange trees: this is a garden, not a forest; and its function is to provide seclusion and shadow, shelter from the low hot sky. The Mezquita was built to be a mosque, where the devout gather to pray, and all (all men, at least; I don't know when that decision was made) are free to gather in twos and threes for discreet conversations among these columns.

Córdoba was of course a Great City in its day, roughly a thousand years ago. Seville's Greatness came four or five hundred years later, when the gold from Mexico and Peru was unloaded at its quays — for it was a seaport in those times.

For a thousand years the European Christian nations, having settled the Jewish and Moorish question to their satisfaction, fought among themselves for primacy. What a waste! With grain, fruit, fish, meat, relatively small populations, walkable cities, fairly benign climate, the Mediterranean world could have been a paradise on earth.

Painting, music, sculpture, poetry, cuisine, games — and a peasant class to harvest the olives, of course — characterize this world when at peace. And what interrupted peace, as I understand it, was chiefly the perceived need to protect one's own nation, pre-emptively, from the aggressive intentions of other nations which themselves are acting with similar pre-emptive intentions.

That, and greed for riches beyond one's own, and a manic zeal to convince the rest of the world of one's own system of hierarchal administration.

So Córdoba gave way to Seville, and Spain fought with England, and colonies rebelled, and republics threatened monarchies, and Napoleon tried to impose order on cruelly idealistic anarchy, and a Congress of Vienna sorted things out, and now a couple of centuries later we begin it all again.

And for me the reassuringly permanent pleasures, Contemplation and Comfort, are best found in the countryside and in villages and in the cafés and gardens of provincial cities.

I wish there were a way for small groups of good-hearted men and women to share these pleasures, to converse and think about them and convey them to the next generation. I suppose our travels, across oceans and nations and among friends and family, are our way of doing just that.

And now out into the city to see what today will bring, and this afternoon a drive to Granada for the Alhambra, for me a distant goal since boyhood, when I read about it in Washington Irving.

Night
Granada, 9 November—

SO WE SPENT THE MORNING in the public gardens given the people of Seville by Maria Luisa, a thick canopy of green (sycamore, eucalyptus, jacaranda, locust, acacia, all with their varying shades and textures) high above long meditative concourses of well-packed golden-ochre dirt paths, some quite straight, others artfully winding among the ponds, flowerbeds, and fountains.

This was the grounds of a 1929 (I think) international exposition, and in one corner there are still a few of the national pavilions to be seen. We avoided those, though, walking instead over to the Plaza of the Americas, past the amusing Fountain of the Frogs whose ceramic spitting frogs reminded us of our own, which Lindsey's father salvaged from sosmewhere and gave us years ago.

There weren't many Sevillians in the park — I suppose they have to work: it was a Friday morning, and not everyone is enjoying these Golden Years. One young man, neatly dressed, took a few steps in one direction, carefully composed a photo with a small 35mm camera, then aimlessly stepped an equal distance in another direction, taking another.

An older man sat on a bench with a large portfolio; I suppose he had prints or drawings to sell, but the portfolio was closed. Perhaps he was waiting for bigger crowds. Twenty minutes he appeared again, walking purposefully toward a nursery-school whose playground was animated by laughing children.

We climbed the artificial mount near the Plaza: its waterfall was dry, and indeed much of the park seemed in gentle disrepair, though the plantings were well enough maintained. Some of the tile walls were disfigured by grafitti — swastikas, feminist slogans, other mindless expressions of discontent with things as they are.

(I wonder if the inventor of the spray can is still living, and how he feels about the misuse of his idea. And I wonder how much graffiti can be explained by the ubiquitous presence of advertising texts and informative signs,, which crowd the surfaces of so much of our cities: you can't escape the printed word, which is so often either an imperative or a coy invitation.)

We walked back to our apartment on one of those broad well-packed ochre concourses, hundreds of feet long, set about with orange trees, for in Seville the orange tree is everywhere. And I marveled that nowhere in Spain is boules or petanque or bocce or any version of them to be seen, though these green oranges — and some of them are now turning yellow — are exactly the right size and shape and heft for a game, and the dense soil pavement is exactly the right field. Why is no one playing boules? Another mystery of the Spanish temperament.

In the late afternoon we drove here to Granada, across two hours of undulating flat landscape, mountains off in the distance, a splendid red sunset gathering behind us. We entered the city from a highway under construction (or, more likely, repair), and were misdirected, driving through suburbs of apartment towers, then onto a ring road, and finally up toward the Alhambra, and ultimately within the Alhambra, which surprised us all.

For our hotel, the America, is inside the Alhambra walls. It is the first hotel I've stayed in, I think, that might equally have welcomed Henry James, or perhaps even Washington Irving. Our room is perhaps fourteen feet square, quite big enough for its three single beds (for Eve is with us), with a Santa Fe ceiling of exposed beams, heavy dark wood headboards, and a magnificently furnished bathroom whose tub even boasts polished chrome wrist-rests.

I type this in a comfortable sitting room full of upholstered side chairs, framed paintings, a vitrine or two filled with ceramics and whatnots; and I wait for Lindsey to descend to have what promises to be a sustaining breakfast.

But what the hotel lacks is a parking lot. Where do I park the car, I asked; First let's check you in, the deskclerk said, And then I'll explain.

I think this strategy retains guests who would otherwise choose another hotel. I checked in, and then was told the car park was a ten-minute walk away. We unloaded the girls and the baggage and I drove off into the night — a ten-minute drive, in fact, for the road was circuitous.

It was pitch dark. The sky was overcast and the moon is new — the beginning of Ramadan. Pitch dark. I found my way to the ticket-booth, for you pay for admission to the Alhambra. We had reserved tickets, and after I found my reference number, hidden in the bowels of this handheld computer, I was given the paperwork.

But where is the Hotel America, I asked, and the ticketseller pointed mysteriously toward the entrance gate to the Alhambra.

I'll have to describe the Alhambra later, after having seen it by daylight. At night it is nothing to see, but much to feel — imposing bulks of hedges, trees, and walls looming overhead and crowding in from the sides.

The gravel crunches underfoot, and there is always running water to hear — unseen in the night, but fully present. Paths and steps are occasionally illuminated, but the lamps are set at ground level, throwing no light up into the sky. And many of the steps are in fact unlit, and you want to feel your way carefully.

The girls had unpacked, and the little painting of a teacup that Patrick let me make in his studio was on my bedside table as always, telling my protective spirits where I'm sleeping tonight, and it was time to walk down into the town for dinner.

And one of these days I'll tell you about our eating these days: but now it's time to see the Alhambra by daylight.

Alhambra

Calle Jamerdana, Seville, Nov. 10—

I BEGIN BY CORRECTING myself: Henry James most likely did not stay in the Hotel America, as it was converted from a private house into a hotel only seventy years ago. The house itself of course is much older, and very pretty; this is a hotel for the short list.

I won't attempt a description of the Alhambra; you'll have to read a guidebook. I'll simply tell you what our impressions were. After breakfast — not as substantial as I'd hoped, only a couple of rolls and coffee with milk — we walked up to the Generalife gardens, past huge castellated walls of clipped cypress trees, through endless formal beds bordered by clipped myrtle and planted in alarming red salvias, or mixed bedding plants.

The gardens are divided into "rooms," all bounded by the clipped cypress hedges say ten feet high, open to the blue Andalusian sky (about which more later), now and then opening suddenly onto a vista, or peering through a "window" in the hedge into another room with its pool, or monocolor planting, or group of tourists posing for a photo.

Then there are long *allées*, always geometrically set out, with long long sightlines through arched cypresses or past arcing jets of water. And at one end of the entire garden is an outdoor theater, the backdrop composed of tall dark cypresses behind the stage which looks west over the pit and the orchestra. The effect at sunset must be extraordinary.

The Generalife was the summer or weekend palace of the Caliphs who otherwise lived in the Alhambra, which we toured next, a series of rooms and halls and gardens and patios. It was built fairly cheap, out of tiles and plaster and wood, say seven hundred years ago; but the surfaces, walls floors and ceilings, are magnificently detailed, ornamented everywhere — avoiding realism, of course, forbidden by the Prophet, but relying instead on the flowing Arabic script and by geometrical fascination — with the Pythagorean theorem, for example — to symbolize the seven heavens in the marvelous stalactited recessive ceilings, and to relieve what would otherwise be vast expanses of smooth white walls.

One room bore a plaque: Washington Irving lived in it while writing the book that impressed me nearly sixty years ago, a book now dismissed as "a highly romanticized view of Andalusia" by my own highly pictorialized guidebook (one of the Eyewitness series).

(Irving also lived around the corner from our apartment, in Seville.)

One can only speculate, dangerously no doubt, on the affinity of the medieval Moorish mind for these hypnotic tiles, figures, labyrinths, gardens. Contemplating these interiors forces the mind inward. I prefer the gardens, which lead the eye outward and onward, inviting the mind to follow along.

The Christians had their differences with the Moslem mentality, and in some cases set their own architecture, rather heavily, atop previous building, as if to suppress it. I've already mentioned the surprising example of this in Córdoba, where a Gothic cathedral is set down within a darkly contemplative mosque.

And at the Alhambra Carlos V, who confusingly began his career as Carlos I, was unwilling to occupy these moorish buildings, and had his own palace built by a student of Michelangelo.

The result, the only building remaining by this gifted architect (Pedro Machuca his name was), is one if the finest buildings I've seen. I have to learn more about it. I don't know, for example, when it was finished: begun early in the 16th century, it seems more like a product of 18th-century Enlightenment than high renaissance — but these are subtleties beyond my information.

From the outside the palace footprint seems to be a perfect square, but once you enter you find an enormous central open area, perfectly circular, nearly filling the building, open to sky and air for light and ventilation (which must be essential in the summer).

The staircases and galleries linking this square and circle are utterly fascinating, and the ratios of the two very high storeys, the thirty-two columns supporting the loggias, the pavement of the central patio — all these are utterly rational, a huge contrast with the lyrical, hypnotic, insinuating effects within the Moorish buildings.

We walked down into the old town, having a glass of wine outdoors in a plaza featuring a really terrible American singer-guitarist at one end and rather a good Irish bagpiper at the other, and then we took a cab back up to the parking lot and drove out of town, losing our way only once, and onto the highway home.

Again we drove through a sunset, this one extraordinary. Clouds were piling up in Art Deco layers, tinged first with orange, then the pink of a Provençal rosé, then deeper shades of carmine and red, always against an oddly lucid turquoise blue sky, with the dark distant mountains silently watching as they have for millions of years.

I read recently of a Spaniard who warned a child against going to Holland, "where the sky is too close to the land and there is no room in between for men," and I thought about this enormous and enormously energetic Andalusian sky, as high and eventful as New Mexico's, but tonight at least even more theatrical and busy.

We are close to the end of the continent here, to Gibraltar. These skies are the theater of winds from the Alps and the Sahara, of currents from Turkey and the Caspian beyond.

Eve telephoned her roomates to say we would be going out to dinner and a show, and to tell them to go out and look at the sunset. Too late: they were already up on the roof photographing it.

We had a quick nap, then pork-cutlet Solemilla tapas, then watched the late flamenco show at Los Gallos — wonderful male singers and dancers, so-so women, at least to my taste. And then, at one-thirty in the morning, through the still active Seville alleys to our apartment and bed.

Further excursions
13 Nov 2002—

SENTENTIOUSLY QUOTING SHELLEY I stand next to amused Eve in the portico of the *servicios*, waiting for Lindsey. My name is Ozymandias, King of Kings, I intoned; Look on my works, ye mighty, and despair.

It seemed appropriate. We had just toured Italica, the ruins of Trajan's town, established a few thousand years ago by Scipius Africanus. There wasn't much to be seen but the local Coliseum, with its sad tunnels from which lions and gladiators once emerged to meet the spectators; and a few floors, once-wonderful mosaics now fading in the bright Andalusian sun.

Everything is so transient, and a damn good thing it is. Even the television set in our apartment fades to black within a few minutes of being turned on. You turn it off, turn it back on immediately, and it looks normal: but in a few minutes it's black again.

Still we all try to leave our marks, me with these observations typed at the breakfast table and carried in my pocket until I find a telephone, others with their damn spray-cans.

Abplanalp, of course. Thanks, Tom, for reminding me. How could I have forgotten the marvelously named Abplanalp, friend of Nixon, inventor of the spray can? He did it for DDT, not paint, but it's still his fault, all these graffiti everywhere.

What is it with these Republicans and their oddly named friends, Ablanalps and Sununus, that they continue to think their unnecessary inventions will fail to find their socially negative functions?

Italica was beautiful, its lawns and groves an oasis in the dry brown autumnal Andalusia landscape. How this country needs water and trees! We drove to Cádiz yesterday [Monday], through fields just harvested and in some cases tilled — lots of cotton in the south, and some kind of grain, I'd say. The fields are tawny:

brown, tan, beige, even grey, under that pale blue daytime sky, hazy yesterday with the promise of moisture.

Cádiz is a pleasant town, the old city (very old, the oldest, they say, in Europe, though that's hard to believe) completely filling a small headland, the sand-spit leading to it now crowded with 14-storey condos and apartments.

We parked on the waterfront and walked through a public garden, then along the esplanade, quickly reaching the center of town, a quiet spacious plaza fronting the cathedral. There we had lunch — tapas, of course: tiny squids deep-fried whole (looking just like an alarmed squid in one of the Italica mosaics); salt cod; ox tail.

I think. All these tapas places begin to run together, though in fact they are all quite different, each excelling in one or two things — clams, or pork-cutlet, or ham, or cheeses.

One of our favorites, Las Teresas, stands out for its spinach-and-ceci. Another, whose name I forget, down on the Plaza Alfalfa, has unforgettable sausage.

In every case Lindsey has a white wine; I have a Manzanilla. Two, in fact: they're small. Eve has her lemon Fanta, and is quite happy so.

And now it is Wednesday evening and we are in a hotel in Salamanca, thinking about — where to eat dinner. Today's drive was through wonderful country, due north from Seville through Merida and Carceres.

It began, this country, looking like California down around San Juan Bautista, with eucalyptus and oaks on hilly plains. Then we climbed into higher country recalling the Mother Lode, and here were long reaches of sparsely planted olives and cork oaks, the trees very old and ill-tended, chiefly there, I suspect, to provide shade and food for the livestock — huge black bulls destined for the bull ring, I'm afraid; and free-ranging pigs, big but lean, destined for the tapas bars.

We drove into the high plain of Extremadura, and then into a range of mountains, climbing to nearly 1200 meters — 4000 feet — and into a fierce tempest whose winds nearly knocked me down when I got out to buy gas.

Fortunately it was a following wind: had we been driving into it I think I'd simply have quit for the day, the rain was driving so hard. But it blew over, and we pulled into Salamanca about five o'clock, and here I'm able to send and receive my e-mail, so this will catch you up.

Along the way we were pleased to get a phone call from Hans — we've been concerned about the Dutch storm of a few weeks ago, but apparently Apeldoorn came through well, though there are many trees down in our beloved Hoog Veluwe.

I'm not responding yet, individually, to most of you who have written from far and wide — New Mexico, Australia, England, California — but we welcome your greetings, and will be back in touch all too soon. Tomorrow we'll drive through Bilbao, where one of us greatly wants to see a Gehry museum, and with any luck we'll spend the night in France.

We should reach Paris by Saturday. If you need to reach us we'll be getting e-mail daily, and there's always the telephone in the other pocket:

Sheep
Hondarribia, Spain, November 14—

WE TURNED OFF THE FREEWAY — yes, it *is* free, in that part of Spain — and drove through a dusty little uninteresing town, Baños de Cerrato, outside of Palencia, because there, according to my eagle-eyed guide, who had studied her Green Guide, was the oldest Christian church in all Spain, built in the seventh century by visiting Visigoths.

Two double-backs at roundabouts and we were on our way — except that just as we crested the overpass across the railroad tracks we encountered a slow dark-haired man in a wool sweater and baggy wool pants, a dog, a puppy, a donkey, and several hundred sheep, all slowly but relentlessly headed our way.

I did one of the few intelligent things I do in such situations: I stopped. My camera was out of reach, but Lindsey's was near enough. Perhaps we have the Kodak Proof of this: time will tell.

In the meantime it feels good that such moments still obtain.

As for the church, well, it was soberly splendid in its small way. We have chanced upon ancient romanesque churches enough in our travels, in France and Italy and even Holland, but they've all been much younger, say half a millenium. This one was dated 661, and parts of it — the columns, for example — were older yet, brought in from pillaged sites elsewhere, no doubt.

And next to it was a spring from at least the same period, said to be good for the kidneys, but we didn't put it to the test.

The drive from Salamanca was fairly uninspiring at first. Salamanca itself is of course fascinating (and thank you, Hans, for insisting that we give it some time!), with its Roman bridge, and its splendid Plaza Mayor.

I've idly thought for years about making a study of piazzas, or *places*, or plazas — urban squares enclosed on all sides by buildings. I've been fascinated by the geometrical proportions of façade-height to square-side; by the kind and degree of light falling on the square; by the texture of the pavements; by the position and orientation of these squares within their communities.

I have collected some favorites: the main square in Timisoara; the plaza at the Winter Palace in Petersburg; the Place des Vosges and even better the Place St.-Louis in Paris (the latter in the 10th), the Campo San Marco; and so many others, I'm sorry, I don't have my books and maps with me. The Healdsburg Plaza, of course, finally once again completely enclosed.

Well, the Salamanca Plaza Mayor is worth any of these, but it was severely compromised yesterday by a number of temporary exhibition spaces set up, plastic-window'd tents offering kitchen cabinets and livingroom carpets to the eager buyer. What can the local tourist board be thinking of, we wondered, destroying — though only for the moment — a timeless architectural masterpiece in order to attract a few commercial exhibitors.

But of course this was the original purpose of these piazzas: markets. As there is only a difference in social level between spray-can graffiti vandal and graphic-design neon artist, so there is only a difference in acceptance between these trade fairs and the street-markets of twenty years ago, or two centuries, or millenia.

(I had pointed out the small enclosures in the Roman ruins of Italica, the ones on the periphery of the villas, facing the cross-streets: these were the shops, I explained to Eve; they probably sold tapas, and wine by the glass, and maybe lottery tickets.)

We have driven from Seville to Salamanca to Hondarribia (on the Atlantic, on the French border) for two strategic reasons: to visit the Guggenheim in Bilbao, and to avoid Madrid. The latter was my idea; the former was my co-pilot's. I will spare you my opinion of the Bilbao Guggenheim — many of you will be able to imagine it — and mention instead a couple of serious matters neglected until now in these reports.

The first involves the driving. From Seville to Salamanca, or nearly there, we drove a two-lane highway winding along next to a superhighway under construction. This was frustrating. We made fairly good time, but Spain is a very big country.

(Collection of countries, I should say. Chris Alexander is right, in his magnificent book *A Pattern Language*: there should be a thousand nations, and Spain would easily comprise a handful of them.)

From Salamanca to Burgos, though, we were on divided four-lane highway, and free of tolls. We had to begin paying after that, and it's been about 25 Euros so far — and the Visa card is inexplicably rejected here, though it worked on the pay-roads in eastern Spain. Go figure.

We clip along at about 120 to 130 km/h, which is about 75-80 mph, and this makes these long drives manageable. Today's weather was thankfully much better than yesterday's, and the scenery only slightly better, so we didn't mind driving so fast.

From Burgos on, though, the countryside has been much more beautiful. We saw snow; we saw trees; we saw romanesque churches off the road. Endless ploughed fields, where hay and sugar beets and God knows what else had constituted the monoculture, gave way to poplars and river-valleys and pines and smallholdings, and I began to think once again that there was hope for humanity and its way of dealing with God's green world.

The other mattter, of course, is the food. Last night in Salamanca it was a little restaurant where we had modest but tasty food;

I particularly recall the stuffed peppers.

Tonight, in our hotel restaurant, it was a big salad — again — and, for me, three little lamb chops, again with red peppers, for we are in Basque country. And with it a bottle of clean semisparkling white wine made right here, and afterward a little digestive of some kind of mountainberry, a sort of Basque equivalent of Beerenburg.

Well. I type this fast, while Lindsey relaxes in the tub. Tomorrow will be a long day, driving up to the outskirts of Paris. It will be a relief to put Spanish aside and slip back into bad French. I have no idea where we'll be in twenty-four hours. But it will be pleasant, and appropriate; and it will bring us one day closer to home, and that's beginning to be attractive.

* * *
*

"the oldest Christian church in all Spain" (p. 56)

Paris

Paris

17 Nov 2002—

WE ARE IN PARIS, and happy to be here, for several reasons. Yesterday's drive was the longest and fastest of the trip: 824 kilometers, over 500 miles, in nine hours elapsed time.

And it wasn't bad. Lindsey drove most of it, letting me look out the windows in pleasure at the unfolding French landscape, or out the windshield in terror at the back ends of trucks.

It sounds like you didn't like Spain much, David said at lunch today, and I guess that is how it sounds. In fact I have mixed feelings. Córdoba was the highlight, apart from seeing and being with Eve — nothing compares with that, of course.

I liked eating (and drinking!) in Spain, though I was prejudiced against it for stupid intellectual reasons having nothing to do with experience.

But there are such things as national mentalities, and I'm not drawn to the Spanish ones, at least not so far. I guess I simply like what I know, and resist getting to know what I don't. A sad turn of events for a former avant-gardist, no?

Anyhow we arrived in Paris about six-thirty, driving into town easily and pulling up in the courtyard of our friends Barbara and Philippe, who live in a spacious calm apartment on the top floor of a former Steinway piano factory building in the Seventh, around the corner from the Rodin museum.

We returned the car today. We had driven about six thousand kilometers altogether, a little over thirtyfive hundred miles, getting our money's worth. Yesterday we pushed it to a steady 140 km/h, which is fast for such a little thing, and our fuel economy suffered, and so did we, because gas which is 80 cents a liter in Spain is 1.10 a liter here in France. Oh well.

We dropped Lindsey's photos off a the Bon Marché down the street and drove to the Gare du Nord and returned the car, and then walked down to the Place République and a little further to meet David L. for lunch, but the place he'd chosen, a crêpe restaurant run by a woman from Brittany who is also a photographer, Jour de Fête the place is called, was closed, its name having been a bad omen I suppose.

So we lunched at a completely ordinary little place and had duck confit with french fries and a bottle of red and a bottle of water and afterward, for me, a glass of prune brandy, and it was nice to be eating French bistro food again after all those tapas.

(I'm not complaining about tapas. I love them. But it's nice to change off.)

Then we took a cab to the Trocadero to see a huge retrospective of the paintings and drawings (and poetry too) of Francis Picabia, a favorite of mine, a buddy of Duchamp's and a fine painter and even better draughtsman, and there was his portrait of Gertrude Stein, sitting in front of the Bilignin landscape and draped improbably in a striped toga of some sort. Which of course reminded me of the Stein lecture I give a week from tomorrow, in Oakland.

I found a copy of the comic-strip version of the first volume of Proust's *A la recherche du temps perdu* for Barbara and Philippe, who didn't know about it for some reason. And they are playing for me the sound track of a Spanish movie they like, *Parle avec elle*, an Almodovar movie, and it ends with a Purcell lament, which reminds me of a lecture I gave in Aix a few years ago, a lecture that was sprinkled with dirges.

So we are leaning into the return home and getting back to work. I have CDs to make — the lectures, and some music. I have George's book to prepare. I have these travel notes to flesh out and explain and improve and illustrate.

And what will we find, I wonder. I am able to read newspapers again, barely, and find new threats from Bin Laden, and new confusion about Iraq, and suspicions about Russian-Chechen histories, and continued warnings about the role of poverty, widespread poverty, in the unfolding international situation.

Some friends wash their hands of all this, feeling helpless. Others follow it all with a certain realism, or maybe fatalism: we must all get used to a few years of terrorism, it seems, of never knowing whether an airplane or a soccer stadium, or a museum, or a cathedral may not be the next target.

Except that the technology has changed so alarmingly there's nothing really new here; Europe has dealt with this for years. England and the IRA; France and the Algerian-sympathizer plastiquers, Israel and the suicide bombers.

You must be tired of reading these musings, and God knows I resent being distracted by them. I want to observe food and drink, people and landscape, art and history; not this constant press of impending events.

But in many ways I feel we're in Europe in 1939, during the "phony war," except this time it's a phony peace. No one here seems to like the current official American stance, but no one knows what alternative there can be. We all wish things would simply go away, but people here think there will be war, probably in January, and no one can really imagine what kind of world it will lead to.

But it's time to walk around the corner to dinner with four Chez Panisse friends who happen to be coinciding tonight, and to walk back through the lovely Paris mist, bracing but softly luminous; and then to dream, again, perhaps, of helping my grandfather trim the plumbago, or talking to Terry about how we do or do not write our music.

What is your country?
Rue Babylone, Sunday morning —

SOME PARIS INSTITUTIONS change very slowly: but they do change. The old *restaurants du quartier*, the neighborhood restos, gradually descend through the generations. We have long liked Au Pied du Fouet, where the regulars still have rolled-up napkins in a case at the back of the tiny dining room.

But we don't go there this time. Barbara and Philippe, who live next door, say it has changed, the owners are usually in a bad mood, the servings are smaller and the prices higher, and so on.

We went last night to Thoumieux, an old-fashioned brasserie near the Invalides. Zagat gives it a solid consistent thirteen (out of thirty!) for food, decor, and service; but David L. had recommended it, having eaten there recently with Mort Rosenbloom, who wrote that interesting book on the Olive.

So David T. booked it, because I'd called him on a lark asking for a recommendation, and he said by coincidence two other Chez Panissers were in town and we could join them all for dinner.

Thoumieux is a nice half-hour walk from Barbara and Philippe, where we're staying, but I hadn't allowed for two or three conventions of European street-numbering:

• If there's a block on which there are no buildings, or even two or three, as there are in front of Les Invalides, the numbering simply stops for those blocks and picks up where it left off when the buildings reappear; and

• numbers apply to buildings, not individual occupants of the buildings, so there are rarely more than eight or ten numbers to the block, rather than 100 as is the case in the more metric (in this case) United States; and

• there is no reason to believe that if you are standing in front of 96, say, then 97 will be directly across the street; it may be a block or two away.

So we were a little late, but no matter. David T. and Randall were well in charge: they settled in Paris six months ago, and are quickly becoming expatriates.

David T. was a chef at Chez P. — three times, in fact, as I recall, over the years, and a gifted one: but his heart is clearly here in Paris, enough so that he's willing to be chef once more, in his home, once or twice a month, for groups of a dozen or so, as a way of paying some of the bills.

(There is a long tradition of occasional-restaurant-in-one's-home here; I don't know if it obtains in other cities.)

David L. had said to us, at lunch, So, you travel a lot, what's that all about? I thought about that a little all afternoon and wondered what one might answer; I think about the travels my mother made in her last fifteen years — much more courageous than our travels: to Peru, to China (two or three times), across Siberia on the railroad; finally up the Nile, her last trip.

Then at dinner David T. said And what is your country, Charles? And I said quickly Not the United States, I am not happy with the United States. I am a Californian, from Sonoma County.

But it's funny how Paris turns out to be so easily everyone's second home town. It was Virgil Thomson's home town; it was Gertrude Stein's. It was Picasso's.

Even John Cage, who began so absolutely a Los Angeleno and ended so determinedly a New Yorker, even he received his conversion, you might say, his baptism into Modernism, in Paris. One never thinks of Cage as a Frenchman. But he was so close to Duchamp and to Satie, who were themselves both Norman but also converted or baptised, I have to find a better figure of speech, in Paris.

For years friends thought of me as a Francophile, though in fact I never thought of aspiring to Frenchness. What I admire about the French is intellectual vigor, analytical clarity, elegance of wit — qualities I will never come close to, because I am all American and rustic to boot.

And Paris is the French Great City par excellence, perhaps the Greatest of all Great Cities. It is not marginal, as are Moscow and Vienna; and unlike London and New York, it is international and cosmopolitan without insisting on global domination.

Anyway we had dinner at Thoumieux, if that's what it was called, the six of us, admiring the restaurant's cat and her comfortable way of accepting Randall's elegant Yorkshire terrier, and joking about the sometimes absentminded service, and overlooking the ordinariness of the food (though to tell the truth my *gigot d'agneau* was pretty good).

And then we walked home, Lindsey and I, leaving the others to the Metro, and got to bed about one o'clock. And today we went with Philippe to the flea market at Clignancourt where I found a book on Picabia, just what I need; and then a visit to my niece, the daughter of my Australian brother John, who has married a Parisian she met in Thailand, and has now settled with him and their 15-month-old son Hugo in a vertical six-room flat in the Kremlin-Bicetre just outside Paris.

They have just settled here and are beginning their life, and it was a pleasure to see youth and promise and good looks and enterprise and even perhaps a modicum of optimism. Ana is not an expatriot; she is an Australian married to a Frenchman. They have the entire world available to them, and that is what seems different to me these days, different from the world Lindsey and I made our life in.

In so many ways history is a constant swing between poles, many pairs of poles. One of these pairs is internationalism-localism, which operates in several ways. Lindsey and I were always local, and I think our children are as well: but the next generation has inherited a world easier to move about in, with consequent benefits as well as drawbacks.

I'll stop here. I promised myself: no politics today. It's Sunday. But tomorrow maybe I'll report an interesting observation of Philippe's.

Flea Market
18 Nov 2002—

PHILIPPE IS A COLLECTOR, but it was not for his collection that we went to the *Marché aux puces*, the famous Paris flea market. Of course if a bronze athletic trophy should appear, one he needed to add to his collection, that would be just fine: but not likely, as his study is already crammed with dozens of hurdlers, footballers, tennisplayers, swimmers, boxers; big ones and small, often in triplicate or quadruplicate, marvelous sculptues owing something to Degas's horses and dansers but devoted implacably to their everday purpose: the celebration of athletic prowess.

Instead, Philippe was picking up a couple of Art Deco lamps, industrial ones salvaged from a factory that had recently been shut down and whose materiel was being retailed by a group of shopkeepers at the Clignancourt market.

He led us, though, first, through the market. Here you will find everything, he said, except what you are looking for; and it's true that I did not find the Noguchi book for Richard, but a biography of Picabia jumped into my hands.

You come here, Philippe said, for new ideas, for new ways of seeing and doing things. Yes, I replied, that is why the Surrealists loved the Puces, for its collision of meanings and appearances. I almost expect to see M. Breton around the next corner.

We went to the Maison Coloniale, a small house of three storeys, a room to each of them, crammed with things from French Africa (and, to tell the truth, some other uncertain origins): zebraskins, a human skull, ostrich eggs, a tin bathtub, snakeskin tables, elephant tusks, daily-life things from colonial times.

It was not the furnishings, the objects on sale, but the treatment of the walls and ceilings, the division of the interior spaces, that spoke the most to Philippe, and to us besides.

We had lunch in a little café. A woman took our orders; another stood behind the counter cooking and serving out. A man in his beautiful late thirties stood in the crowded dining room surveying things, wearing a beautifully curled thick black mustache.

A young woman at the next table was in loud conversation with her somewhat older male companion: You are all egoists, you men, she announced.

Philippe turned, startled, to look at her, and she stared directly into his eyes. You too, she said, You are an egoist, you are all egoists. Philippe shrugged and we returned to our own conversation, about what might become of the world — I won't write about politics again here! — and about love and passion.

He and I disagreed, lovingly and passionately. He feels one harbors passions, that they develop and then die. I believe that passions do not develop or die; that they pursue an independent life of their own, choosing one of us or another for a temporary lodging, then abandoning us for another human shell better suited to their immediate desires.

Picabia's life-work is an illustration of this. The head is round, he wrote, to permit the thoughts inside to continuously change direction.

(The split infinitive is not a problem in French.)

I got up to visit the WC, but chairs and tables touched on every side and it was impossible to move through the room without inconveniencing the diners.

Excuse me, I said to the young woman, hoping she would hitch her chair forward a bit. Can't you go round the other way, she said. No, I said, pointing out the numbers of people who would need to move to permit a circuitous approach to the WC; excuse me for being egoist, it's a question of bodily need.

It sounded cleverer, I thought, in my improvised French. She blushed red, suddenly aware of her outburst, and hitched just enough to let me by.

When I am in France I feel that everything is *bien regulé*, well regulated and adjusted, completely forseeable and logical, though often just a bit *louche*, just a little sideways. This is particularly true in Paris, of course, because the grain is so rich, the textures so detailed.

The texture of daily life, of walks through the streets, visits to marketplaces, overheard fragments of conversation, consists of familiar bits constantly falling into new and surprising configurations, like those collages Picasso and Braque discovered to express their Cubist rationalaity, which were immediately subverted by the Dadaists to prove the failure and absence of reason; and then again subverted by the Surrealists to announce the primacy of the Unconscious.

It's all here and I love it, and it is also a reminder of the continous presence of the Pagan in a world that for two thousand years has been contested by Jews, Christians, and Muslims, not to mention priests, soldiers, bankers, merchants and politicians, but I will not write about politics today.

Peristalsis
20 Nov 2002—

THE LINE MOVES FORWARD fitfully. Tired, I lean against one of those metal barricades you see all over Paris, they look a little like old-fashioned iron bedsteads, a series forms a fence directing the long queue outside the Grand Palais, I am comfortable, one heel resting on the lower bar, my arms stretched out either side along the upper, I look out across the crowd toward the silver-grey sky beyond the browning golds and yellows of the elms, I guess they are, across the street.

The queue doubles back on itself several times. The couple ahead of us are French; they murmur occasionally to one another; the woman, faded but pretty, limps a little.

The couple behind us are American. He speaks quietly into his mobile telephone, apologizing for inquiring about the result of a conference held last Monday, then dialing again, switching to fluent but accented Italian, and arranging a lunch appointment for next Wednesday.

His wife juggles her Paris streetmap, the *Herald Tribune*, and a thick book he had carried until the telephone business began. He hangs up and congratulates himself, in a deprecating way, for doing business while on queue; she smiles tolerantly.

A hundred feet down the line a group of a dozen or so lurch forward a few steps, and the line moves fitfully forward again. A space opens behind them; another group notice and move forward; the space lurches back our way, like a bubble of gas in an intestinal process.

Once inside we are in a similar process but less linear; the Matisse-Picasso show is in a series of large square or rectangular galleries, some of drawings or prints, most of paintings with a few bronzes ocasionally set about the center of the room. Great knots of people gather to read the wall-texts; others cluster with their earpieces in front of key items.

We sit on occasional benches looking at the tops of familiar paintings, old friends. You can tell the Matisses: they do not recede, staying quite on the surface of the canvas, and there is always green, frequently too much.

The other difference of course is that Picasso is Spanish and an immigrant; Matisse is French and at home. Matisse's work is almost never dark; Picasso's is frequently. Picasso is frequently violent or at least active; Matisse is at rest; even though the traceries of his grilles, his tendrils, the limbs of his nudes wind sinuously across the surface, the result is always tranquil, repose.

We get up to re-acquaint ourselves with the lower halves of the canvases and move into the next gallery. Suddenly we are through and at the postcard room; then the bookstore; then the cafeteria for a cup of tea; then the checkroom to reclaim my camera, checked perforce, even though there would be no way of photographing a painting in that crowd.

It's the hot ticket just now, this Picasso-Matisse. Advance bookings, which finesse that long queue, are sold out through November. But though there are some great paintings here (not to mention the sculpture), and a few items from private collections that we've never seen before, there's something wrong with the idea.

The show doesn't have the surprise, the analytical discovery, that a similar show had a few years ago in Fort Worth (of all places). It's just a compendium, lacking the backbone, the brain, and the heart of the fine Picabia retrospective we saw yesterday.

My feet hurt and we take a taxi back to the rue Babylon. The cab moves easily across the Seine toward the Invalides where Napoleon sleeps beneath that glorious black-and-gold dome, lit by a shaft of golden light that continues up into the now darkening sky; then slows into the Blvd. St. Germain before easing into the rue du Bac.

Earlier we had walked down the St. Germain on our customary last-day-of-trip errand: searching a couple of empty cardboard boxes for the books and maps and pamphlets we've picked up.

And we had walked down the rue du Bac to the Bon Marché, the great department store, where Lindsey has had her film printed to avoid fogging by the X-ray machines at the airport, and where the Romanians gather begging near the doorway to the Grand Épicerie, the swankest grocery store in Paris.

One of Lindsey's photos is of the living-dining room on rue Babylone, where I sit typing this, a quiet spacious room with a fireplace, couches, a piano, the dining table. It overlooks the quiet courtyard, an island of modest *Luxe*, perfect *Calme*, and sober *Volupté*.

In the photo Sourisette the beautiful blue-grey cat is gazing out from beneath the dining-table, one eye gleaming red, the other greenish-gold, a Picasso cat in a Matisse room. Barbara was enchanted with the photo and we leave it with her. She will be back soon and we'll drive across the Seine to the Place Victoire for our last European dinner for a few months.

Paris: les Invalides

Epilogue: a week later
26 Nov 2002—

JET LAG NEVER USED to bother me, but here I sit at five thirty in the morning listening to the owls a week after that last Paris dinner.

It was at Chez Georges, by the way, a fine old Paris brasserie that we should have visited years ago, though it has by no means lost its character. I had a dinner of my dreams: frisée salad, that wonderful invention, curly endive dressed with a little vinegar and bacon and a poached egg, a dish I always think of as quintessentially French and which always reminds me of Tom Guernsey who used to make it for brunch at Chez Panisse in the old days, and calf's liver again with bacon, served with French fries of course. Not perhaps the healthiest dinner, but carefully adjusted with a bottle of good red, and eaten in good company.

Barbara drove us first to the Harlequin theater where Philippe was attending a book-signing, and then he drove us on away from St. Germain and over the river and right to the Bourse where Chez George is. He was a little excited from the signing. The minister of culture was there, well the ex minister, the government is changing, all the old crowd are out and watching in some disarray from the wings as the new rightist government, completely consolidated for the first time in decades, takes hold of the country, as is happening in so many countries these days.

Philippe and Lindsey and I had had our conversations about politics, of course. He says there are four possibilities now for the world: it can become a Confucionist-style communism dominated by China; it can become converted to an Islamic empire; it can go toward a Soviet kind of dictatorship of the proletariat; or it can become democratic, in the Toqueville sense. The models are China, Saudi Arabia, Russia, and the United States.

He's talking about global administration, of course. The trick will be to allow local nations to exist within that administration, and this is what the European Union is practise for, I suppose.

In the meantime, he points out, we just have to live with the threats of terror. You Americans, he says, you have your elected president (the fine points of the election in question elude generlized discussion), his office is conceived in a manner to deal with these situations, now you must sit back and let him do the job he was chosen for, and if you don't like it in two years you can vote him out.

We drove past the hotel, in the French sense, the town-house which has served as the headquarters of the Socialist party these many years; it looked forlorn. But at dinner all this was forgotten; Philippe leaned over to the next table to talk to a Swiss couple in town for a few days, they always come to Chez Georges to eat; the waitress who had been there for fourteen years handled us all with grace and humor, apologizing that they didn't have a *vielle brune* (a dark beer) when I asked for my dessert for a *vielle prune* (an aged plum brandy); I pointed out that I had an old brunette of my own sitting across the table, *Oh mussieu*, the waitress said, disapproving my lack of gallantry, but I was much pleased at using a pun right out of Raymond Roussel in a Paris bistro.

And then the next morning the taxi ride to the airport, up the Champs Elysées, past the clothing boutiques with names like Naf Naf and Lacoste and Marlboro Classics, past the automobile agencies and the bistros; then out into the environs and past the chain hotels, the Formule 1, the Bleue Marine, the Holiday Inn; and into the not filled Airbus and across the water and the ice and the hours and the movies (Woody Allen; *Bourne Identity*), and home.

There had been the anxiety dream in the morning: my lecture had been printed, but the title was completely changed, the content Wastelanded; and the editor had included a letter advising me to get a decent haircut; and the publicity was vague as to date, time, and place. So I was clearly headed back to work.

Well it is a beautiful autumn here in Sonoma county; I have never seen the foliage so splendid, vibrant and full of nuance. There was one big rainstorm; all the dust is washed away, but everything dried off immediately, there is no mildew, no browning of things.

We have been down to Berkeley twice already, and to Napa once to see Joe Ortiz's quirky and loving *Bread, the Musical.* The Lecture, *Why I Read Stein*, went very well, thank you, and its book is splendid, Sumner Carnahan was a sensitive and sensible editor and Michael Sumner an inspired and resourceful designer. (The book is available at the usual online bookstore sites.)

There are about seven hundred photos to look through, and now an e-mail from Holland asking if I'll give a lecture on Duchamp next time I'm in the country, and these dispatches to get into some kind of print form for friends who resist e-mail. And now the sun threatens to break through, and soon we'll be on our way once again, third time in a week, to Berkeley, and… dinner, of course.

* * *
*

Ávila: the city walls (page 94)

To Spain again, February 2005

Time Warp

Hostal San Lorenzo, Madrid, Feb. 7—

IT'S A LONG TRIP FROM Healdsburg to Madrid, so we always break it in Miami. Florida is such an interesting state, and you can't beat Miami and especially Miami Beach for a bit of sunshine and amusement en route to so cold and serious a place as Madrid. So we always break the trip in Miami; we started doing that yesterday.

The red-eye out of San Francisco was bumpy and uncomfortable; I think American Airlines is reneging on their well-publicized more humane seat configuration, and God knows the food isn't even as good as it once was, let alone really what you might call basically good. But we landed safe and sound at Miami only half an hour late, and found our Thrifty Rental car without having to resort to anything as demeaning as helpful public information. Which seems as yet unconsidered in Chad County.

But from there things looked up. A friend had suggested spending part of a twelve-hour layover having brunch at the Delano Hotel in Miami Beach; the hotel itself has been rescued by Philippe Starck (famous for his weird retro chair designs) from shabby gentility and transformed into a witty postmodern wannabe Thirties Deco palace, and the kitchen is said to be looked over by Claude Troisgros, whose brother Michel staged a while Chez Panisse and now runs the family temple in Roanne.

We sat under the ceiling looking out toward the pool and, beyond that (if we could only have seen it through the wandering semi-nude readers of the New York *Times*), the cerulean green Atlantic; and we took our ease and a couple of Mimosas, and consulted our menus and the oddly clad fellow diners, and had an enjoyable couple of hours.

I usually dress up for travel; it's one of my few concessions to fashion. I looked like a retired college instructor from a private liberal-arts college, which is in fact one of my roles: Harris tweed sport jacket, Italian silk tie, conservative blue button-down shirt, black trousers and shoes. I dressed so mostly because I would be unable to change before checking in at my Madrid hotel, where I wanted to look substantial, since I'd be running up a substantial debt. But it was not the prevailing dress in Miami Beach.

Didn't matter. The main thing about this town, at present, is that you can be anyone and look like anything and fit quite into the scene. We parked on a side street and walked the Lincoln Avenue Mall, which runs from the imaginatively named A1A, Florida's beachfront highway on which all the posh hotels are sited, west toward the sound separating Miami Beach from the city of Miami. I can't tell you anything about Miami; I've only driven through it. (Well, I can tell you one thing: it's perfectly flat.) But I do have a few things to say about Miami Beach, or more specifically the Lincoln Avenue Mall.

The first thing that strikes you is that you've walked into a time warp. I doubt a building has gone up along this mall since the Japanese bombed Pearl Harbor. The best buildings are streamline moderne; the worst aspire to it. Where there used apparently to be a street — Lincoln Avenue, in fact; in its day an Auto Row, to judge by the remaining Cadillac Building — there is now a pedestrian mall, unfortunately interrupted at the end of each block by a stoplight permitting two lanes of traffic in each direction.

Along the mall is a curious assortment of chain boutiques, souvenir shops, those odd emporia of computers and cell phones and CD machines that seem to spring up in tourist centers, second-hand clothing shops, *gelaterie*, restaurants serving pizzas and the like, a white gospel church, one decent bookshop, and the home of the New World Symphony, directed by Michael Tilson Thomas.

The mall is furnished with fountains, café seating, a number of vendors of juices freshly prepared from fruits clearly brought in from sustainable local airports, and tall palms, one thicket of which was peppered with noisy green parrots. I wouldn't eat under those trees, and fortunately wasn't asked to.

We killed a bit of time, bought a Spanish-language phrasebook, and ambled over to the Delano for our Mimosa and a lei-

surely consultation of the menu. For forty-eight dollars each it proposed, beyond that drink, as much as we wanted from a rather
elaborate buffet: cereals and pastries, omelets and sausages, braised
duck, or steamed salmon, or roast veal; waffles and pancakes and
the like, and a long salad and hors d'oeuvre station. I had a few
oysters on the half shell, wanting to go light since the previous day
I'd been laid low by a pre-flight flu; and a nice salad of flageolets,
and another of eggplant and zucchini and peppers; Lindsey had the
same minus the oysters but with seaweed. I followed with duck
confit, braised with a Chinese-influenced selection of vegetables,
with a slice of roast veal just to see what it was like, and Lindsey
had truffled eggs Benedict.

I'd been entertaining myself watching people. A short young
man in whites walked in with a much taller blonde in a skin-tight
red dress; the top of his head came about to her Adam's-apple. Another elegant young lady applied mascara to herself a table or two
away. A number of older diners ignored their spouses by sharing
with them the Sunday *Times*, but at our next table six young beau-
ties giggled over their iPods and cell phones. An intense young
man in a bright red tee shirt seemed to have an eye on every detail,
and when he noticed me observing him he was right at our table:
May I be of some help to you, sir?

I explained that we were by way of being in the restaurant
business from time to time, and I always enjoyed watching a good
manager. He beamed at that: perhaps he'd been concerned I was
sent in disguise, as Zeus or Wotan used to be on occasion, to be
sure things were running the way they were meant to. We chatted
for a while, and he talked freely about the joys and perplexities of
attempting a fine dining operation in a locale too humid to bake
bread, too laid back to provide attentive or even particularly competent help, and too rich to house a clientele that didn't already know
everything about how such places should run other than the fact
that they really knew rather little, and that that came from unreli-
able sources in the media.

Well: the food wasn't bad. It wasn't up to Troisgros in Roanne, but it was better than I'd expected. We had dessert — a rice
pudding for me, a humid Key Lime Tart for Lindsey — and went

back out into the time warp on the mall, convinced more than ever that a part of the upper East Side of Manhattan was passing itself off as the Santa Monica of the 1950s.

I write this in a nice little hotel room on the Calle Clavel, just off the Grand Via, where one guide-book warns us street robbery is more prevalent than elsewhere in Madrid. It's been quite a first day in this promising European capital, until now innocent of visits from Lindsey and me. Our friends Hans and Anneke flew in from Amsterdam to spend the week with us, and we celebrated by going out to dinner at two o'clock, at a neighborhood *restaurant du quartier*, as the Parisians used to say, which Thérèse discovered a trip or two ago, and which has since appeared in Frommer's.

La Fuencisla is a small yellow room, square, with about eight or nine tables, opening off behind a bar on Calle San Mateo, near the Tribunal Metro Station — an easy walk, even in a light rain, from our hotel. I stepped in authoritatively and eyed the room: only two or three tables busy. The waiter asked how many we were and promised we'd be seated immediately. Then he asked my name.

I thought at first this was uncommonly sociable of him, and was on the point of asking his in return when I realized he assumed we'd reserved. We hadn't; it had never occurred to me. It's Monday; it's past two; just give us a table. But there seemed to be some consternation, and he consulted with an enigmatic presence who until then had been silently reading a newspaper at one of the tables.

This fellow suggested that we be admitted even without a reservation, and nodded to a service table until then stacked with cutlery and folded napkins. We took our seats and looked at the menus.

The waiter had heard me speak English to Hans and Anneke (and Lindsey, of course), and proudly pointed to the English translations in the menu he handed me. But it seemed to correspond inexactly with what the others were looking at, which suggested fixed-price daily specials. But today is Monday, and what the hell is *cocido*? It became clear that none of us spoke any Spanish at all, that we hadn't done our homework, and that no one here was about to speak Spanish to us. (The same had happened earlier at the airport, except at the tourist information desk and the Thrifty office).

Much mime and bad guessing and second-guessing began to restrict the possibilities until Lindsey asked, with some point, if we hadn't bought a phrasebook for precisely that sort of information. And in fact the Harper Collins Language Survival Guide, in spite of its British bias and a few typos, is worth having, and particularly for its food pages. There it was: "*Cocido*: stew made with various meats, vegetables, and chickpeas." We all four had it, of course, preceded by a bowl of perfect chicken-noodle broth and accompanied by a dry dry Rioja 2000, and followed by the inevitable flans and an exceptional espresso featuring Segafreddo coffee. Cost per couple, fifty-five Euros.

After a nap we took a taxi through the rainy traffic-jam hour to the Queen Sofia Museum, a truly great regional museum of twentieth-century painting and sculpture, particularly strong of course with Spanish names: Saura, Tapies, Picasso, Gris, Gonzales, Miro, Dali. This is where Picasso's *Guernica* has found its apparently final resting place, and the sight of it brought tears to my eyes — it's hard to look at this just now with an American passport in your hip pocket; any number of residences in Iraq must have looked like this in the last couple of years.

And the bitterness of this realization was enhanced by the series of documentary photographs taken by Robert Capa during the Spanish Civil War, when "liberals" were fighting and dying in a futile attempt to preserve their country from the arrogance of an authoritarian, nationalist, bible-thumping and backward-looking "leader" who played on his country's fear of Modernism, internationalism, liberalism, and social justice for all.

But I digress, and it's time to fold six feet of fatigue into a bathtub designed for one of Goya's dwarfs. We'll see how that works out.

Crash of tongues, date with death
Hostal San Lorenzo, Madrid, Feb. 8—

IT'S COME TO THIS: we're standing at a glitz counter on the fourth floor of the Corte Inglés department store, speaking English among ourselves and French to a Spanish woman about buying tickets to a Dutch orchestra concert tonight here in Madrid.

This because none of us, neither Hans nor Anneke nor Lindsey nor I, can manage in Spanish. The language is fairly accessible via print, when the print's large and close enough to make out. But when it is spoken it is exceedingly difficult to deal with. For one thing, it doesn't sound like it looks. What we call Saragossa, and the Spaniards spell "Zaragoza," sounds something like "tharrahath," the "h" a heavy breath. And so it goes.

Well, the Concertgebouworkest concert was sold out weeks ago, so we'll do something else. There's no shortage. We slept like innocents, unholy ones, and woke up at 8:30 refreshed, and spent two hours planning our day, finally settling on a walk, not a long one, to the Prado. The museum clearly needs a week. I could cheerfully spend an hour examining Jan Breughel's five little paintings dedicated to the senses, and there are many more significant things than that. The Van Dyck portraits are amazing. The Rembrandts. The Rubenses, many of which lack the fat nude females for which he's best known, and for which I scarcely forgive him.

Eyes grow glassy in a place like this, but you sure can learn a lot about painting. For one thing, you can watch it being done; there were four or five people working away at their easels, copying details or entire canvases; some nearing the end of their futile occupation, others just beginning their canvases, sketching out the broad lines of the composition in *grisaille* (more often in brown or sepia washes) to be covered later with their dutiful and attentive but somehow less masterly homage.

One copy was particularly useful, for it had been made centuries ago, of Rubens's *Adoration of the Magi*, before he enlarged and changed the original painting. More lessons here: how he became more dramatic and more insightful by slightly adjusting the postures and gestures; how he learned to direct the viewer's eye along the lines of his composition. And how the copyist was unable to capture the master's dramatic lighting, and how he utterly gave up trying to paint the kneeling King's ornately embroidered coat, and so would I have, had I even got anywhere near that far.

After literally rinsing out my eyes I found the paintings had trained them — or perhaps it was the exercise of looking first at the grand compositions, then the tiny print on the labels, when we wanted to figure out what the hell exactly was going on in these mute but richly filled reports from several centuries ago. How people dressed, how they looked, what they ate, how they danced, how they gardened, how they furnished their homes, whether they were nobles or clerics or peasants — all that is more and more fascinating. And above all how they differ from us, principally technologically; and how they are the same, above all emotionally. I couldn't help thinking of Capa's photos of the Spanish Civil War when I looked at Rubens's panoramas of lustful Greek centaurs and the like. Joy and misery, and the few serene moments that lend meaning to the violence they convey, hardly ever change.

There's a particularly ugly painting hidden away in a small room where the elevators discharge, an enormous painting of Salome's dinner party, at the moment she shows her father the grisly head of St. John the Baptist. Painted in the early 17th century, it's as disgusting a portrayal of anti-Semitism as I've seen: every face but the Baptist's is shows as ugly or deformed or supercilious or depraved. You could imagine it having been painted in Germany in the 1930s.

Lunch in the museum café, not bad; then a walk to the Corte Inglés for that language lesson in Babel. And, finally, a telephone chip, so I now have a working phone, may it serve me well, and home to rest for an hour. And then for the evening business: we walked down to the Puerta del Sol, a beautiful plaza whose ensemble of buildings, elegantly matched, form the oval façade to a large busy intersection; and then down through the Plaza Mayor to the Teatro Albeniz, imagine tildes and accents, to buy tickets to tonight's show. And then retrace the steps to our second typical restaurant du quartier, this one recommended by, of all people, Rick Steves.

The Casa Labra Taberna (12, calle Tetuan, behind the Corte Inglés and down the street from Juan Gris's birthplace) is where in 1879 the Spanish Socialist Party was founded, and it looks like a worker's hangout, and I think it is. Busy bar on the street, restaurant on the side, casual sit-down tapas joint behind the bar in what looks like a onetime checkroom, with high railroadcar hatracks running all round the room. Here we had delicious salt-cod tapas, and tuna on a toothpick, and mixed salads, and finally Fino. When I asked for a Fino the previous night the waiter informed me that in Spain the word was spelled with a "V," v-i-n-o, vino. No, Fino, I said, vino de Xeres, Sherry wine, not vino. No, he insisted, is vino with "V", and brought me a red wine.

But here in the worker's bar, only a few hundred meters further south but far enough, there is both vino and Fino, and I had the Fino, and then just to make sure a Manzanilla, and they were the right stuff.

I wanted it because after all we were going to a flamenco-type show. *Carmen, Carmela*, it was called, a drama-in-dance conceived and choreographed by Antonio Canales, who played Don José, with two singers, a guitarist and a percussionist behind the scenes, and a prerecorded tape of many guitars, a flute, and a chorus to present the key items of Bizet's score, and two really good singers; and another male dancer, Diego Llori, as Escamillo; and Lola Greco, apparently the daughter of José Greco, in the title role.

Canales changed the story a bit, to get rid of Micaela who I never like anyway, and the third act, which I always sleep through; and to end with a brutal and abrupt surprise. Much of the evening struck me as contrived and jimmied together. But much was valuable: Bizet's score revealed again its nervous intensity; Merimée's plot led Love to its inevitably cruel end with clarity and grace; the singers — Herminia Borja and Jose Valencia — stepped forward to participate in the action honestly, intensively, sympathetically. I was reminded of all sorts of things: my despair when I was jilted by a girlfriend, fifty years ago; the desperate lovers kissing on benches in the Atocha railroad station down the street, the illfated young husbands and wives in Capa's Civil War photos, Romeo and Juliet and all the rest.

    And then home, after a nightcap, and to get the mail, and so to bed.

Rococo rant
Hostal San Lorenzo, Madrid—

WHAT IS IT WITH BOCCHERINI? We listened to six of his string trios tonight — there didn't seem anything else to do so early as 7:30 in the evening — and while the music was clear and melodious and by turns spirited and affecting, fifteen minutes later we agreed, sipping our tea and mocha and frappuccino at a nearby Starbuck's, that it was pretty lightweight stuff. And in fact I couldn't recall a single theme, not even the ones that he'd returned to over and over again in a couple of rondo-finales.

    They were played beautifully, by three young Russians who have taken jobs in one corner or another of the present Spain. The violinist, Yulia Iglinova, is in the Royal Philharmonic of Galicia; the violist, Yulia Malkova, is a soloist in the Madrid Symphony; Anton Gakkel was in the Tenerife Symphony Orchestra for three seasons, and is now, with Iglinova, in the national radio orchestra.

    It was a free concert, and it was packed. In fact we couldn't get seats in the 300-seat hall; we sat in an overflow 114-seat hall and watched a bigger-than-life-size instant television relay, with impeccable sound, seated in posh, soft, capacious armchairs.

    It was the first of five concerts surveying some, by no means all, of the string chamber music of Luigi Boccherini, who died at sixty-two exactly two hundred years ago, after helping Haydn and Mozart define the idea of the string quartet and quintet. Though he was born in Lucca, much of Boccherini's career unfolded here in

Spain; he died here in Madrid, and was only returned to Lucca in 1927, though I'm sure it hardly mattered to him.

The series is beautifully produced by the Fundación Juan March, otherwise apparently mostly a home to contemporary currents of the arts — there was a handsome video installation scattered across a number of monitors in one of the lobbies, and a series of works on paper from Picasso forward upstairs. There is a fine forty-page program, with an intelligent general introduction to Boccherini and terser but still informative comments on each of the five programs.

In his introduction Ramon Barce discusses the vicissitudes that naturally accompanied Boccherini's dependency on the Spanish court for his income. He worked at first for the younger brother of Carlos III, don Luis de Borbón, who loved music and painting and the fair sex and hunting and was therefore too immoral to take place, even by fatherhood, among the Holy Catholic Monarchs of Spain. And by methods too Baroque to go into in an e-mail he was aced out of any possibility of ascending to the throne and even exiled from court.

Now according to Barce the music of Boccherini reflects some of this turmoil. He says:

> Boccherini's music... takes its place easily within the style and the ethos of the Rococo, where it joins the work of Haydn, Mozart, and the Mannheim School, with an Italian taste for openness, simplicity, delicacy and luminosity. You could think of his music as "celestial," compared with the more complex and severe music of Haydn. ... A light sentimentality is quite present in his slow movements and at times in passages that are deliberately descriptive or evocative, with allusions to the hunt, or the Infanta's aviary, or the pastoral and bucolic world, material common within the late Rococo.

Bingo: the Rococo. Earlier Lindsey was speculating about her lack of enthusiasm for Goya, as he is represented in the Prado. We saw there the famous two Majas, the nude one and the clothed, each of whom wears her head slightly awry; and the series of court portraits — Carlos IV looks like a straw man; Maria Teresa has no room for a brain behind her slightly vacuous expression; even the innumerable dogs and horses seem to lack character.

He could paint accurately and expressively; the wonderful Crucifixion proves that. And even though the more celebrated late political satires are not to be seen in the Prado — no surprise; this is essentially a Royalist collection — Goya's sympathy for the proletariat is obvious in the Summer and Winter canvases of his cycle on the four seasons.

But we agreed, Lindsey and I, that most of the Goyas here are clearly Rococo: light, quick, entertaining, decorative, and little more. Velasquez managed to please his royal patrons without an airbrush; Goya didn't seem to mind. He stands a little too close for my taste to Watteau and Fragonard on the majestic march of painting from Cranach and Giotto to Guston and beyond.

We spent the morning in the Prado, mostly looking at Goya and Bosch and Breughel. Clearly one must book a Madrid hotel for a week to study the Prado. I am far from a connoisseur or even a student of painting, and I can easily walk through a museum in fifteen minutes, especially if it's getting close to dinnertime. But I am an enthusiast of painting, and the painting here is meticulously, passionately, intriguingly seductive. You want to spend every minute looking at these paintings, and then every minute thinking about them, and then every minute talking or writing about them. Everything in the world is here, every aspect of human desire and hope and history, individual or social, violent or peaceful.

The first thing that strikes you is that almost none of these paintings looks like the famous and ubiquitous reproductions. This is partly a matter of size and space and lighting, of course; but color and texture enter into this discussion, and it all adds up to *substance*, substance in italics, beyond or behind appearance. We normally think of looking at or seeing paintings, with our eyes, as we see them in photographs or prints or projected transparencies or, these days, on the Internet. Here in the Prado you do that of course, but these paintings, the best of them, which is to say a good half or more of them, get under your skin, fill your lungs, take over your mind.

In a few hours we'd had enough, the four of us, and we walked out the museum into a beautiful day, chilly but beautifully sunny, time for a walk in the park. We headed up for the Buen Retiro —

what a marvelous name for a park! — and ambled the packed-clay paths among the planes and pines. It's winter; parks aren't at their best, perhaps. But there's cool clean air, the traceries of the bare limbs (trees, of course, not majas), and the cunning architecture of the park, which spreads formal geometry across unpredictably varied topology.

Suddenly we came upon the huge crystal palace, no longer a Victorian greenhouse like the one in San Francisco's Golden Gate Park but a space for exhibitions of contemporary art. Here we found a number of works by a Mexican sculptor named Gabriel Orozco, who closely observed visitors who, like Hans, took up a cue to drive a billiard-ball into the red target ball that swung like a Foucault pendulum from an invisible line attached to the roof far overhead, or a paddle to play ping-pong with Anneke on a cross-shaped table for four with a lily-planted water hazard at the intersection.

Outside there was a larger pond, and then quite a good-sized one, with rowboats; but we were hungry, and walked back into the city to Las Truchas, which had been recommended for its fish. Here we had the local garlic soup, thickened with bread and paprika and a poached egg, bracing and filling; and then a platter of whiting and anchovies and squid and daurade, lightly battered and fried, perfect with a pitcher or two of local light-bodied but flavorful white wine, and completed with a huge baked apple.

And then a rest, and the Boccherini. I'd have liked to go on after that to a flamenco show, but was outvoted; we'll get to that tomorrow. We'll get to the Titians and Tintorettos later, too; if not tomorrow, then next month, at the end of this tour. You can't do everything, is perhaps what Goya and Boccherini were lamenting; not in this imperfect world. You can try, but Mister Bosch showed us pretty vividly today, in his *Garden of Delights*, what that can lead to.

Whole lot of taste
Hostal San Lorenzo, Madrid—

I'M SURE THERE ARE MANY Madrids, and we've only given them three days, which has brought us two museums, five or six restaurants, a hotel, and two concerts, most of which you've heard about. Madrid is a huge and sprawling city, probably as big, geographically, as Los Angeles: but except for a late-night taxi and one tourbus ride today, taken mainly to sit down for an hour or so, we've walked everywhere.

So we can only talk about a small part of town, centering on the famous Plaza Puerta del Sol, more or less the geographical center of the old city, halfway between the Royal Palace to the west and the Prado Museum to the east. Madrid has its Paris-type boulevards, but they do not radiate outward from nerve points. Four lead like the spokes of a flattened X out of the Puerta del Sol, but none leads north and south. The streets are otherwise narrow and rather helter-skelter, for the city lies aslant, with no predictability to the grades.

Nor are there any concentric circles remembering ancient city walls, for Madrid isn't particularly ancient. The Royal Palace lies at the western foot of its gentle slope, its *champs-de-mars* leading down to the river Manzanares, and the position would not be easily defended: this was clearly the palace of a royal family that feared very little attack. Spain seems to me in many ways similar to the United States, and this is one of the ways: its history seems one of consolidation in relative isolation, from Roman times to the discovery of the New World; and then one of administering a far-flung empire again from this secure relatively isolated position on its own continent.

The empire was definitively lost only a couple of centuries ago, and the aftermath is still unfolding — witness yesterday's car-bomb reminder, apparently aimed by a faction of Basque separatists at the King's participation in an important art fair with an international guest list. Spain is a constitutional monarchy with a relatively weak center administering to a number of semi-autonomous regions, many of them the relics of former independencies with distinctive national cultures of their own: Barcelona-dominated Catalunya, speaking its own language; distant Galicia; to the south Andalusia whose own sub-regions respond, no doubt with occasional local grudges of their own, to Seville.

To complicate things further, the Spanish monarchy overlapped for many years with others. It tried to own and run the Low Countries for a century or two, and the Dutch "G" retains the harsh aspiration of the Spanish "G" and "J." It was allied to the Kingdom of Naples, and was therefore close to the discovery of Pompeii and Herculaneum, whose decorations were immediately taken up by a court already fond of chinoiserie and various American motifs. There were of course various connections between the Spanish monarchy and the French. We Americans too easily think of distinct European nations as having hard and fast boundaries and clearly defined languages, as we are beginning to think of our own regions as being either Red or Blue: but these matters are never descriptions of steady states; they always refer to dynamic processes flowing easily or turbulently within a very complex fluid — except that there's nothing you can usefully think of as a source, and nothing that we know of that will be a vast final pacific ocean.

Anyhow we traipse up and down the very center of this slanted city, usually on narrow streets, protected by bollards from the little cars and taxis — there are no big vehicles here — and looking out for green-uniformed men and, occasionally, women, pushing motorized sidewalk-washers with rolling cylindrical brushes and snorkelly flexible snouts. (They clean the pavements at the expense of fouling the air.) The streets are amazingly crowded, and everything you've heard about the Madrid timetable is absolutely true: lunch begins no earlier than two and may continue past five, and dinner is unthinkable until nine.

The Madrid we know is a shopping town. There are sales everywhere just now; it's the season. I would advise touring shoppers to spend January in Rome; that's the month the government decrees the shops all have their sales. Then move to Madrid for February. You have small boutiques and enormous department stores. The Corte Inglés isn't content with every floor of an enormous building; it spills out into hardly less enormous annexes across this street and that; and you can get anything you can think of there.

If for some reason you want to reject the "values" of your parents' generation, and stay away from this Nordstrom-Magnin-May Co.-Macy's perfection, then for the other part of the Madrileño's life — entertainment — there is the local Fnac, which peddles everything electronic, from MP3 players to home theaters, as well as everything media-related, from books and magazines to DVDs and tickets to movies, theater, and concerts. And don't forget the cameras and telephones.

So the streets are jammed during shopping hours, then fall silent during the "siesta" which is not a siesta at all but eating-time. I suppose this is the result of the weather: it must be beastly hot in the summer, when you hide from the sun for hours; how could you change your pattern for the few months of bitter cold weather in winter? So we go about in our chic black surcoats and scarves and gloves at night, shopping until nine o'clock, then nibbling tapas and sipping our wine until midnight, when the shows begin. The youngsters, I'm told, roll up the day at five in the morning. There are two days to every day.

Still, you wonder, what does Madrid really look like? It looks like architecture. Perhaps because it's courting the 2012 Olympics, it is cleaning itself up with a vengeance. The relatively few plazas do not serve as chaotic parking-lots, as piazzas and places do so often in Italy and France: they've been hollowed out underneath, and steep, narrow ramps lead to multi-level parking structures neatly out of sight. There are sidewalks only on the few wide boulevards, and these sidewalks are often very wide indeed; but they are not lined with trees except along the magnifcent Paseo del Prado which defines the western boundary of the central city.

What there is, to fascinate the tourist eye, is the architecture. The Gran Via, the Calle Mayor and the Calle de Atocha are lined with immense and delightful buildings, from the late 19th and early 20th centuries I'd say, all of an even height. (There are tall buildings only in the suburbs, with one unfortunate exception — probably the one that suggested the imposition of a limit, as the Tour Montparnasse did in central Paris — out at the Plaza de Colon.)

These buildings are uniquely harmonious, contributing a playful sort of dignity, or a sober sort of eccentricity to what would otherwise be too masonry-dominated a city. The façades are full of relief and detail, but the styles are fully achieved and arrived, with an integrated character entirely their own: these buildings need no fake Corinthian capitals or sly Chippendale architraves. Postmodernist historicism seems banned from the center, and while there's plenty of elegant wit there's no heavy joking, no one-laugh architectural effect. You can walk these streets and look at these façades for hours without getting bored or tired.

This morning we went to the Royal Palace, where we spent two or three hours walking through the rooms home to the Spanish monarchs for the last quarter-millenium. The ceilings are painted by Goya and Velasquez, among others. The immense building is designed inside and out to the Italian taste, by Italian architects, only toward the end suffering some redecoration along French lines, Empire or Directoire or, in the end, in a previous king's billiard room, in a sort of romantic Gothic kitsch, the ceiling mural having been paneled over to make the place look like a secular choir in dark carved woods.

There was a lot of taste here, a whole lot. You can be sure this was a decadent period in Spanish history: the royal family didn't have to do too much beyond hunt and dance and listen to music and, of course, eat and drink. There was an extensive bureaucracy to run things, to the extent they could be run, and anyway the old empire was being sold off or traded away or lost to skirmishes for independence, rather as if a formerly wealthy man were finally to let his servants have the damn country house anyway, he'd rather stay home in the city and play cards with his cronies. I may be simplifying things a bit.

All this taste may have led to a few medical crises, judging by the extensive pharmacy we toured in one corner of the palace, with rooms filled with beautiful porcelain jars and glass bottles containing spices and simples of every sort, along with more than a few pure chemical elements and compounds. I suppose the exploitation of Latin America and, to an extent, southeast Asia brought many of these botanicals to Madrid. They did not apparently do enough for the weakening inbred Habsburg line; fortunately, the present Borbón family seems both more stalwart and more sensible in its enthusiasms.

A rest atop the tour bus refreshed us for dinner, which we took at three o'clock or so in a restaurant near the Plaza Mayor. (This perpetual disjunction between spelled and sounded Spanish almost made me type what you always hear: "plothamy yore".) This was, for Lindsey and me, an unwise but irresistible combination: olives, bread with tomato and olive oil, creamy salt-cod bacalao, creamily tuna-filled red peppers, and roast suckling pig, washed down with sangria, then a fine 1999 Rioja.

Afterward, inevitably, a nap; and then out again this evening to see what was happening in the tourist district down by the lovely early twentieth-century cast-iron San Miguel market. We settled for something simple: anchovies in vinegar and oil and a plate of Manchego cheese, both always dependably flavorful and clean and interesting, with a glass or two of Fino. And then a taxi home.

Tomorrow we leave Madrid. We rent a car, pack our bags, and struggle out through the city traffic, about which I refuse to worry further at the moment, and head for Ávila, which manages to contain the bodies of both Torquemada and St. Teresa. That must be energizing. We'll see how it goes down.

Secular, sacred
Hotel Torre del Clavero, Salamanca, Feb. 13 —

OUT OF MADRID along the Gran Via, through the Plaza de España where (as I understand it) the skyscraper is that took fire this morning, and through disorganized sprawls of suburbs, then into the Sierra. Spain is transversed by a number of these Sierras, or ranges. The word is related to the word for "saw," and refers to the many similar-sized peaks, set more or less in line, like the teeth of a saw; it's a familiar geographical feature and therefore word to Spaniards, and so was naturally applied to similar ranges in Mexico.

More to the point, the word also contributes Serrano ham, ham from pigs from the mountains. Well, the word doesn't contribute the ham, the many delicatessens and department stores and bars and cafés and, of course, restaurants contribute the ham. There is a chain of stores called the Mesón de jamón, I think, unless it's actually the Museo de jamón, I don't recall at the moment. It's been a long and hard day.

The hams hang high and low in the Museo, unless it's the Mesón (itself a transliteration into Spanish of the French *maison*, but enough etymology for today). How much do they weigh, Anneke wondered, so I asked a shopgirl: Oh, about four, four and half kilos, she said. Some of these hams go for as little as nine Euros the kilo; others range up toward forty. The ham is of course absolutely delicious — salted and air-dried. The best comes from the bars in Seville, I think, where it hangs for days directly over the bar, profiting from the blue cigarette smoke.

There was snow on the peaks, and before long we saw it alongside the road, in the shadows to the north of the rocks and trees. The country began to remind me of that north of Flagstaff, high desert with pines; and then we dropped down to the plain to the north, and before long left the toll highway for a national highway to Ávila.

What a city! The capital of its province, with perhaps forty thousand inhabitants, it is said to be the highest city of any size in Europe, and to have the best-preserved walls. It's entirely encircled by these walls, sturdy high ones composed of the warm beige sandstone of the region with occasional infilling of rubble and smaller river-run stone — perhaps there were times when the walls had to go up more quickly.

The walls are punctuated by tall cylindrical towers, castellated at the tops, exactly as you expect watchtowers to look; and the city is entered by way of four or five gates. Or it is if you're a local. We are not, so we parked in an underground garage a block or two from our hotel, and carried and wheeled our luggage along the sidewalk, then over a road paved with river-run stone — noisy wheeling, that — and through the main gate and around the corner to our hotel, itself just around a corner from the cathedral.

Ávila's main industry seems to be Saint Teresa, who was born here, but ran away as soon as she could — unsuccessfully; she was nabbed a few kilometers out of town and brought back. I'm conflicted about St. Teresa; I've always been attracted to a concept of her that came to me from Virgil Thomson's setting of Gertrude Stein's *Four Saints in Three Acts*; but that concept has little to do with either reality or history, as far as I can tell.

We toured her museum yesterday morning, after a sound night's sleep in a very quiet city. The museum is in the basement of her convent, the convent she established with the help of her friend St. John of the Cross — they founded the Carmelite order, famous for its bare feet, though Anneke pointed out that one of the relics in the museum bookshop, along with St. Teresa's ring finger (complete with ring), was the sole from one of her sandals. (She did not have terribly small feet.)

I was fascinated by the excellent facsimiles, in this museum, of Teresa's writings. Her handwriting was fast and fluid but very graceful and amazingly clear; once used to the long "S" and a couple of other eccentricities — of the Spanish of her time, not of hers — you could read these manuscripts pretty easily.

And she wrote a lot, and apparently read even more — in Latin *and* Castilian, the bookshop attendant told me proudly, and in books of all sorts. But however much she read and wrote, she is responsible for much more: a quarter of the museum seemed devoted to various editions of various translations of her work and commentaries on it, along with similar literature on a number of saints who trained for their profession under her influence. Some of these are quite recent, and one, born Edith Stein but known now as another St. Teresa, died in 1942 in Auschwitz.

I relate more easily to books than to ancient fingers. Generalissimo Francisco Franco kept Teresa's finger, presumably with the ring and in the present crystal reliquary, on his bedside table: I would not be able to do that, not even if I were Generalissimo. Some of St. John's bones are on view, too, and that somehow seemed indecent; I don't think they were meant to be so publicly laid bare; it doesn't fit the virginal concept I retain of this particular saint. But, as Teresa so famously wrote, *todos pasan*, all things pass.

I have the impression Ávila is a conservative town, politically. A prominent escutcheon on one of the walls mentions Franco's contributions to the town: his name is writ big, the very first word, though it's true the remainder of the first line is chiseled bare. Or, rather, covered over with a layer of cement: perhaps the city fathers are hedging their bets, and remain ready to restore Franco's title when necessary.

Conservative or not, it's a pleasant city. Our hotel was new last year, installed in what was already an inn centuries ago — the columns in the dining room retain iron rings to which horses were formerly tied. From the wall I looked down on another building only a few yards away, a building almost identical to our hotel Las Cancelas: I wouldn't be surprised to see it turned into competition in a year or two.

On arriving in town, a little past noon, we walked the walls — thankfully not more than a tenth of them, all that are open to tourism. This was a chore: the steps up are narrow, high, and uneven, and the pavement at the top is also uneven. But the views are marvelous, more so when you admire the architecture inside the walls than when you look beyond to the extramural outskirts, or even to the bleak plains at the north foot of the Sierra.

Ávila is all made of the same warm beige stone; only the Bank of Spain chose to find something more symbolic of its power, I suppose, a whitish granite of some kind; and its false classicism is as inappropriate as its color. Otherwise the architecture is rather humble, the few new or newish buildings carefully suiting their neighbors. But the cathedral is a surprise, made of blocks of stone mottled liver-and-white, giving the building a headcheesy quality with I find oddly pleasant, particularly as it articulates some quite splendid Gothic vaulting.

We slept one night in Ávila, taking our dinner at a place said to be both high in quality and local in flavor. It was okay. I could have given Ávila a day or two more, but I would have gone on to explore another restaurant, I think. But dinner was pleasant, and the walk home, at midnight, kicking a frozen softball-sized ice ball along, passing it back and forth among the four of us, was hilarious.

* * *

We left Ávila about noon, after spending the morning at St. Teresa's and then having yet another *boisson*, as I always call them, in a very pleasant bar-café on the Plaza Santa Teresa (what else?) outside the wall, on a huge "Plaza de Italia," so called I supposed because of the arched portico along one side, though the other is walled by two particularly unfortunate new buildings.

The road to Salamanca was fast when we weren't behind trucks, one lane in each direction, with enough curves and dips to rule out passing when you particularly wanted to. And we did. There were only two or three towns along the route, and they were not interesting. The countryside was mostly open, and when we later learned the area is famous for its beans it became clear why nothing was going on: the fields are fallow where the country is cultivated; other stretches were dotted with heavy oaks and no doubt populated by pigs — let's hope they somehow get to the Sierra before they become ham.

I could spend a week in Salamanca. We've been here before, but only overnight; on this trip we've spent two nights and seen a fair amount — my God, I'm tired — but have a lot left unseen. Last night we went out to a concert by the regional orchestra, a multi-European affair, strings from Russia and northern countries, to judge by surnames, and winds from Spain; conductor from Colombia. We heard the Mozart wind Symphonie Concertante and the Tchaikovsky Serenade for Strings, each played for the first time by this thirteen-year-old orchestra, and played very well indeed, in a hall seating 1200 with splendid acoustics — a big wooden box of a room with a small balcony, rather the shape of Amsterdam's Concertgebouw, the sound utterly transparent and alive.

If Ávila's business is the church, Salamanca's is the university. Its university is the oldest in Spain and one of the oldest anywhere. Salamanca's spoken Spanish has the reputation of being the best, like the French in Tours, or the Italian in Firenze, or English in Healdsburg. And Salamanca draws students from all over the world, and the students draw non-students, and the non-students draw bars and cafés and bookstores and the like.

The shopping is hip and elegant, and the café life is wonderful. I have made a hobby of squares and *piazze* and *places* and *pleins*, and Salamanca's Plaza Mayor is hands down the most handsome I have seen, exactly the right dimensions, perfectly consistent, quite detailed without being busy, and marvelously lit by a caressing sun through the day and subtly placed artificial lights by night. There is no traffic in this square other than pedestrians, and the pedestrians are anything but pedestrian. Today, Sunday, we admired elegant and conservative people of our own age at noon; then after dark when we returned we enjoyed a mixed population of younger generations, children included.

Today we also explored the cathedrals — Salamanca has two of them, side by side — and the University, and a museum devoted to Art Nouveau objects; and of course we had dinner, and *boissons* now and then, and heard music in the street, and so on. But I have gone on long enough. Tomorrow we drive to Segovia for the night, and the next evening we drop Hans and Anneke off at the airport and move on to the third stage of this little tour of Spain.

Mag ik de zout?
Hotel Infanta Isabel, Segovia, Feb. 14 —

ON THE DRIVE FROM SALAMANCA to the Madrid airport we stopped off again in Avila, for three reasons:

• to look for a book we may have left there in our hotel, but *no, lo siento, señor, no es aquí*, it wasn't there.

• to ask the whereabouts of Barca de Avila, which a friend recommends as a particularly nice country village, but *no, lo siento, señor, no es la via al aeropuerto*, it isn't on the road to the airport; we'll have to find it some other time.

• to have for God's sake something to eat. Our breakfast was the one we had yesterday, in our hotel, at the breakfast buffet, where among all the offerings we take a cup of coffee with hot milk, a glass of orange juice, a clementine, and a piece of toast. I, minding my greater need of caloric input, being so much bigger and stronger, have in addition a croissant stuffed with chocolate. Chocolate is insidious stuff; one grows to depend on it. No matter: it's good for you.

But such a breakfast only goes so far, and afterward we had a strenuous morning investigating the absolutely marvelous San Esteban church and monastery; whose cloister is one of the most affecting I've seen; whose monumental staircase contains in its railing an eccentric and quite moving statue of St. Mary recumbent, lying at about a thirty-degree angle upward (the angle of the staircase), resting on her elbows and looking ahead dreamily as if she were conceived by Edward Burne-Jones in the late stages of the 19th century instead of four hundred years earlier; and whose nave is perhaps the most perfect such we've seen, quite high in proportion to its length and width, magnificently daylit through its high square lantern-dome, and completed with an elaborate reredo composed of a thousand pieces of wood, intricately carved, then magnificently gilded — the sort of thing that would be far too much if it were not in an interior so otherwise modestly chaste.

I would say that regardless of the two cathedrals, regardless of the breathtaking library in the University, regardless even of the Plaza Mayor, which I think is the most nearly perfect outdoor living-room in my experience: if you can see only one thing in Salamanca, let it be San Esteban.

Anyway. We then had our coffee with Hans and Anneke, and went back to the hotel to pack and check out, first securing a hotel in Toledo for Wednesday and Thursday. And then to their hotel to pick them up, and then back along the now-familiar highway to Ávila.

I was mistaken if I suggested a few days ago that this highway was bordered simply by fallow bean-fields. They are wheat-fields; it's perfectly obvious from the occasional grain elevators scattered about. For maybe forty miles the two-lane road winds through rolling wheatfield country, before rising into the sparse oak-lands and scattered farms; and then pines begin to appear, and the snow is more evident; and before long we were again at the Four Posts where St. Teresa was apprehended by whatever relative it was she was running away from, and then Ávila.

The tortilla in the bar Santa Teresa, in the Plaza Santa Teresa, is delicious — it manages to be both firm and soft, yielding and structured; the eggs are almost deeply browned on the outside, but still moist and delectable on the inside,with tiny cubes of potato and shreds of uniquely sweet onion to deepen the plot.

All they need is salt. The others were rather jammed into the corner banquette we'd chosen two or three days ago on a similar visit, so I approached the bar, waited to be waited upon by the nice pert young man, and, when he asked *Dica*, which means literally "talk to me," I answered:

Mag ik de zout?

This is not Spanish. It's pure Dutch, a construction I learned a long time ago. *Mag ik de zout* means, literally, "May I the salt"; the final word, *hebben* (have) being understood.

This happened simply because we'd been having fun talking among ourselves, Hans Anneke Lindsey and I, and of course we were talking in English, but it's always a little in the air that their native language is Dutch, they say "when" for "if" and occasionally pronounce "yellow" as "jello" and things like that, and when I talk to them I'm always thinking, part of me, a teeny part of me, in what little Dutch I know. So out it came, or, as the Dutch would say, outcome it did, and the waiter looked at me and, what else, waited, until I explained myself.

Then at the airport when I asked the Eurocar clerk if he spoke English he said Of course, and spoke it better than do I, but with a familiar accent; and when I asked where he'd learned it, why, in Netherlands, he said. Oh, I asked, *sprekt U nederland?* And then we both wisely gave it up, though it was clear he was better than I in Dutch and Spanish and at least as good in English.

I am sorry to report that the approach to the Madrid airport is inscrutable, enigmatic, recondite, concealed, withheld. The signs high above the highway each offer a number of numbers: A1, A6,

M40, M11, and so on, all in sizes ranging from barely adequate to invisible, and all interspersed with various irrelevant destinations, some hundreds of kilometers away, along with meaningless abbreviations of other apparently meaningful phrases and various icons and graphic assistances.

When the sign pointing out AEROPUERTO does finally appear it is not overhead where all the other damn signs have been but hunkering down alongside the shoulder as if while hitchhiking it had noticed a familiar car approaching and it were desperately trying not to be observed. I can't imagine who decides to order, or fabricate, or choose, or place such signs. They are an offense to right-thinking drivers, let alone those of us wondering whether this lane or that goes to short-term or long-term, or private car or tourbus or rental, or domestic or international, or whether that tractor really wants to cross the road, or the guy in the Mercedes in the rear-view mirror cares whether he totals both his car and yours in his idiot compulsion to negotiate this maze.

Well. We finally found the rental-car place and parked, and I found a push-trolley and we loaded Hans and Anneke's luggage; and then we trekked to the terminal. This did not involve any sidewalks or ramps, oh no it did not, it required our crossing four lanes of maniacal traffic without pedestrian crossing or stoplight or even a warning sign. And before that even we had to leave the parking lot, which involved getting under or around one of those wooden gate-arms that may swing up to let you through, or may not. In our case it did not, and we managed our way around, and were better off than the hapless group that was coming the other way, and saw the gate miraculously rise, and hustled through, only to gather in alarmed sympathy when it came crashing down the last minute on one poor fellow's head, knocking him to the ground. They all looked like so many disciples and hangers-on at the foot of the cross in one of those paintings at the Prado, and we looked on in reverential and shocked and useless sympathy while they gathered the poor man up and dusted him off and continued their miserable flight out into the rentalcar parkinglot.

* * *

But tonight I am writing about *eating*. We dropped Hans and Anneke off in the terminal, having pushed the cart from one end to the
other and back before finding the right place — the Madrid airport
being the most customer-unfriendly I have ever found, either in its
highway approaches, or its parking lot, or even within its passenger
accommodation facilities, there, I'm already using that kind of
offputting language. And then we negotiated our change of car,
from the spiffy Audio 400 that Eurocar gave us, with a free upgrade,
a car that easily did 140 km/hour, to a Hertz Kia, of all things, that
will only do 120 with great effort and then on an even grade and
with the benefit of luxury cars breathing down its neck.

And we drove here to Segovia. I had thought, judging by the
two guidebooks we have with us, that this would be rather a simple
town: but it is not. Finding our way to the hotel, right on the Plaza
Mayor, took us through a number of roundabouts and tight corners
and two conversations with bystanders. We pulled up in front of
the Hotel Infanta Isabel and checked in, and after we looked at our
room we stretched our stay to two evenings and canceled the reservation I made for tomorrow at a desperate halfway point between
Madrid and Toledo; we don't have to do that. This hotel is spacious and quiet and pretty and we intend to rest for a day.

And then a walk down the main (pedestrian) street to a restaurant highly recommended. We'd phoned en route, desperately
hoping to get a table this Valentine's Day, when restaurants are
crowded, and were thankful to get one at the unfashionable (indeed
unheard-of) hour of eight o'clock; and we got there a little early to
make sure, and nursed a Fino until twenty after or so, and then
took our table in an empty dining room and presided there alone,
the two of us and our courtly but friendly waiter, until we were
done, or nearly. We had a mixed salad and Castilian soup, in
which I've been specializing — broth, garlic, bread, paprika, and
egg. And then we had suckling pig.

And, wonder of wonders, the table had a salt-cellar on it, and
for the first time in Spain so far the food of course needed no salting.

And with it a bottle of delicious Alizar (tempranillo) 2002,
with a very quick violet nose and quite a bit of tannin but very

friendly indeed; and then a baked Alaska for Lindsey and some soft floral sheep's-milk cheese for me, and so to bed, after writing this.

There have been things left out, notably storks. But they will have to wait.

Storks and sephardim
Hotel Infanta Isabel, Segovia, Feb. 15 —

STORKS, YES. Hans and Anneke were excited and delighted when we checked into our hotel Friday night — nearly a week ago! — to discover stork nests on the roof of the Ávila cathedral, visible out the high window of their room. We hurried in to take a look. I remembered how pleased and surprised a fellow was on a street in a small town in Holland, two or three years ago: he was walking toward me, a big smile on his face, and when he drew near he said *Ooievaar!* and I looked the word up as soon as I got into my room, and found out he had seen a stork; and I immediately went downstairs to relay the news to our host, and he rushed outside himself to have a look.

Storks are good luck, they say. I was pleased to find one grazing, I suppose, on a small lawn in a desultory town on the German side of our walk across Holland, later that week. But I've never seen more than one in the wild. Here in Ávila the sky was lousy with them, as Lindsey's father would have said. There were nests on every bell tower in town, often three or four of them, many in iron bowl-shaped cages installed there for the purpose.

They migrate between Africa and Scandinavia, I read, and make their stop here in the Spanish mountains for their breeding season. As we walked the Ávila wall we watched them wheel about in the sky, apparently enjoying themselves, perhaps in a sort of courtship dance — I don't know; they weren't talking. They weren't even squawking. They do have a call of sorts, which they make by clacking their bills together quickly several times, sounding like a stick dragged quickly along a picket fence. It's a pleasant sound, really, particularly since it's generally so far away.

At the end of our effortful stroll along the city walls we descended into a small park, where two stork couples had built nests in the top of a tree — perhaps they couldn't afford the more desirable perches on bell towers. Why were bell towers preferred, I wondered; perhaps there's something about the vibrations that they like, Lindsey suggested. Another stork enigma.

Since it's early in the season a number of them were still a-building, and we often saw a stork flying overhead with a stick or a piece of rope in its bill — never, as far as I could see, a diaper-slung baby. At other times we saw them simply perching, often on one leg, sometimes with their wings held out stiffly as if to dry. I wondered what they must have thought of the many magpies hanging about, who looked like stork midgets, wearing the same elegant black and white; but the storks seemed to take no notice of them at all.

Ávila was lousy with storks; Salamanca was lousy with storks; but we see relatively few of them here in Segovia. It may be that it's simply too damned cold. Segovia isn't that much higher than Ávila, if at all; I could look it up but I'm too lazy; but it's in an exposed location, perched on a rock island in the midst of rolling plain, and to the east and south are those mountains, some rising to seven thousand feet or so, and they are covered with snow down to their feet. I've asked a number of locals if this weather is normal, and they all assure me that it is: *es frío, Segovia*.

This may be why the stern Alcázar, which is the Spanish word for castle and not for movie theater, was used most recently in its checkered history as a military school. It had been built for a royal residence, back when Segovia was capital of Castille. (Isabella the Catholic, better known to us Americans as Isabella the wife of Ferdinand and therefore co-sponsor of Columbus, was given her crown here, not far from our hotel, the Infanta Isabella.)

(Another parenthesis, if you don't mind: *alcázar* seems not a Spanish word at all, but an Arabic one taken up by the speakers of Castilian — which is what the language we call Spanish is called hereabouts.)

When the capital was moved elsewhere there seemed nothing

better to do with this gloomy fortress of a castle than turn it into a prison, and so it remained for a couple of centuries. Perhaps the prisoners all finally froze to death: in any case it was turned into a military school for the artillery, and the museum here offers lots of swords, daggers, crossbows, blunderbusses, mortars, and other instruments of mayhem, along with stone cannonballs. And, more to my interest, models and detailed drawings of apparatus needed for measuring the size and shape of these things, and the force of samples of gunpowder.

For among other things the place was a laboratory for the production and improvement of military chemicals, particularly gunpowder. And then, inevitably, the whole place took fire, and burned for three days and nights, giving the locals only time enough to escape with their lives and the holy vessels and books.

(You could write a disquisition on the Siamese-twin relationship of chemistry and war, but I won't; I'll just hesitate long enough to point out that peacetime chemicals seem to concentrate on agriculture and are proving as mischievous as the wartime ones.)

The Alcázar was rebuilt, and the inside looks pretty convincing. Rick Steves says the whole thing has a Disneyesque air to it, but I disagree: this Alcázar is nothing like Miami Beach. Or even San Marino. The residential rooms have been put back to what they may have been during the early days, and the ceilings in these rooms are entrancing. Ditto the friezes and the sculpture.

But oh my God this castle is c o l d . We could stand it no longer, and rushed back to our hotel, stopping along the way for chocolate and *churros*, those deep-fried strips of extruded pastry that serve for doughnuts in this country.

Later the sun came out, though tiny flakes of snow continued to drift, and we tried another tour on foot. Like every other city we've visited on this trip Segovia is fascinating for its architecture, much of which is as early as the 15th century — magnificent houses with truncated towers, reminiscent of the old residential architecture in Verona, for example, except that almost every important façade is decorated with obsessive repeated textures (as is the Casa de las Conchas in Salamanca, and Salvador Dali's house in Figueras).

Usually these are simply sgraffito designs, though they are mostly done in the negative, the figure raised above the ground. Sometimes, though, they stand out in a much heavier relief. The champion is on a house that serves now as an art school, its façade studded with pyramidal forms. The guidebook refers to this as symbolic of a woman's veil, but I'm not so sure. I think they may have been meant to deflect cannonballs. I was pleased, though, to notice a woman's jacket on sale in one of the many nearby boutiques, a quilted jacket whose puffs were very similar to those pyramids.

We walked down the hill to look at Segovia's famous Roman aqueduct, and were pleased to find a fine enlarged copy of the famous she-wolf suckling Romulus and Remus, given Segovia by the city of Rome to celebrate the double millennium of the aqueduct. Does our country ever think of giving little presents like this, I wonder; have we for example given the French anything to commemorate the help they gave us in our quest for independence from England? Don't know. Have to look into this.

We climbed up the other side to have a look at the aqueduct from the top. It's an amazing structure, still able to function, I read, though it hasn't really been used for a century or so. But the wind was blowing, the sun had drifted away, and we were getting hungry. We took refuge at a bar where we could thrust our fingertips under a sort of steam-table containing basins of tapas, and I asked what they were and was told in incomprehensible Spanish, excuse me, Castilian, so I pointed at this and at that and particularly the little roast potatoes and the meatballs, and Lindsey had a glass of good white wine (chilled! Imagine that!) and I had a tinto, because there was no sherry in this bar, we are not yet in the south.

And so we thawed out a bit and stove off hunger with a good-sized plate of tapas. The bill was three Euros twenty. When I expressed surprise the bargirl was concerned; she apparently thought I was complaining about being cheated. She pointed out the wine list prices. Yes, I said, but what about the tapas? Oh, they come gratis with the wine, she said. So we complimented her on her nation's values, which put food at the service of wine, and home we went to contemplate a last Segovia dinner.

Segovia, like all of Leon y Castile, relies on pigs. Roast suckling pig is on every menu; ham is ubiquitous; even the wonderful *sopa de Castilia*, garlic soup with bread and a poached egg, tastes of lard. So we thought we'd go to a Sephardic restaurant we'd noticed, though Lindsey did point out that the menu included *cochinella*, roast suckling pig.

And I started with the Castilian soup, because this one was different: it had quail eggs in it rather than the usual chicken egg. And it was good, though I thought a bit more tripey than I've had elsewhere.

Afterward, though, we went ethnic. Lindsey had couscous, made with chick peas and rice as well as the couscous, and a fine assortment of vegetables, and dressed with fine green olive oil flavored with parsley. And I had *Markla hlua*, chunks of beef braised with orange sections, tiny white figs, raisins, and spices, served with rice with a little saffron. It was not my usual fare, but it was very tasty indeed — I could have been in Venice.

Dessert? Six dates, pitted and filled to overflowing with almond paste moistened with cream and liqueur, and in the middle a scoop of tangerine ice cream, really a gelato, drizzled with raspberry sauce. I ate it up, every bit of it.

Mentioned by Michener
Hotel Pintor el Greco, Toledo, Feb. 17 —

STORKS HAVE GIVEN WAY to partridges, and snows to cobblestones. We saw our first partridge at a gas station ten kilometers out of Toledo, where we'd stopped so I could get out of my jacket — infernally hot here, I thought, not having opened the car door since leaving frozen Segovia. And what's that, I asked Lindsey, a partridge? It's some chickeny kind of bird...

She peered at it through the binoculars and confirmed that it was. Partridges had been on our minds. We have to eat partridge before we leave this country, she said the other day, and I thought to myself Yes: man can not live by suckling pig alone. But we did not expect to see partridges walking around calmly like this.

As we got back on the *autovia* we noticed an enormous partridge farm. Ah, so: this is an escapee. The history of Toledo is a history of sieges and escapes, and this lonely partridge, soon no doubt to be recaptured and prepared for his end (and Lindsey's sustenance), is a trivial but touching testament to this history.

Our hotel, for example, is near the calle del Transito, and near the two surviving synagogues. I step outside and stroll across the street to the bluff from which, according to James Michener, a mob of Christian Toledans, inflamed by an anti-Semitic sermon, threw all the Jews they could find, having dragged them out of synagogue and slit their throats.

I asked about this in the gift shop on the corner. Oh no, señor, there were no Jews murdered in those years, they all either converted or went away. There's something in a book about that, but it isn't true.

Well, is it true, I continued, that during the Civil War, back in the 1930s, there were many executions here? Yes, señor, that is true, there were many many people murdered here.

That was in 1936, when the country was torn between liberals and leftists who wanted a democratic republic, of all things, and conservative and theocratic Loyalists or Nationalists, as they were known, who wanted to continue with the disengaged sort of autocracy that had been Spain's method for the previous century or two.

Toledo, the religious seat of the entire country, was a conservative city. A group of Republicans were brought in from Madrid to change the town's political opinion, and they rounded up as many conservatives as they could easily find, brought them to this same bluff, and shot them, afterward tossing a number of the bodies down on the same rocks.

As you know, the Loyalists ultimately lost. When Franco finally took firm control the situation was reversed, and Toledo took its revenge; anyone whose jacket's right shoulder showed signs of wear was assumed to have been a rifleman for the Loyalists; all such were rounded up, taken to the same place, and given the same treatment. Thousands of rightists murdered by leftists, thousands of leftists murdered by rightists.

When I was a boy, sixty years ago, Spain was an enigma. It was vaguely allied with Germany and Italy, though officially neutral; and it remained isolated from Europe and the United States until fifty years ago, as isolated as Albania, or more recently Libya. Things began to change when the US traded food aid for military bases in the early 1950s; but didn't really change until Franco finally died in 1975. When we first visited Barcelona, for example, in 1976, Catalan was still barely spoken, and the police all carried submachine guns.

Today Toledo looks like any other touristy European city. The museums are full of Japanese tourists and grammar-school students, who troop around with clipboards and dutifully write essays about this El Greco or that. The shops are full of ceramics and needlepoint and swords and leather goods, some of which may be manufactured within a few score miles, for all I know. Menus are in four languages. It is often necessary to speak Spanish, which I do very badly indeed, but that was true in Salamanca and Segovia and even Madrid — Spanish must be a very satisfying language; it seems that few who grow up speaking it as their native language bother to learn any other.

The name "Toledo" has always stood for one of only two things to me: scales, or an El Greco painting. Scales, because so many seemed to have been manufactured, when I was a boy and began noticing such things, in Toledo, Ohio: and perhaps to commemorate that fact there is indeed a Calle Toledo Ohio in this city.

The painting, of course, is the famous *Storm Over Toledo*, which has always led me to believe, foolishly, that Toledo stands on a cone-shaped mountain, occupying most of it, rising above an otherwise bare plain.

Might as well assume all the Apostles had unnaturally long faces and fingers. Toledo does rise above its surroundings, but the hill isn't that simple: we're constantly walking uphill and down. I think the Cathedral, which is big and made of stone, may have

been forming a big dimple in the middle of town, the way the Ant-
arctica ice sheet has depressed that continent unnaturally. (Is the
stone under the ice unnaturally dense, I wonder; and, if so, will it
rebound when the ice melts?) The streets around the cathedral
take implausible angles, often reverse angles, in their urge to lead
either up or down, never flat — contour lines had not been invented when this town was laid out, presumably by the Visigoths.

The streets are also, at least in our quarter, quite narrow — often too narrow for cars, which is a blessing, as you don't like the
things sneaking up on you from behind. And the pavements are invariably cobblestone. All this leads to another effect Michener mentions: the town can be infernally loud. You'll hear someone walking down the street outside your hotel with a drum, for example.
Why should this be? Why would anyone walk around town in this
day and age mindlessly beating a drum? And it's not even particularly good drumming; it has no real beat; there are no flams or
paradiddles, just mindless thumping.

The schoolchildren are quiet enough when they're scribbling
at their clipboards — sweet and intent, in fact; it's a pleasure to see
whole pages being filled with their impressions of the paintings in
front of them. But once out on the street, which provides a wonderful acoustical enhancement, their shouts are competitive, demanding attention. Now and then they don't notice your ear is
scarcely a foot away, and they'll shout right into it, leaving it ringing
for minutes afterward.

It's an aspect of a curious detachment I've noticed between a
number of people here in Toledo and the people around them —
perhaps because they've been doomed to live among a vast number
of tourists, though I don't recall noticing this detachment in Venice.
(Of course there may be no native Venetians at all; the workers
there may all be commuters from the mainland, for all I know.)

Shopkeepers and baristas, for example, when giving you your
change, or a cup of coffee, or whatever knickknack it is you've
bought, rarely set it on your side the counter. They put it down as
if it's intended for their own use, and you reach across the counter,
one elbow raised to keep the damn shoulder-bag from slipping to
the floor, the book you've had tucked into your armpit thereby

loosed to fall in its own turn, you can't lift the cup and saucer because someone else is crowding in, you can't simply slide it toward you because the counter has a cunningly infernal change of level built into it causing an invisible step to interrupt your action, the coffee slips over the lip of the cup, the spoon falls to the floor...

* * *

I mentioned Michener. Lindsey's been reading his *Iberia*, a combined travel-history he published back in the late 1960s, and she handed it to me to read the section on Toledo. What a fascinating book! I'd never read him; I always thought of him vaguely as some kind of political reporter, something like the John Gunther whose *Inside...* series were so prominent among the Book-Of-The-Month© Club selections that turned up now and then on my parents' bookshelves, and which I never read, perhaps because it seemed as if they were something I were supposed to read; or perhaps it was the obligatory © that turned me off.

But Michener, it turns out, is the author I always seem to want to be, combining personal experience with a little real knowledge: except that his experience is so much more interesting than mine, being completely beyond my ever sharing (if only because it took place in a time never to be recaptured, and ever so much more fragrant than my own); and his knowledge so much more extensive.

He tosses off a parenthetical paragraph early on, for example, in which he daydreams about an ideal college education, which would require the student to spend his first and fourth year studying one brief segment of history.

> ...he would immerse himself in the world culture operating at that period in time, and to do so he would study the art forms, the music, the contemporary understanding of geography, the philosophy, the religious convictions, the economics, the travel, the architecture, the writing and the daily life of the peasant. And he would be obliged to explore in depth the half-dozen nations or principalities which best illustrate the significant meanings of the age being studied.

Michener chooses A.D. 70 and the fall of Jerusalem, 1832 and "the passage of reform in Great Britain," some date when Greece and Rome were in confrontation, and another in the Middle Ages "before dissolution of old patterns had begun" as the four periods most fruitful for such study, and they seem pretty good choices to me.

Suppose our present Administration were well grounded, for example, in the period during which Christianity definitively defeated Hellenism; or that of Alfonso the Wise; or even — Michener's own choice — the 1530s, when Francis I, Henry VIII, Carlos V, Martin Luther, Suleiman I, Ivan IV, and Akbar were presiding over France, England, Spain, the Reformation, Turkey, Russia, and India, and the world as we knew it until, say, ten or twenty years ago was being built. (He leaves out China and Japan, which seems a pity.)

Lindsey bought the *Herald Tribune* the other day, and in it we learned that Arthur Miller thought, among other things, that the mass of humanity had no real awareness or understanding of the forces that manipulated their destinies. I doubt that was true in the 1530s, when even the peasants understood both the stakes and the methods involved in the international struggles to impose new patterns on the chaos that had followed the dissolution of the old ones.

It's happening all over again, but it's odd to think of Tony Blair as a Henry VIII, or Jacques Chirac as a Francis I. Mr. Putin may have ambitions to be an Ivan, terrible or otherwise; and for all I know George Bush may think of himself as a Habsburg. That would explain his determination to bankrupt the country with wars and corruption.

Oh well. We had a nice day today; we saw the synagogues, poor things, they started out as mosques, converted to synagogues, then to Christianity, each time apparently losing a little of their beauty along with their principles. One of them was ultimately a barracks for Napoleon's troops, and you know how that ends: target practice on the cornices, peeing in the corners.

We investigated the El Greco Museum, full of fascinating paintings; and the Santo Tomé Church, where his *Burial of the Count of Orgaz* still hangs where he installed it, a marvelous painting. We munched Manchego and a little more ham in our room, and then strolled the town some more: the Museo Santa Cruz, always being reshuffled apparently; the fine cloister at San Juan de los Reyes, whose handsome church is sober and beautiful enough to have hosted the tombs of Ferdinand and Isabella, if only political considerations hadn't taken them instead to Granada. And in a half hour we go out to dinner; and tomorrow we drive to Córdoba, for so many years the real intellectual engine of Iberia, and the site of a splendid garden. And then my mood will improve, and Life will assert itself over death and politics; there will be bacalao and sherry and the good Andalusian life; and we'll spend the weekend with a beautiful granddaughter.

Andalusian weekend
Calle Duende, Seville, Feb. 21 —

A LONG HIATUS in these dispatches, and today I'm afraid we have two of them. You may not feel the need to catch up, but I do.

Castile and La Mancha have given way to Andalusia, but the weather is still cold, cold. It's odd to be so close to Africa while still enjoying the Norwegian air. There are orange trees everywhere, with sour but pretty fruit hanging on every branch, but the air bites.

In fact you enter Andalusia, coming from Toledo, through a fairly high notch in a range of low mountains that define the country pretty definitively. Spain is a nation, but it is not a country; it's a collection of countries. The reports in yesterday's newspapers, for example, on the results of Sunday's nationwide referendum of the European Union and its new constitution, gave the results by province in a way that seemed more meaningful than our division of our own nation into blue states and red states. Galicia, Catalonia, and Andalusia, not to mention the Basque country, have distinct individual cultures that extend, somehow, to political "values."

But while Andalusia is mountainous it is Southern. We spent a night in Córdoba, in a pleasant hotel not far from the principal tourist attractions, the Mezquita and Alcázar, and the night life in the streets seemed easier, more open, more leisurely, than it does in the north. And the Mezquita is clearly an Arabic building, an enormous mosque deceptively concealed behind a plain stone wall, perhaps twenty feet high, that completely surrounds the equivalent of four city blocks.

Inside you come first to the entry garden, a wonderfully symmetrical grove of orange trees designed to calm and ground the urban mind; and then you enter the mosque itself, another grove but this time of evenly spaced stone columns sustaining a seemingly endless succession of perfectly drawn arches, evenly striped red and white. It is rather dark and quite quiet, even when crowded with visitors. It goes on forever, the arches and columns drawing you into a meditative stroll with no particular goal in mind.

I suppose the devout Muslim would have had as his goal the intricate prayer room. A more secular person, me for example, prefers to stroll, admiring the calming effect of the regular rhythms of columns, arches, and interior spaces; and to note the propriety of conversation here, quiet conversation between twos or threes of persons marveling at this place.

During our visit, though, Mass was being celebrated; for in the time of Charles V the Christians celebrated their rout of the tolerant Muslims by tearing the ceiling and roof off a small section of the Mezquita, near the center, and building there a Gothic cathedral. This was set about, Sunday, with signs asking us to respect the spirituality of this odd intrusion, and we did, but we noted the ironic effect of ranks of clerics in their medieval-inspired costumes, speaking of tolerance and humility in a flamboyantly decorated and rather proud cathedral, surrounded by the quiet decorum of the egoless mosque whose architecture, having only a very subtle goal, substitutes calm and meditation for architectural striving and drama. It's a perfect expression of medieval order giving way to the beginning of modernity, and Charles V was right, I think, to shake his head sadly when he saw the then-new cathedral, murmuring "We've ruined it."

The Alcázar garden put me back in spirits, as it has before. It's the outdoors version of the indoors Mezquita, with rows of neatly clipped topiaries, principally enormous cypress columns and mushroom-shaped orange trees, and long narrow pools, and regularly distributed beds. Winter is not perhaps the best time to visit, but the bones show well and the cypress are newly shaved, and the lower light throws defining shadows highlighting this ingeniously arranged series of garden rooms.

Then we drove to Antequera, for no particular reason except that we'd never been there, seventy-five miles or so across plains, then rolling fields, into one of the subcountries into which Andalusia's numerous ranges of hills and mountains assign its agriculturally productive regions. The map sprinkled this area with symbols I took to stand for pine trees, in low mountain forest of some kind, but they turned out to mean olive trees: we were in the heart of olive country.

Antequera lies at the northern foot of the Sierra Nevada, Andalusia's highest range, and has been populated for millennia. There are three "dolmens" on view, for example, one of them really not a dolmen at all but a marvelously constructed, perfectly dome-shaped burial chamber under a mound of earth. These are oriented so as to exit northward and aligned toward a curious and imposing natural feature, a small rock mountain whose profile suggests a human head lying on its back, slowly settling into the flat plain around it. It's impossible not to attach significance to this feature, and among that significance is the sudden realization that Surrealism is based in nature, that Yves Tanguy and Salvador Dali painted versions of landscapes that only slightly heighten bizarre interpretations that are in fact innate in certain geographies.

Next morning, on to Ronda, a town I wanted to visit for its bridge, a stone affair only a hundred feet long at the most but spanning a gorge at least a hundred yards deep. It was truly frightening to look down into this abyss, but looking across was very pleasant indeed, especially from our table at lunch, a long one in an interesting restaurant successfully bringing traditional foods into a modernized presentation — much more successfully than was done by Charles V's architects.

And then on to Seville, the delayed goal of this trip, and a night in Eve's apartment, and next day, yesterday, our transfer to our own. And with that I'll close, lest in describing our present situation I end on too negative a note.

Seville: the river, which is so wide and slow-moving (p. 130)

Internet apartment
Calle Duende, Seville, Feb. 22 —

I'M SURE OUR LANDLADY is a very nice woman. I found her attractive, in fact, immediately, in our telephone conversation yesterday, when we arranged a time to get the keys and the instructions concerning our new *pied-à-terre* in Seville. Her Spanish was measured and forgiving, pitched in a low, melodious voice; and she quickly responded to my own halting and clumsy speech: We can speak Engleesh, if you prefair; I speak Engleesh, but slowly, and in the Engleesh style.

Fine, I said, may we meet at two o'clock? Yais, undair the clock of the ceety hall, my hair ees blonded.

When we got there, five or ten minutes late, we found a young woman with stylishly unkempt blonded hair; with her, a terrier on a leash, who was getting acquainted with another terrier on another leash, held firm by another stylish young woman.

We paraded then down the calle J. Guichot and up the calle Jimios, me wondering all along where our calle Duende might be as it wasn't to be found on any map, and then we came to an abrupt halt in a pile of sand, scaffolding ahead of us, cement mixer to one side, wheelbarrows and hard hats and jackets scattered about.

Our landlady said something to herself in a language I didn't quite catch, and then observed that this was very strange, as everything had been perfectly normal just two or three days ago.

Astonishing, I thought, that so much destruction and so little reconstruction could have taken place in just a few hours of work, for yesterday was Monday, and I was reasonably sure these sturdy, sullen workers had not been laboring over the weekend.

We picked our way past a building that has been completely gutted, whose wall on the calle Duende side has been newly erected, those children's-toy hollow bricks stacked up within the bearing girders. Some, to give the workers credit, had already been stucco'd; part of the stucco had dried and already been painted. But there is clearly a lot of work left to do, and the job's clearly been under way for weeks.

We stepped across hoses and extension cords and steel cables and dodged workers and wheelbarrows and scaffolding and continued down the passageway, for the calle Duende is nothing more, it is not a street, it's a mere passageway and a dead-end one at that, with the door to our building at the very end. On our way we looked apprehensively up at wheelbarrows of freshly mixed stucco being hauled aloft by those steel cables.

Once we climbed the single flight of marble stairs to our apartment things began to look better. Sitting room, kitchen, bedroom, bathroom; television, stereo setup, twenty-five biographies in Spanish ranging from Alexander the Great to Salvador Dalí. Air conditioner: we will hardly want that. The apartment is freezing, but will soon warm up, we're told.

Washing machine, microwave, twoburner range, toaster, electric whipper thing.

We gave the stylish young woman our money and she left, taking her terrier with her. Then we discovered there was no hot water. I found a switch, finally, that apparently would turn on the water heater. Then we discovered that the toilet had an alarming desire to fall over on its side, like a spavined horse.

Well, "Duende," of course, is what all flamenco artists have to have if they are to portray their sense of the tragic with any authenticity. We might have seen this coming.

It's all right. We intend to use the place only for sleeping and resting our tired feet. Seville, like every other town that seems to call us on this continent, is paved with cobblestones for the most part, at least the most part we're interested in. The streets are narrow indeed, fewer than half wide enough for even a small car to negotiate. On those streets that do have automobile traffic there may be a sidewalk, but it's likely to be too narrow to walk on comfortably; two abreast is impossible, and if someone comes your way one of you must step into the street, avoiding those steel bollards that only come up to mid-calf height.

We are near the Plaza Nuevo, a fine rectangular plaza behind the Ayuntamiento or City Hall, very near the fashionable shopping streets Tetuán and Sierpes, and not far from the Cathedral and Alcázar. We've spent our first twenty-four hours walking, eating, drinking, sleeping, walking. I like eating in Seville: we generally avoid restaurants, taking breakfast in a bar, lunch at a sidewalk tapas joint when we can find one in the sun, then tapas again later if we feel like it.

Yesterday, for example, we went with Eve for tapas at Los Coloniales, where we must have shared nearly a dozen plates of things — potatoes, peppers, pork, quail eggs, fried zucchini, spinach croquettes, ham, several small glasses of sherry and so on, for about thirty dollars. Breakfast is our usual: coffee with hot milk, toast with butter or jam. In the neighborhood bars this costs about five dollars for the two of us, and I have a second coffee.

We were last here in November, a year or two ago. February is a different season. There are plenty of oranges on the trees, as noted a day or two ago, but the deciduous trees are bare, the banana trees severely frostbitten, the roses mere sticks. In a month things will be different; in two it will be glorious. I would not recommend Seville between November and March, but we're here for museums and bars and the Cathedral, and the promise this weekend of rainstorms doesn't particularly bother us.

Today we were advised to visit the Casa de Pilatos, which some eccentric built in the early 16th century on the supposed plans of Pontius Pilate's house in Jerusalem. It is home to one of Spain's noblest nobles, and their are no nobles nobler than the Spanish; and the rooms and gardens that were opened to the public — upstairs by guided tour only — revealed a fine sense of spatial taste, with a series of rooms looking in on one another and out onto one or another garden, all set about with that geometrical sense of order, clarity, and calm that seems so Spanish, yet so unlike the violence, surprise, and immediacy that form an equal component of the Spanish temperament.

(Maria Rosa Menocal's fascinating, occasionally maddening account of Spanish history from Muslim times to the Inquisition, *Ornament of the World,* takes as its given the idea that no man or nation is worth much that can't hold two opposing concepts simultaneously. This idea comes to one's mind repeatedly here in Spain, and counters nicely an article in yesterday's Herald Tribune, describing the great care the European Union has taken to allow only six heads of state to speak to President Bush during his visit here, and each of them to discuss one topic only.)

We were advised to visit Pilate's House today, because Tuesday is the day it's open free of charge. But of course this is true only for citizens of Europe. We often find this to be the case: an American passport (but for that matter also one from China or Norway or Zimbabwe) rules you out of this cultural largesse. And, of course, since the house was free to so many, it was very crowded, primarily with Spaniards.

So I stood on the edge of the crowd as it moved from room to room, looking out over a sea of dark-haired heads — little blonding here! — all at about the same height from the floor, say five feet six, looking rather like a flock of dark sheep, with an occasional Dutchman or German or American sticking up like a skyscraper. They say Spaniards of a certain age are all short because they were starved during their childhood, during the terrible Civil War era: but I notice that even the youngsters crowding the bars, or walking quickly by twos and threes, jabbering into their cell phones, are considerably shorter than those I'm accustomed to.

Admirable as the Casa de Pilatos is, not to mention the fine paintings, tapestries, and furnishings in its rooms, it was the gardens, and the way they related to the building itself, that impressed us the most. A number of ground-floor rooms have large open unglazed windows looking out onto courtyards and gardens, and as you stroll these rooms and gardens things keep changing configuration, just as life keeps changing as you make your way along. Fountains, doves, the voices of children, murmured conversations in corners reveal the astounding silence that contains them: you can't believe you're just off a narrow cobblestone street winding between hard-surfaced stucco threestorey buildings.

* * *

I called this dispatch "Internet Apartment," but that doesn't mean we have any internet connection here. Our first day, in fact, was partly devoted to finding a way of connecting. One after another promising lead failed to pan out: Oh no, the boss doesn't let people connect their laptops. Sorry, the computer's down today. Oh no, I'm afraid that place has gone out of business. No, the café's closed on Mondays, and only open otherwise from four in the afternoon until eleven.

Finally I went down to the place I used a couple of years ago, whose only disadvantage is that it's a bit of a distance away, though a pleasant enough walk, and close to a couple of bars I like, Modesto and El Toboso. So here we are back in touch again. Tomorrow, with any luck, I'll let you know about Seville's Museo de Bellas Artes, which I've wanted to see for years. In the meantime, I think I'll see if that water has heated up yet.

Getting bearings
Calle Duende, Seville, Feb. 23 —

PERHAPS BECAUSE I grew up in the country, where I was allowed to ramble a bit on my own, and it was useful to know at any moment what direction home lay, I'm never really content unless I know which way is north. And I've always thought of myself as having a pretty good sense of direction, so when it fails I get unhappy. Downright anxious at times, Lindsey would say. And the fact is the fine instrument is losing its edge, and increasingly I find myself disoriented, especially in the city where the direction of shadows isn't always handy, or at noon, or in latitudes more extreme than I'm used to, or in foggy weather.

Seville is particularly cruel, because many of the maps, and all the maps we find ourselves using much of the time, are wrongly oriented. Well, not really: in fact they're properly oriented, for they put east at the top, as was the convention for many centuries. But the convention changed long ago, and I'm used to north being at the top, and the result is that on our first visit here a couple of years ago I got used to the idea of a sideways Seville, the old city on the wrong side of the river, the river flowing in the wrong direction, everything all bollocksed up.

So I've written EAST prominently in the top margins of the maps, and as we walk through town I try to remember to tell myself what direction we're headed. It doesn't help that there are almost no parallel streets in this part of town, or that the river forms a sort of diagonal, or that few streets continue in a straight line any longer than necessary.

This contrasts with certain elements of the Spanish temperament. One of you wrote recently that you like the Spaniards for being "tough, not in a bad way, but they are very direct which I... found refreshing after Paris, certainly."

Well, yes. Yesterday I got lost for the first time: I was on an important mission, to buy tickets to a flamenco concert, and I was so intent on getting to the box office quickly that I took one wrong turn after another, and finally had to resort to stepping into a shop: *Habla inglés? No.* Um, well, okay, (continuing in bad Spanish) do you know Ximenez de Enciso street?

She was gorgeous, elegantly coifed, expensively dressed, and her two friends were equal to her, and they all looked at me with a certain amount of disdain. Then she answered, her monosyllable beautifully modulated, rising patiently: *sí...*

Silence: and then I had to ask: *donde está*; where is it? She floated toward the front door of the shop, stood in the doorway, and indicated a street with her chin: Take that street, the next right, and continue straight on.

I thanked her and shambled my way out of the shop, feeling myself grow smaller and smaller as I walked away from them.

* * *

I've been reading, among other things, a fascinating little book by Eugenio d'Ors, *Tres horas en el Museo del Prado*, written nearly ninety years ago and never out of print in this country. The premise is of course both stupid and brilliant — you have to be able to keep two conflicting ideas in mind simultaneously. The book is written as an engaging conversation with an ideal newcomer to the Prado, "young, intelligent; with an instinctive good taste and not confused by too much art doctrine."

D'Ors chats enthusiastically about the pictures in the Prado, taking as his point of departure an idea he attributes to the sculptor Adolf Hildebrand, who, when studying "the problem of form" in art, decided that form always embraced two values: one architectural, the other functional — terms for which d'Ors substitutes "spatial" and "expressive." Another kind of orientation. And d'Ors decides that painting occupies the central position among the arts, because it is uniquely balanced midway between the two values: architecture clearly crowds the spatial extreme; music the expressive.

D'Ors then strolls the Prado, finding Mantegna excelling at the spatial end, El Greco and Goya at the expressive, Velasquez brilliantly balancing the center. It's a nice kind of thread to string through these galleries, offering a third, objective reference point to triangulate the usual direct picture-to-viewer statement. It's only one way to do this, of course, but it's clear and coherent and often gives d'Ors a chance to make a brilliant observation, as when a painting of Claude Lorrain's recalls to him Baudelaire's memorable lines:

> *Tout n'est qu'ordre et beauté,*
> *luxe, calme, et volupté...*

(Nothing but order, beauty, light, calm, voluptuousness...)

I tried carrying d'Ors along with me today in Seville's Museum of Fine Arts, a rambling old structure climbing stairs and turning corners around three or four courtyards, with a decommissioned church in the middle to house an absorbing series of religious paintings by Murillo. The museum is heavy on the Seville school, whose stars are Murillo and Zurbarán, but it begins with a marvelous collection of 15th-century paintings and sculpture, on religious themes of course, whose depictions amount to almost photorealist portraiture.

What's disarming about this realism is that while the subjects are clearly representing one kind of religious emotion or another — maternal love, innocent childhood, the agony of martyrdom, the torture of self-discipline — and while the faces involved are so individuated you could pick them out if their models were to pass you by on the street, still the expressivity of this work transcends mere emotion of the moment. Perhaps because this work was done before the Reformation, it is content to portray a more or less factual account of its subject-matter: there's no propaganda here, no insisting that its own point of view is the only permissible point of view.

As the commissioners of these paintings grew richer, more powerful, and more competitive with one another — and fewer and fewer, intermarrying as utility companies do these days — and as the perceived need grew to correct Protestant error and remind the faithful of their obligations, painting grew bigger, bolder, more "dramatic." There's no Baroque like Spanish Baroque. Further north of course the extremes of this "expressive" style, centuries apart, are El Greco and Goya; here the extremes are reached by lesser painters.

Here the extremes of the Baroque are not so much in the paintings as in the subjects painted, culminating in an amazing series of huge canvases depicting great florid blustery absurd baroque carts, carved into fancy scrollwork, glistening in white and gold, and carrying dozens of ladies in billowing drapery, squeaking along, I'm sure, on their great wooden wheels over the cobbled Seville streets, drawn by teams of eight or ten horses each. The cost of these things must have been incalculable, and the resentment of the poor, on seeing them, must have been bitter indeed. Voluptuousness of a certain kind, I suppose, but precious little calm or order, and to my eye not much beauty either.

I can't tell you where this Seville school wound up, because the last three rooms of the museum were, maddeningly, closed for reinstallation. The entire city is undergoing reinstallation, it seems. I've already complained about the hotel being built down our street, if you can call it a street; there's cement dust everywhere. You can hardly find a street outside of the very center that doesn't have some piles of sand and sacks of cement and buckets clittering up and clattering down, as Joyce says somewhere.

The big squares in front of both the City Hall and the Cathedral are fenced off with that ugly plastic meshlike stuff everyone uses these days, apparently for the installation of the grandstands that will be needed in a couple of weeks during Semana Santa, when religious floats — the inheritors of those mad Baroque cars — fill the streets, attracting penitents, priests, and gawkers by the thousand.

But the contrasts then take hold. You turn a corner and find a street whose houses could be a stage-set for Rossini's opera about the Barber of this town. Around another corner a stone church hunkers down stolidly as it has for eight hundred years. Above it all the Giralda watches the sky, recalling the Moorish kingdom that was here half a millennium before Peruvian gold was even dreamed of.

We walked up to Eve's quarter a little after nine: the streets were crowded; in the plazas men and women, young and old, prosperous and poor, stood at the little tables outside the bars, drinking their beers and sherries and conversing animatedly. An hour later, as we walked home, the streets were absolutely silent; everything shuttered tight. The city seems to follow unstated rules and hours, no matter its unpredictable and evasive orientation.

Networking
Calle Duende, Seville, Feb. 24 —

DON'T YOU THINK LIFE has more purpose, a greater sense of validity, when each day has some little goal to be met, some challenge to be overcome? I think so too. I've already noted some of the challenges of our apartment — in case you've forgotten, here's the letter I just wrote to the rental agency:

> I would like to tell you how we find conditions in our apartment on the calle Duende.
> The apartment itself is very nice but there are a few problems. The toilet is not attached to the bathroom floor and it is often in danger of falling over on its side. This is very uncomfortable.
> The electricity goes out if we are trying to use both the toaster and the microwave. This makes breakfast difficult.
> There is not enough hot water to make a bath, so we have to heat water in a pan on the stove in the kitchen.

If these things were taken care of the apartment would be very nice. BUT.

The building next door is under complete renovation. All day long we hear the noise of the workers, tractors, air hammers, and the like. Also the air is full of cement dust. We must keep the windows closed all the time.

When we walk down the Duende to arrive or leave the apartment we must step through piles of broken tiles and concrete. We must also be careful to avoid being hit by falling wet stucco as it is being put on overhead.

The situation is so bad that we have decided to go away for the weekend, from Saturday until late Monday.

Yours,

I went out a couple of hours ago to find the rubble piled up higher than usual, and more cement dust than usual swirling around the passageway and into the open kitchen door of the little restaurant across the Duende. I also found two cops, one looking a little mystified, the other a little upset. I asked him if he spoke English, and when he said he didn't I told him that I'd rented an *apartado* here, that *esto es todo muy mal*, very bad for one's health. He agreed, with a serious look on his face, and stepped into the building that's being renovated to have a talk with someone.

When I came back from my errand things looked better, but that doesn't mean much, because by then the work had stopped for the night. We'll see how things look tomorrow. It's a good thing it's cold weather, because we can't open the windows here; the rooms would be entirely filled with dust.

I'd gone out to see about renting a car for the weekend so we can get out of town. We're seeing a flamenco show Saturday night in Jerez, and another on Monday night. Jerez is a short drive away, and we could simply return home both nights — but Eve has the weekend off: why not do a little more touring?

And that brings me to the heart of the matter of goals and purpose: finding a place to do some internet research into hotels and the like. The internet has revolutionized all this, as you know. For one thing, there are at least two excellent websites offering highway advice, mappy.com and viamichelin.com. Of the two I marginally prefer mappy, which is very fast. You can get distance and driving time between any two points in Europe, with toll estimates if you're driving toll highways; and you can also get maps showing just where your hotel is.

Well. In order to browse the internet, not to mention get your e-mail (and load up the inboxes of your friends and acquaintances with material like this), you have to be on line. There is no phone in our apartment, other than the one in my pocket, so my usual Earthlink dial-up connection won't work. Each day therefore has involved a trek to one internet point or another, and I've already told you about that; some are open, some aren't. I've found only two reliable ones, Internetia on a big street to the southeast of here, say ten minutes' walk away, where I can attach my laptop with a cable; and the Plaza Café, not quite so far away in the other direction, where from four pm to one am I can go online wirelessly (but not on Monday). Plaza is free; Internetia costs about two euros an hour.

Today for the first time I tried Plaza, and was annoyed by the music though not by the obligation to have a fino while getting my e-mail. I forgot to turn off my wireless thingy when we left, and when I opened the laptop back here in the apartment... guess what? I'm online. I have no idea why. There's a wireless network in the area called "3Com," and I'm on it, a free rider. After all those treks.

We spent the morning working the flea market, the Thursday market along the calle Feria. This is a pretty dispiriting affair, with scores, maybe hundreds of people, mostly men, standing or sitting behind an array of stuff, or junk, or detritus, or things, often laid out on an old sheet or something of the sort, or occasionally set out on an improvised table of some kind.

There's the stuff you expect to see just about anywhere — telephones, tape cassettes, cheap auto tools, kitchen equipment and other household items of dubious functionality. One guy had a quite impressive line of what looked like brand new automobile tires. Most of the stalls, though, contained assorted junk. A lot of it would interest interior decorators, I'm sure: old doorknobs, drapery hardware, tiles from the entries of demolished buildings, assorted lamps and sconces.

There were shoes both new and used, jackets ditto, tired flamenco dresses outworn or outgrown or simply abandoned. There were old photographs and postcards. One stall had a number of old handwritten papers of various kinds, and I was struck once again, for perhaps the hundredth time, how much more elegant handwriting was fifty years ago, a century ago, four hundred years ago, than it is today. Technology brings us better pens: fountain pens, ballpoints, felt pens; it does not improve our handwriting.

At the end we debauched into a few blocks of very ordinary stores — work clothes, hardware, small groceries. There was a covered market, with several produce stands featuring pretty attractive fruits and vegetables, a small fish market with eight or ten stalls, a meat section. Then another block of work shirts and underwear and shoes and socks, and then, surprise, a right turn, another block, and the Basilica Macarena, behind the principle gate to the city from the north.

Here there is a particularly affecting Virgin on the altar, with human hair and diamond tears; and here in the museum is an enormous gold-leafed float, big enough to carry a dozen life-size polychrome statues, intensely lifelike: a Roman centurion, a couple of assorted petty criminals, lawyers, witnesses — and, during the fourteen hours this float is carried through the streets of Seville, during Holy Week, the life-size statue of Christ being sentenced, that now occupies a secondary place in the church. Secondary, because here in Seville — and in much of Spain, I think — it is not the Redeemer on whom religious practice centers, but on His Mother, the Holy Virgin.

The float, the museum attendant told me, weighs *dos milles kilos*, two tons; and it requires forty strong men to carry it — all of them hidden beneath the float's voluminous red skirts; all of them with pads on their napes and shoulders, and lifting and carrying the thing on signals rapped out on the pavement by a supervisor with a stout jangling staff. Fourteen hours they carry this, unable to see where they're going or where they've been, and able to set it down only now and then, when the procession is held up by some unseen event, or has to negotiate a particularly tight corner.

The float is not that old — no more than eighty years, I think I recall. It's made of wood, with detailed realistic carving all over, all of it representing passages from one Testament or the other, lovingly carved and gilded; and on it ride the lifesize carved polychromed statues, perhaps a dozen of them.

Upstairs there's another float, this one demountable so it can be taken downstairs, reassembled, and carried in its turn out the wide double doors into the street and down toward the Cathedral. This one is a forest of silvered columns, elegantly turned, slender yet enduring; for it will carry the Virgin. And in display cases around the float are immense embroidered capes the Virgin has worn in parades past, each more sumptuous and costly than the preceding. The amount of money, time, and dedication here is beyond comprehension.

We looked at all this, and looked at one another, and walked out into the sunlight, unmoved. I was baptized myself, nearly sixty years ago, so am technically a Christian: but nothing in any of this speaks to me, moves me. The guidebook suggested I look about me, seated before the Virgin on that altar, to see how many of my neighbors would be wiping tears of their own away: and in fact it was true, and they weren't all women or impressionable youth, either. But my eyes were dry, and not only dry, but fatigued. It is all more than I can comprehend. There's a curious kind of foreignness to it; it's as if I were studying the life-systems of a different species.

Quiet time
Calle Duende, Seville, Feb. 25 —

ACROSS THE RIVER, then, finally, this morning, to take a walk recommended by one of the guidebooks in the Seville quarter known as the Triana. Seville, the old city, grew up as an inland seaport on the broad Guadalquivir river, and though the river silted up so badly centuries ago that all port activities had to be moved downstream — to Seville's regret, for gold and silver were still coming in from the Americas in those days — the river still makes an imposing presence here.

In the last century, for example, there were two world's fairs held here, an ill-fated one in 1929 that saw some splendid national pavilions built, now being used as government offices, and a more successful one in 1992, whose pavilions are being used as private corporate headquarters for the most part, though some have been transformed into various tourist venues.

But it was not this Magic Isle, as the '92 fairgrounds is called, but to the older Triana that we wanted to explore. Here is Seville's oldest still-consecrated church, Santa Ana; and here is the center of Seville's still-thriving ceramics industry, responsible for the tiles you see in almost every doorway, and the plain or fanciful finials gleaming in their luster glazes on the corners of so many rooftops.

After crossing the river, which is so wide and slow-moving as to be almost an endless lake, we strolled its banks for a half-mile or so, walking on tamped granite clay, enjoying the fresh air, playing a few minutes with a blackbird who cheerfully improved upon whatever I whistled to him. On the river there were a number of racing shells, most of them for solo oarsmen and -women, and an occasional tourboat churned by, its upper deck crowded with visitors whose heads all turned in unison this way and that as a voice, unheard by us, pointed out one sight or another.

We browsed the ceramics shops, of course, and found much we liked. But nicely glazed fountains are hard to carry on the airplane, and it seems more logical, if we're going to buy such things, to buy them in Mexico. I contented myself with an interesting piece of tile I found in a dumpster. This wasn't hard: Triana, like Seville the other side the river, is undergoing an incredible amount of renovation.

I asked a woman in a ceramics shop why. She was glazing a border tile, and I asked how many more she had to do: *Muchos, muchos*, she said, handing the one she'd just finished to her husband, who tossed it rather casually I thought onto a stack while she reached for the next. It's a job for a building being reconstructed, she went on. Times are good; lots of people want apartments or homes or shops in Seville, and everything that's built or rebuilt or restored is done in the traditional manner.

The activity, as I've mentioned earlier, is intense. You walk past 18th-century façades of threestorey buildings and suddenly realize that's all they are, façades, braced from the front or behind, waiting for an entirely new building to take place behind them. And large plot or small, there's likely to be amazingly deep excavation going on behind. We looked down into a hole bigger than the cathedral yesterday — I'm skipping: it was in Jerez de la Frontera, not Seville — where there will be an underground parking lot of immense proportions.

The underground parking is everywhere, under many of the plazas. This is fine: you no longer see jumbles of autos parked in plazas, as you so often do in France and Italy — unless in the last year or two the same kind of thing is going on in those countries. Perhaps it's a European Union mandate; or perhaps it's subsidized by Komatsu, who seems to make all the enormous earth-moving apparatus we see everywhere.

Metros, too. They're building one in Seville, beginning apparently with the stations; one's going in right outside the venerable Alfonso Hotel at the Puerta de Jerez. I don't know how they can do this without running into classical antiquity, and indeed there's a huge dig across the avenue from the Plaza Encarnacion where what must originally have been commercial development has been transformed into archaeology.

I read the other day that the mayor of Venice, of all places, wants a subway of his own, at least to unite the airport with the old city. Because of the danger of subterranean vibration to the ancient city, built as it is on pilings in mud, the proposal is to put the Venice terminal a little offshore; perhaps people would get there by boat — in which case why not simply continue taking the boat to the airport, as is done now? The mayor says the subway will reverse Venice's alarming loss of population, down from 250,000 to sixty thousand since World War II: but wouldn't a subway simply enhance continued commuting, by workers, from the mainland? But this is Venetian business, and I'm in Spain.

* * *

Speaking of rebuilding and the like, Lindsey wants me to assure you that in fact our apartment is not a dump. The toilet is loose; the hot water is scarce; the circuit-breaker blows readily: but these are minor matters. How much time do you really spend with the toilet, after all, or with hot water, compared to the amount of time you sit on a comfortable couch in a nicely decorated room, reading Michener or d'Ors? Not very much.

During the day the place is nicely lit, indirectly, by the sun. I make the breakfast we like very easily in our little kitchenette. The bed isn't all that bad, and the apartment is beautifully situated, two minutes from the Plaza Nueva and the Ayuntamiento, five from the Cathedral. So don't get the idea we're in a dump. I guess this means: don't take my complaints too seriously.

And speaking of the Cathedral, it was very interesting to contrast Santa Ana with the Cathedral today. I think of all the cathedrals I've seen this one in Seville is by far my favorite. (Of course I may be wrong here, because I don't really recall St. Stephen's in Vienna well enough. That has to be revisited.) Seville's cathedral is, first of all, huge: someone famously reported that you could lose Notre Dame in it. The legend is that when it was built, six hundred years ago, the planners said "let's build a cathedral so huge everyone will say we're completely insane." The ceiling, at the transept, is something like 150 feet high. The columns are nine feet on a side, and they are roughly square in cross-section, but so cunningly carved and fluted that they seem round.

Today as on most winter days it was sparsely populated. A few groups were being herded by their tourguides, in German, or Japanese, or Spanish, or English. Adolescent girls stood around talking on their cell phones, which get good reception in this huge stone building. Americans clustered around the tomb of Cristobal Colombo, as he is called here — I always think of him, from the old jazz tune, as Mister Christopher Columbus, [who] sailed the sea without a compass.

The Sevillians were crueler than the Córdobans, who simply tore a few columns out of the Mezquita to install their Renaissance cathedral inside a pre-existing Muslim mosque. In Seville they completely destroyed the mosque that was there. I don't know if there are any drawings of the mosque as it was: I'd like to see them if there are. At least they had the good sense to leave the orange-grove in place, and appropriately on the south side of the cathedral. What a wonderful thing these groves are! Symmetrical, calming, a home for birds, easily cared for, and a reminder of Nature in an environment that is otherwise nothing but stone, stone, stone.

Santa Ana, on the other hand, is a comfortable size, a neighborhood church. It's proudly cared for: we got there a minute or two after closing, and at least a half dozen women and one or two men were already at work mopping the floors and dusting. I asked a woman how old the place was: Oh, señor, very, very old, the oldest in the city, much older than the Cathedral. And indeed it is; Columbus very likely worshipped here, or stepped in at least. One of the main streets in this part of Triana is named for Rodrigo, his watchman, who was the first European to catch sight of the New World, at least on that particular day in 1492.

* * *

Tomorrow we go to the country for the weekend, so today we make arrangements. I don't know what happened to the Sheres who used never to make reservations: these days we seem always to be booking hotels in advance. With age comes uncertainty. I thought I'd found a Jerez hotel on the Internet, the Torres, but though I booked a room (or thought I did) they never confirmed, so it's back to the tourist office to find another.

The boy behind the counter remembered me from a previous visit: it's always a good idea to make an impression. I told him our predicament, and he suggested that since his boss was away he could call for us, though he's not supposed to. He did: no answer. He booked a room at another hotel, and gave me a list of car rental offices around the corner.

So tomorrow it's off to Arcos de la Frontera and Jerez, and then down to Tarifa for an attempted sighting of Africa, and then on to Cádiz. Rain is predicted there, but it could be worse: they're actually suggesting possible snow in Seville!

Tip of Europe

Hotel la Mirada, Tarifa, Feb. 27 —

ACROSS A FEW MILES of dull greygreen water, under heavy fog that alternated in fact with pretty stiff rainstorms, we could see the Rif Mountains of North Africa. Tarifa. It's a place I've always wanted to see, one of the key geographical sites — the southernmost town on mainland Europe. It's not the southernmost town in Spain: there are two towns across the Straits, odd enclaves on the African continent, and one day I'll visit them too, but they'll have to wait.

We drove here this morning from Jerez, where we'd spent the night after seeing Israel Galván dance in the Feria de Jerez. Galván is one of the bright young Turks, in the old-fashioned expression, on the flamenco scene, bringing his thorough knowledge of the traditional forms and his consummate mastery and discipline with his own body to an art of his own, not always appreciated by flamenco connoisseurs. And I have to admit I don't get it at all myself, partly because I know nothing about flamenco.

For one thing, flamenco is a dance which connects feet to earth. Every other dance form I know of attempts the opposite, works at minimizing the fatal pull of the earth on our weak and fragile bodies. Flamenco does not merely stamp the feet, though it certainly does do that; it roots the body through the feet, through the floor, into the earth, much as the flamenco singer denies the conventional artifice of "beautiful tone" and opts instead for what is often a hoarse, nasal, complex sound whose pitch, even, cannot be precisely identified — though it always seems to respect pitch, as the anticipations and delays in a fine performance of a Chopin piano piece always respects the beat, though the notes may rarely actually fall on it.

Galván's performance brought Merce Cunningham to mind, though Galván's a relatively young man, near the beginning of the important, perhaps even historical part of his career. He has the same mastery over tiny parts of his body as well as his entire body. He can pivot and turn faster than seems possible and then come to a dead stop, each fingertip placed dramatically, extending the frozen lines of motion that seem to connect the center of his body to every corner of the hall, every riveted eye in the audience, in a web of invisible lines of force.

Well. We saw his performance, which lasted an hour or so, and then stopped in a nearby bar for some tapas — olives and capers, cheese and tuna, fino and then, as a treat on a Saturday night, a glass of *anís*, that wonderful Spanish anise-flavored liqueur, a cross between Chartreuse and *pastis*, neither of which is an unpleasant thing in itself.

Toward the end of the glass a beggar came through the café. (We were standing at a table outside on the sidewalk, along with dozens of others.) He came directly to me and spoke immediately in an odd German-flavored English, asking for money to buy food. My first instinct was to brush him off. I give money routinely to musicians on the street, and occasionally to begging women; I even give money to the guy at the entrance to Trader Joe's parking lot. But beggars who move through restaurants and bars annoy me.

Of course I immediately saw the reason for this: a certain shame or, short of shame, embarrassment at my good fortune in having coins in my pocket and a glass of *anís* in my hand, when this poor fellow had virtually nothing at the moment, and the prospect of even less tomorrow. So I fished out a euro for him and he went on his way to the next table with hardly a thank-you.

At one point he went into the bar, approaching a couple of tables, but soon enough he was shooed out, and stood disconsolately on the outskirts of our terrace. Then he moved in again, and then I lost track of him. But before long Eve nudged me and indicated him with a nod: he was standing out on the sidewalk, and he was being lectured by a guy who'd been eating two or three tables away from us, accompanied by a couple of women.

The man spoke to him sternly but with no trace of anger or even irritation. He was younger than the beggar, considerably so, but he spoke to him like a father to an errant son. That was striking enough, but even more so was the beggar's attitude. He stood quietly, listening attentively, not returning his lecturer's gaze, looking down at the pavement instead, but neither defensive nor evasive. He listened politely, with only very rare vocal responses; and after what seemed four or five minutes the conversation was over, the young man moved back to his companions, and the beggar disappeared down the street.

I've looked at so many paintings of biblical scenes lately, at so many conversations among saints and sinners, that moments like this one, living moments revealing the reality of the lives of strangers, take on a painterly kind of drama — and of course the nocturnal light enhanced this, throwing the distance into an unseen but somehow nestling background, the bright light spilling out of the café picking out the two faces, especially the whites of the eyes.

There'd been another such moment earlier in the day, though it involved no seen persons. We'd overshot a turn into the day's first goal, the hilltop "white town" of Arcos de la Frontera, and we found ourselves on the top of a hill, looking back at the town over a valley a mile wide or so, fertile and carefully farmed, quite lower than either we were or Arcos was.

We'd pulled off the road to turn around to go back, having found a dirt road that led very quickly to an abandoned, half-destroyed building. The view was so beautiful I turned off the engine to get out to take some photos. The place was littered with detritus — broken glass, rusting cans, broken tiles. The building was interesting, and we poked our heads into the rooms, standing open without doors or windows, and I climbed up the external staircase to the roof, which probably had originally been the floor of a second storey.

I don't know what the building was originally meant for. There was a row of bowls cast in concrete in one room, and I thought perhaps they'd been intended for successive treatments in the curing of olives. What was equally interesting was the question of how the building had come to its present condition. It looked as if it had been shelled. Perhaps it was a victim of the Civil War: it could well have been that old. I'll never know, of course.

Places like that always make me feel a little sad. It was undoubtedly built in a spirit of optimism: a place better than its builder had known before, a place where he would work and live, a place he would pass on to his children — and here it was, destroyed, beyond salvage, and its builder and other occupants gone and forgotten and unknown. Buildings like this function in their landscapes as skulls do in those "vanitas" still-lifes: they reveal the transitory nature of the things we cherish and depend upon.

Tarifa is a completely different thing. We took the coast road here, though it doesn't really follow the coast. From the compellingly rolling hills around Arcos we'd descended to the immense flat delta on whose margin Jerez and, indeed, Seville are built; and today we continued along the eastern edge of that delta, but soon the road struck out east and south and into foothills again. The country reminded me often of the California coast, especially the San Mateo county coast; and when we finally drove into Tarifa Eve said Ah, Santa Cruz, and I thought to myself Ah, Pismo Beach.

Tarifa is in fact a windsurfing capital, but today's weather, miserable much of the time, discouraged all but the hardiest. There was one stalwart fellow on his sail plank in the Mediterranean, and fifty yards to his west a row of a dozen or so men (and one or two women) on their surfboards in the Atlantic. Tarifa stands on the point demarcating the two, on the north shore of the Straits of Gibraltar. (Gibraltar itself is far enough away, to the north and east, as to be invisible from here.)

We walked through rain squalls from our hotel, two or three blocks from the old city wall, into the old city, looking for something to eat, and spent a couple of hours in the one restaurant that seemed to be open. There's a sizable Italian community here, we were told, and we had the kind of meal we are used to, and have missed these last few weeks — a bowl of chicken noodle soup to start, a green salad, and a plate of spaghetti with tomato sauce, washed down with a bottle of cheap red wine.

The place was full. Old people, young people, a couple of babies, a few other tourists. The service was uneven, and the poor girl whose job seemed to be chiefly clearing away plates no longer needed was lectured a couple of times, once so severely she turned her back on the room, resting her hands on the bar. Look, Eve said, she's crying. And she was, and she avoided showing her face to the

dining room for quite a while, and then when she did it was clearly
a bit swollen.

It had stopped raining by the time dinner was over, and we
walked down to the beach, where we saw the surfers, and then we
walked out across the mole to the Isla de Palomas, inaccessible once
you're there because apparently dedicated to some kind of military
or law-enforcement purpose. The place reminded me a bit of Biar-
ritz, though much less tony; or of places along the southern Dutch
coast, or the west shore of Danish Jutland. There are concrete bun-
kers half-buried in the dunes, and the shell of an improbable castle,
small but arrogant in its symmetry, trying to decide whether it's
Gothic or Victorian. Like that building outside Arcos it was empty,
probably abandoned; but it had not been shelled.

Before turning in for the night I went out to get a bottle of water. The hotel's dining-room and bar are closed today for the
weekly *descanso* or day of rest, which inevitably falls, in these small
hotels, on the one day we choose to book, but there was a nearby
bar. There I had a small *anís* and watched the local scene. A
shaky-looking guy, clearly a local, had a second glass of Spanish
gin, a tumblerfull to which he added a bit of inexpensive white
wine that arrived in a small screwtop bottle.

Two girls sat at the bar smoking and talking, often laughing at
something, drinking soft drinks and nibbling at tapas. A couple of
families were eating at tables at the back of the room. Then an
interesting-looking man came in, wearing an old zipper jacket and
a red baseball cap. The bartender handed him a bottle of beer and
a glass, without having been asked, and then a dish of olives, and
the fellow silently and seriously addressed this meal.

Before long another group of four or five people came in, men
and women, clearly all together; but as they went to a table at the
back of the room one man stopped to greet the man in the red cap.
This man was about the same age, early thirties or so, and similarly
dressed, but wore no cap; his head was shaved as close as his beard;
his high round forehead gleamed; his face was unusually flat, and
his wire-rimmed glasses gave him a serious but poetical air: he reminded me of photos of Jaime Sabartès, the poet who was Picasso's
friend and secretary for many years.

This man went right up to the other, who swiveled around on his stool, and they began an intense, serious, but clearly very friendly conversation. Their hands rested on one another's shoulders in a gesture that was confidential, affectionate, yet serious, and it seemed as if their conversation was resuming from one that had broken off, the day before, or a week before, or years. It was as if they'd been reunited after a separation unforeseen, unavoidable, dramatic perhaps, but accepted as one of those things that happens in this life.

I finished my *anís*, ordered my liter of water, paid my euro and a half, and went back to the hotel.

The Barber of Seville
Calle Duende, Seville, March 1 —

AWAKENED BY THE LILTING sound of Andalusian jackhammers we got regretfully out of bed at nine. I had an appointment, made last Friday, with a highly recommended razor artist in Triana.

The recommendation came from the acquaintance of a good friend, a fellow (the acquaintance, not the friend) who plays guitar, loves flamenco, and knows Seville. We've followed a few other recommendations of his, concerning restaurants, with mixed results. One or two of his descriptions were right on the mark, but concerned places we already knew about, the Restaurant Modesto and, across the street, Toboso.

Another place he recommended was fascinating for four or five truly gargantuan and truly grotesque fish hanging by their gills from hooks in the refrigerated display-window, but the menu was both more elaborate and more expensive than we've wanted to deal with, and also, oddly, listed veal Stroganoff (who eats that in Seville, anyway?) for a euro more in the English-language menu than it did in the Spanish-language one.

The one recommendation he made not connected to food and drink was a barber in the remote recesses of Los Remedios, a neighborhood beyond Triana, on the other side of the river. I walked there quickly Friday, but a passel of little boys had got there before me, and the barber recommended I return later. I clocked the walk home: forty minutes.

This morning I took a cab. This was trickier than usual, for the Plaza Nueva, a short block or two from our apartment, was completely surrounded by do-not-cross fencing, and its taxi ranks were in total disarray. Two or three of the fine tall palms in the Plaza had either blown completely down yesterday, when we were away between Tarifa and Jerez, or were leaning so precariously that they had to be taken down.

The six square white pavilions that had been set up early last week, and that had turned out, when I checked on Friday, to contain a good-will tour from Krakow, introducing Polish sausage and lace to the patient Sevillians, who after all have very fine charcuterie and textiles of their own and hardly need these exotic imports, mandated no doubt from Brussels by the European Union, looked forlorn this morning, closed up, soggy in the rain, and windblown. Perhaps the weather didn't seem so bad to the Poles, who, last time I'd seen them, were in native costume and wielding fiddles and accordions along with their beer-steins. But it was pretty wretched weather to me.

Anyhow I grabbed a taxi and headed for a haircut, badly needed, as the last one was in Rome, in November. "Last year," today's barber observed, and I agreed, yes, last year, not the November before that one.

He was deft, this barber, doing all his work with a small pair of scissors, only finishing with the razor. He didn't once sing Lan lan lalero or any of that other Figaro stuff. In fact he and I, the only ones in the shop at the impossibly early hour of ten o'clock, listened to his radio, which was playing a selection of classical piano music from Málaga, impressively played, and curiously both sober and flamboyant — a combination of which Spaniards seem uniquely capable and, therefore, particularly fond.

I walked back, clipping ten minutes from my record, as this

time I knew where I was going. The weather was better, damp but not actively raining, and after a weekend of inactivity (unless you count driving) I needed some exercise.

* * *

Yesterday's drive from Tarifa home, stopping off in Jerez for another dance concert, was circuitous. We decided to explore the coast road, which really hardly exists between Tarifa and Cádiz. Where it does exist it's narrow and hardly marked, clearly a track meant for locals to use in good weather. We followed it through one tiny town after another, most of them agricultural towns, some of them — the ones with beaches — clearly resort towns, with more hotels than their size indicates, all of them either closed at this time of the year or hopelessly despondent for lack of customers.

At one point the road disappeared under quite a large expanse of muddy brown water, for things don't drain as quickly as they might hereabouts, and it had rained quite hard over Sunday night. We watched as a car nearly as small as ours came slowly in our direction, indicating the thing was possible. A couple of guys were standing alongside a small truck, recording this brave mariner's voyage with a handheld video camera, and Eve delightedly exclaimed that we'd all be on tonight's news. I asked the driver if he'd noticed any problems, and he gave me a thumbs-up, so we put the car in gear and had at it, slowly parting the sea and continuing our northwesterly course.

I suppose it was a little risky, but the alternative was to turn around and go back, maybe thirty kilometers out of our way over ground already familiar. Besides, if anything happened, we had our cell phones — though mine had dropped its coverage in these boonies, and Eve's was locked into a network in Morocco.

The countryside along this coast is very attractive, often reminding us of the California coast, sometimes the San Mateo beach country, at other times the pine forests around Pacific Grove. It was not at its best, but on the whole I'd rather be there in February than in the summer, when it must be completely overwhelmed with tourists from England and Germany, to judge by the trilingual menus and hotel advertisements

Then we struck northerly, heading for a town called Medina Sidonia, I don't know why — another of the much-recommended "white towns" in the hills and mountains bounded roughly by Seville, Granada, and the coast. These must have been picturesque indeed twenty years ago, when they'd have resembled Italian hill towns, perched over fields and olive groves and connected by a network of simple two-lane roads haphazardly laid out across the rolling landscape.

Now, though, many of them — certainly Sidonia and Antequera and Arcos de la Frontera — are troubled by good-sized outskirts of identically designed and constructed apartment blocks, and some of them are further compromised by business parks and shopping centers, which combine in the Spanish method in what they call "polygons," often composed of rows of two- and three-storey warehouse-style buildings tricked up with false fronts. Not that different, really, from what you see outside so many American towns.

Still, the countryside was really attractive. We slowed down in one town to say hello and goodbye to a horse who stood motionless in the drizzle, oddly having chosen one lane of the town's main street for a little downtime of his own. A one-horse town, I told the equally patient women riding in my car; and they groaned, and we were on our way.

Our way was toward Jerez, and we arrived absurdly early, a little after four o'clock, with nothing to do for five hours before a flamenco show that started at nine. February 28 is a national holiday hereabouts: Andalusia Day, the day on which the region of Andalusia signed papers giving it partial autonomy from Spain. (That was twenty-five years ago, so today's celebration as special meaning, at least to those Andalusians who care about such things.)

Well: on such an important holiday, and particularly when it is cold and miserable, of course everything closes. We parked the car in an underground garage, unnecessarily, and walked somewhat dejectedly about looking for something that might be open, and warm, and dry. We finally found a bar: but, as I eventually told the woman behind the counter, you can't drink sherry for four hours. How can we kill some time in this town?

It turned out that though Sandeman's cellars were closed, Gonzales & Byass, the makers of the famed Tio Pepe, were not. So up we trouped to their digs, and waited a few minutes for the next tour to begin — the last of the day, as it turned out, and only in Spanish.

There were only the three of us and the pretty young earnest tourguide. We rode a sort of tourist train to this shed and that in the huge sprawling facility, and then toured a few more aging parlors on foot, and then sat through a videotaped history of the firm, and finally took places at one of several hundred tables in a huge hall for tapas and sherry. We were given a tenth of Tio Pepe *fino*, which is what I've been mostly drinking here anyway, and a good-sized glass of the softer, sweeter Croft's cream sherry, and a good-sized platter of openfaced ham sandwiches, and slices of Manchego cheese, and olives.

And then we went to the gift shop, where we bought enough things to be polite, including a pocket-sized bottle of their brandy to keep the chill off; and then it was finally time to think about the evening's performance, which turned out to be two parts flamenco, three parts Broadway, as presented by Maria Pages, who manages to find ways for pure flamenco to coexist with jazz dance and show routines.

Her production was everything Israel Galván's was not, two nights earlier — colorful, expressive, narrative, entertainment; where he was austere, formal, abstract, and art. I can't imagine two productions better suited to define the possible range in which the ancient and rather hermetic art of flamenco can be suited to a large general audience, and I'm very glad we had the opportunity to see them both.

And then it was a quiet and easy drive on a nearly empty highway to Seville, and return the car to its street a little north of our apartment, and an *anís* with the car-rental guy who was still up, and home to bed at the typically Sevillian hour of well past two. And tomorrow we're off, by train, to Madrid, for a final visit to the Prado.

Blow, ill wind…
Hostal San Lorenzo, Madrid, March 2 —

LYING ON A HOTEL BED back in Madrid, resting, I think about Seville and what I think of it. We actually only spent five days in Seville on this trip, in our apartment in the center of the old city. In November of 2002 we were there for a little longer, maybe a week altogether, staying in another apartment, in the Santa Cruz barrio.

Two weeks, in the off season, two years apart, hardly give me any authority to have any opinion, of course. The Seville you may have visited is no doubt quite different from the one I know. Most people don't visit in winter. But of course I have impressions of Seville, and I'm about to tell you what they are. If you want authoritative comment perhaps you'd best skip the rest of this.

Seville is Spain's fourth largest city, but it's a distant fourth, with about the same population as San Francisco, a little short of 700,000. Like San Francisco it's the cultural capital (and the political one too) of its region, Andalusia being one of the several Regions into which Spain is politically divided.

If Seville is San Francisco, then Madrid is New York, and Barcelona I suppose is Los Angeles. Perhaps Valencia is Chicago, though I doubt it: but it is the third largest city, and a long way ahead of Seville.

Andalusia should be a rich region, but it qualifies, along with one other Spanish region, for special assistance from the European Union because of its relative backwardness. This of course sets it apart from California, whose economy is the fourth or fifth biggest in the world.

But you don't sense this relative poverty in the Seville streets, at least not those we've been used to walking. Last night, in our last walk through town, we strolled a familiar path between our apartment and our granddaughter's, past shops featuring very expensive dresses for weddings and first communions. *Pundonor* is one of the two traits James Michener frequently mentions in describing the Spanish temperament. It means "point of honor," and it remains a very serious trait; and I think (though I may be wrong) that the purchase of so expensive a dress to mark so serious a social moment as wedding or first communion is an expression of this kind of point of honor.

But as I say this is a Spanish trait, not specifically a Sevillian one, and I'm trying to come to terms here with my feelings about Seville. As we walked the Madrid streets this afternoon Lindsey said she thought she could easily spend a month here, in Madrid; there is no way we could spend a month in Seville. It is too large to be a charming village. I could happily spend a month in a charming village — say, Ars-en-Ré, in France. For that matter we have spent a month at a time in a French village, or in the countryside just outside one, and very happily at that — it's a great way to concentrate on a language, to get some serious writing done, to acquaint yourself more intimately with the provender and cuisine of a worthwhile and unfamiliar culture.

But if Seville is too large to be a charming village, it's also too small to supply a month of metropolitan rewards. I know: one shouldn't ask that of her. But she is a city, after all, with museums and music, bookstores and bars; but those attractions, while they are present enough to intrude on my daily stroll or schedule, don't go deep enough to maintain my interest for more than a week or two. I think I could spend a month in Madrid and never visit any museum but the Prado, though there are four or five other great museums here for painting and sculpture. The Bellas Artes, in Seville, didn't ask me for a return after a visit of only a couple of hours.

In short there's something, well, provincial about Seville. God knows I am provincial myself; in general I prefer provinces to capitals. But I think a province is at its best to its natives, not to its visitors. Every province is rich with detail; its social and environmental grain can be compelling, fascinating even — to a native, who has grown up among that detail, and knows and understands its finest points with the kind of engagement a casual visitor can never hope to attain.

Of course there are aspects of Seville, indeed of perhaps any such provincial capital, that would reward a lifetime of study by a passionate professional, an anthropologist or a folklorist or a theology student. Members of my own family are drawn to Seville for its flamenco, and I can understand their fascination. But I am a generalist, not a specialist, and while Seville is busy enough in its urbanity to intrude constantly on my own thoughts, while I'm there, it rarely surprises me with an unexpected delight.

But here I will contradict myself. When we arrived I was happy with our apartment's situation, a few yards from a magnificent plaza, the Plaza Nueva. This is a fine symmetrical plaza, with a central fountain, newsstands on diagonally opposite corners, planted with fine sycamores and tall graceful palms, and animated day and night — not with café society, there are no bars or cafés in the plaza itself, but with pedestrians who cut across it to get from one place to another, or with young people looking for a little solitude in a crowd, or with the occasional down-and-outer who can find an hour's shelter and anonymity between stints begging or ranting in more touristy areas.

Shopping streets of three different kinds lead into the Plaza Nueva: formerly very posh streets, now gone I'm afraid to department stores and chain boutiques along the calles Sierpes and Tetuan, which are also set about toward the Plaza with cafés and bars; more utilitarian shops, for locals with more basic needs — stationery, say, or hardware — along the Nuñez and the Zaragoza; and businesses catering to business, telephone stores and computer repair places for example, on the south side, where there are also more bars and inexpensive restaurants.

And on various sides of the Plaza are strategic bus stops and transfer points, and taxi ranks. So the Plaza Nueva is a truly metropolitan area, not simply a place for tourists or students. It's a kind of intersection of the various modes in which people occupy their cities: business, commerce, transportation, government.

I'm afraid I took the Plaza Nueva for granted. For example, I never took a photograph of it, or in it — it's too big, really, and too busily furnished, to be able to get a photo that would give an impression of it as a plaza. I suppose I took it for granted because of the very fact that it did not represent what I went to Seville for: it is not a tourist thing. It functions for the native, for the resident. And when we returned late Monday night to Seville from a weekend away, and found that a couple of those tall graceful palms had come down in a windstorm, and the entire Plaza was off-limits, I suddenly felt ashamed of myself for having neglected it in its better days, for having taken it for granted.

Tuesday morning it was a mess. Men were sawing up the downed trees; people were dodging under the caution-tape lines to catch their buses; people like me were scurrying around witlessly trying to figure out where the taxis would be stopping. I thought it would take days to clean this up.

But I was surprised, Tuesday afternoon, to find the Plaza Nueva back to normal. The trees are hardly missed: if anything, their departure has brought the sycamores into greater prominence, and this is a sycamore kind of plaza, palms seem irrelevant to its architecture. Buses, taxis, newsstands, pedestrians were all back in place.

Perhaps the Plaza Nueva stands for all of Seville, and I need to give greater thought to those details. The fragrance of the orange trees, even in February when there are no blossoms and the rain and the cold hardly bring out fragrance. The lovely river. The narrow medieval streets (but they are after all like the streets in any old European city that has not been Haussmannized). The surprising courtyards, glimpsed through doors providently if carelessly left open. The tiles, the tiles: handmade, factory-made, ancient, new, proudly decorating wealthy doorways or filling in, as broken pieces, as rubble in a wall or courtyard suddenly laid bare by construction work.

Seville is going through an awkward period, I think. There's construction everywhere. A subway is being installed. The need to balance traditional architecture and decoration with new construction, humane streetscape with modern business, tourist appeal with concern for the resident — that need is evident, and the strain of attending to it is evident as well.

So I will be more forgiving of Seville. I will undoubtedly want to return, partly to see her in other seasons, partly because I'm curious to see what will happen to her in a few years when the subway is finished, the hotels are up-to-date, and even greater crowds are gaping at Columbus's tomb. I'm curious to see just how this political balancing act will develop.

A perfect day
Hostal San Lorenzo, Madrid, March 3 —

IF YOU CAN HAVE ONLY ONE DAY in Madrid you can do worse than spend it as we did today. Up at nine, *café con leche* and *pan tostada* for breakfast, about six hours in the Prado (with a break in its cafeteria for lunch), home to the hotel for a couple of hours of rest, a brisk walk to the Teatro Latin for a *zarzuela*, a slow walk home afterward, stopping off for a *racion* of ham and another of cheese and a couple of glasses of sherry.

We spent three hours or so in the Prado a month ago, when we arrived here, and it was clear that that wasn't enough. In the meantime I've read a little about it — not as much as I'd have liked, as this hasn't really been a reading kind of month, but a little. Eugenio d'Ors's *Tres horas en el Museo del Prado*, for one, which I mentioned a week or so ago, and won't enlarge on here; and the several pages James Michener devotes to it in his book *Iberia*, which I've also mentioned, though not his comments on the museum.

The first thing to say about this magnificent museum is that almost all its paintings reflect the interests of a single family of collectors. Granted, they were obscenely wealthy; granted, they had a lot of professional help. Velasquez, for example, went on shopping expeditions in Italy, buying up Titians and the like to send back to the king. Still, nearly everything here was at one time really wanted, not merely invested in, or seized, as can have been the case in other museums — the British Museum, the Louvre, the Metropolitan.

The second thing to say is that this is a Spanish museum, and its collection ignores great expanses of art history that didn't, for one reason or another, speak to members of Spanish royalty. There are some magnificent Italian paintings here, because there was a close political connection between the two countries for a number of decades. There are some choice Netherlandish paintings, because Spain owned the Low Countries for quite a while. But French painting is only spottily covered, German painting less so; and the entire collection seems to come to a screeching halt in the early 19th century, having found its historical climax, you might say, in the work of Francisco Goya.

I myself have never been particularly interested in old painting. My own interest was always in Modernist painting, though I have a real enthusiasm for certain painters of earlier ages — Vermeer, for example. I have never spent any time studying the history, the technique, or the iconography of painting before, say, Manet and Degas. This may be surprising to those of you who know I worked for years as an art critic: but it was and remains my feeling that an art critic on a daily newspaper is a reporter first and foremost, and in my time and place — 1967-1987, Northern California — there was so much contemporary work to cover it seemed quite ethical to neglect art that was more conventionally appreciated and understood.

So today's hours in the Prado were an attempt to simply let these magnificent paintings speak for themselves, without guides or earphones, catalogues or commentaries. We took them chronologically, and were completely bowled over at the very beginning, with Mantegna's *Transit of the Virgin* (1461) and Roger van der Weyden's *Descent from the Cross* (1437). I've mentioned Eugenio d'Ors's conceit of placing the art of painting midway between spatial or architectural values and narrative or expressive ones, and these two paintings were perfectly paired in that sense. Both seem perfectly balanced between the two poles, but Mantegna's balance favors spatial form, and van der Weyden's favors narrative.

And so it went. We spent three hours on the ground floor; broke forty minutes for quite a competent lunch in the cafeteria (beef stew, mixed vegetables, fruit, and dessert, with a small bottle of red wine); then spent another two hours upstairs, concentrating on Rubens, Velasquez, and Goya.

Perhaps half the paintings on the walls demanded full attention. The spacing, lighting, and labeling here are optimal — well, the labels could be in English rather than Spanish, but that's an ungrateful criticism. Almost none of the paintings are behind glass; and one can lean across the ropes to almost a nose-length away from the surfaces — particularly useful in the case of Breughel and Bosch, whose paintings teem with fascinating detail.

Most of the greatest painting here is of course familiar from reproductions. But the conditions of this museum emphasize a truth we all know anyway in our heart of hearts: in spite of all the postcards and coffee-table books and tee shirts and coffee mugs, reproductions don't really reproduce paintings. They don't even reproduce what paintings look like. They only reproduce what the subjects of the paintings look like. So it becomes clear, after a few hours in front of these paintings, that except for a few overtly political ones — portraits of kings, or statements of theological positions — these paintings aren't really "about" their subject-matter at all, any more than a movie is "about" its actors. They are about light and dark, color and grey, surface and depth, texture, and the like.

Of course many are fascinating for what they tell us of life in the time and place of their making. So we see Saint Barbara sitting on a comfortable couch in front of a fire reading a book, quite as if private life were the usual thing in the fourteenth century: but it's interesting to see she holds the book — an illuminated manuscript, of course — nestled in a sort of napkin, to protect it, I suppose, from the oils of her saintly hands.

But fascinating as such details can be, it's timelessness, not specificity, that makes a great painting seem immortal. I was fascinated by the number of times painters several centuries apart, with different techniques and media and social situations, would somehow speak to a common interest, as if a narrative had been set aside in one century, with the death of its narrator, and then taken up again two hundred years later when the correct next narrator happened along.

And then there are the different versions of a single painting, like the two versions Titian made of his *Venus and the Organ-Player*, one clearly painted much faster, no doubt as his own copy of the original, when he'd found another purchaser. Or Rubens's copy of Titian's painting of *The Temptation of Eve*.

And, to end this haphazard walk through the Prado, a revision of my view of Goya last time round: on that visit we did not see the Dark Paintings, I'm not sure why; this time we did. Clearly Goya was not one painter but two: the public Goya, who painted to religious and royal commission, is hard for me to respond to. The private Goya, who painted what he really felt about the excesses of his own time and place — Spain, 1800-1820 — was a completely different painter, and his most stunning work is utterly Modern: *Saturn Devouring his Child*, *For This Were We Born*, and that amazing, enigmatic canvas showing a dog's head peering up over the rim of a chasm at the bottom of an immensely tall painting that is otherwise quite blank.

I see I've forgotten to mention Rembrandt and Claude Lorrain. Oh well.

* * *

The zarzuela was *La Tabernara del Puerto*, on opening night, and it was delicious. Zarzuela is operetta with a lot of spoken dialogue, or maybe a better description is spoken theater with interspersed musical numbers, some of them light and silly, others of quite operatic ambition.

There was a good-sized orchestra in the pit (fourteen strings, as many winds, harp, and percussion), and quite a large company on the stage — say seven or eight principals, a number of company actors, sixteen in the chorus, and eight dancers. There were three acts, and the third opened with a scene in which the romantic leads were tossed about in their little sailboat on a stormy sea, ultimately sinking in a flash of lightning.

I'm not sure what the story was, as the supertitles translated only the sung lyrics, and the plot of course advanced through the untranslated dialogue. Beautiful tavernkeeper's daughter, returning sailor, smugglers, drunk old couple, epicene waiter, lovelorn kid, put-upon smugglers; all coming right at the end — maybe. Even that wasn't entirely certain.

What was certain was the quality of the leads, and the enthusiasm of the entire company, and the great glee of the mostly Madrileño audience, who happily sang along with the cast, and laughed at what must have been local or political comments, and roared at the slapstick. Zarzuela, Michener said in his 1968 book *Iberia*, is dying out; it speaks of nostalgia for simpler times; but at the same time somehow keeps a hold in its heartland, which is Madrid. Lehár and Strauss speak to all German and Austrian tastes from their own Vienna, but zarzuela is city-specific. But you can't really spend any time in Madrid without seeing zarzuela, just as you have to see a performance of *The Merry Widow* if you're in Vienna for more than a week. It's a cultural obligation, a tourist tax, and we're glad to pay it.

* * *

The ham, cheese, and sherry were at the corner bar outside our hotel, the Viejo Casco. It's strictly a worker's bar. My order, at the bar, was taken by an old old man, who couldn't quite believe I wanted sherry — this isn't Andalusia, after all; one drinks Rioja here — but got a bottle up out of the icebox and opened it, and passed my order for ham and cheese to the appropriate staff, and before long here it was: as unctuous and resonant a Serrano ham as we've had, and great slices of Manchego cheese slathered with a nice olive oil, and a basket of bread.

The tablecloth was paper, and scattered with breadcrumbs when we sat down; and our rations and sherries were passed to us by a woman customer at the bar, for there was no table service at all. The television set blared away irrelevantly with some German slapstick comedy stuff. The old man sat across the serving area from us, watching us curiously, always smiling sweetly, beaming at us even, and affectionately waving good-bye when we left. I've never felt more at home anywhere on this trip, and I'll never come back to Madrid without stopping in.

Einstein, Machaut, Mantegna, Franco
Hostal San Lorenzo, Madrid, March 4 —

ON OUR WAY THIS MORNING to the Thyssen-Bornemisza Museum, about which more here later, I stopped to take a photo of the Madrid skyline on the Calle de Alcala — specifically, two gorgeous bank buildings, one with a couple of bronze three-horse chariots on its roof, the other with a sparkling copper dome.

A young man, say in his thirties, smiled at me and said something about how beautiful Madrid is, and we struck up a conversation. He turned out to be Venezuelan, and like us is flying home tomorrow. He's not happy about it. "I'd like to come to Spain," he said, "I feel better here. My country is not in a good place at the moment. The people are — well, they're violent. They don't want security, or stability, they want violence."

I thought about that as we continued our walk. Lindsey mentioned the surprising turnabout in Spanish social history that came with the death of Franco, when Spain finally began to take its place among the modern European nations. It had tried to do this before, of course, in the 1920s and '30s, but the economy was too unstable, Europe was in disarray, and the peculiar ruling trio in Spain — military, church, and wealthy landowners — didn't want to risk a socialist state. So there was a civil war, a particularly cruel and bloody one of course (that being historically the Spanish way), and Generalissimo Franco emerged from the chaos, a Spanish version of Italy's Mussolini except that he had the brains to resist foreign adventures. By and large the Spanish population preferred stability to civil war, even though the cost was both severe economic hardship and almost complete isolation from the rest of the world; and Franco remained the Spanish way until his death thirty years ago.

But, as Lindsey pointed out, Spain has taken her place among the modern European nations. I think she is still in rather a difficult position, Spain I mean, squeezed between rather a secondary position within the European Union, on the one hand, and potential serious threats at fragmentation at home, with the Basques, the Catalans, and the Andalusians continually rocking the national boat, in different degrees of course but still enough to weaken the national center.

These thoughts began to talk to some other things I've been thinking about, ever since an acquaintance e-mailed the other day to ask what I thought of the next season's concert programs just announced by the San Francisco Symphony.

I wrote back that I didn't think much of them. There are three I'd like to hear, but the rest are either too familiar or too downright weird to be attractive. And after all I'm a composer, among other things, and there isn't a single living American composer listed on these programs, let alone California composer, and I find this simply disgusting.

Like it or not, we live in the modern world. No social institution can thrive, or even I think survive, if its response to the complexities and stress of modern life is to try to ignore them, to pretend that life can go on in the familiar nostalgic way. This is true for governments, for educational institutions, for museums, and for orchestras. It is even true for restaurants.

It is true that the Prado, which has preoccupied me so much these last few weeks, is a brilliant and powerful museum of painting that stops with Goya, who laid down his brush nearly two hundred years ago. But across the street we find the Thyssen-Bornemisza Museum, whose chronological range begins in the Fourteenth Century and extends to just a generation ago; and down the street there's the Reina Sofia Museum, dedicated to the Twentieth Century (and the home now to Picasso's *Guernica*), and this makes easy a conversation among all these paintings, with Mondrian, say, responding to Lorrain, and Mantegna to Monet, and Degas to Velasquez. All you have to do is walk a few hundred yards and buy your ticket.

You can't do that with orchestral music. Well, you can, of course, if you just listen to records: but that would be like seeing these paintings via postcard reproductions. They're an *aide-memoire*, nothing more.

Why are there so many painters, and why do they paint so

many paintings, and why are so many of them so damnably fine? Well, for one thing, it's because we're very much aware of them beginning six hundred years ago. If an institution like the San Francisco Symphony were to do its job properly it would offer a Machaut mass from the time of Chaucer, or the great Monteverdi Vespers from the time of Shakespeare (to switch from a painterly comparison to a literary one), at least as often as it trots out Handel's *Messiah*.

Stravinsky, some say, is music's Picasso, and the San Francisco Symphony is giving us Stravinsky next season, on rather an attractive program: *Le Rossignol* combined with *Oedipus Rex*. But most halfway sophisticated Americans are familiar with two or three generations of painting, even (or more likely particularly) American painting, beyond Picasso: and San Franciscans are aware of a dozen Bay Area painters since the death of Picasso; but not of Bay Area composers.

When a society's cultural institutions ignore its own living creative spirit, what kind of future can it face? Isn't it precisely in the great Continuity from one generation, from one century, to the next, that civilization consists? And what is Art for? Surely one of its most significant functions is to keep alert both the individual's and the society's awareness of what is now fashionably called "values," namely the preoccupations and observations and responses of imaginative and creative minds as they evolve with the fabric of the time and place they share, and share with us.

Lindsey was also talking, today, about the discussions in the press of the centennial of Albert Einstein's publication of his theory of Relativity. Imagine: there was a time when Relativity seized the popular imagination; and now our society is content to be led by people who believe in literal interpretations of religious books two and three thousand years old, and reject scientific warnings of environmental dangers.

* * *

Well, we went to the Thyssen-Bornemisza, and there we spent three hours and more on the permanent collection, which is quite magnificent, beginning with Italian 14th-c. primitives and running on up to de Kooning and Rauschenberg; and then we went to dinner at El Cenador, a restaurant that had been particularly recommended, and there we ate very well indeed, though relatively simply: a leek-and-cheese tart, then bacalao in tomato sauce, with ice cream for dessert — honey and *anís* ice cream for me, *leche merengada* for Lindsey — and then we went back to the Thyssen-Bornemisza for a special treat, a show of a dozen or two portraits by Hans Memling.

When I mentioned having a few favorite pre-Manet painters yesterday I mentioned Vermeer. Memling is another, of course, as is Cranach, and Durer, and Van Dyck — are they all portraitists? Perhaps they are: portraits by these painters are particularly moving, perhaps because they conform to the proposition Eugenio d'Ors presents, which I also mentioned yesterday, that first-rate painting somehow balances (I'll use my own terminology here) formalism and expressivity.

(Well, a couple of other favorite painters come to mind here, and they're not portraitists at all: Hercule Seghers, who has a delicious small landscape in the Thyssen-Bornemisza; and Jan Sanraedam, who is no more evident here in Madrid than is Vermeer.)

One of the problems with our usual understanding of concert music — "classical music," to use the misleading but universal term — is that it is almost completely dominated by a German standard repertory that has swung far to the extreme of expressivity. You could argue that this was the first example of a tendency that's set in among most of the performance arts: in film, pop music, even in fashion, things are getting noisier and sexier and more violent with each passing season.

In the business of orchestral music one result has been the evolution of the huge symphony orchestra that's needed to play, say, a Mahler symphony; and all these people have to be paid, so audiences have to be correspondingly big, which means that machinery has to be set up to persuade potential audiences that it's the big noisy music that they want to hear, which in turn means that they tend also to be persuaded that the subtler music, or the music from eras with other values than the big noise, are what they do not want to hear.

In my opinion the result is an increase in the violence of our society, which is not good. Violence is an understandable response to stress and complexity, but it is not a healthy or productive one. It exacerbates problems and makes more difficult their solution, instead of examining them and finding and instituting corrections. I suppose Franco's Spaniards were right; an isolationist and nostalgic evasion of modern society is preferable to violence; but in today's world it is no longer possible.

So I say, let postmodern performance comment on the primitives; patiently allow technology to erode received values and thereby evolve the next steps in human cultures; rest now and then with a tourist's nostalgia for the picturesque but don't neglect a sustained commitment to meeting the challenges of the real world. And be careful, you especially Charles, about too complacently insisting that others agree with you!

Aromas and flavors
Eastside Road, Healdsburg, March 7 —

YOU SMELL LIKE SPAIN, Eric said, as we got into his car at the San Francisco Airport. Yeah, I said, sweat and stale cigarette smoke.

No, he said, it's more than that, I've often noticed it before, when people arrive from Spain, or when I land there — there's a characteristic smell. It's partly sweat and cigarette smoke, but there's a certain perfume, something that means Spain.

Maybe. I'd been wearing the same wool sportcoat, a Harris tweed, for a month. In normal weather it would have had a few days off, and maybe even a dry cleaning, but the weather was never normal. It had been C O L D . It was freezing when we left Madrid, Saturday morning; I stowed my topcoat — wool, of course — in its travel bag just before getting on the airplane. Otherwise it was wool sweater, wool sport coat, all the way home..

Wool, a little sweat, ham, cigarette smoke, and no doubt the scent of sherry — I suppose there are those who would take offense at the combination, maybe even some of you reading this; but to me it had grown familiar and even somewhat pleasant, the smell of being alive and even enjoying myself. Paintings and music are fine, but for intimate pleasures there's nothing like scents, fragrance, aroma. Alice B. Toklas named her second book *Aromas and Flavors*, and as a title it's hard to beat.

Still, when I stepped out of Eric's car to open our gate, stepped out into a night that while cool seemed positively balmy after this Spanish vacation, a deep night, no moon, plenty of stars overhead, and the scent of new green grass on the hillsides, the cattle sheds a mile to the south, the peach and plum and nectarine trees in bloom — I was home. I could smell so many of the details: the shale on the road, the decomposed granite patio, the damp teak patio table, the rosemary blossoms, the laurel tree when I brushed against it. Home.

Time to give you a roundup of hotels and restaurants and a few other comments. I give all telephone numbers in groups of three, though custom varies in Spain; called from outside Spain, they must be preceded by the country code, 34.

MADRID: Tourist information offices are on Plaza Mayor and, nearer the Prado and the Atocha train station, on the Carrera de San Jeronimo. The most useful map proved to be Streetwise Madrid, one of those stiff plastic fold-out maps, best used in good light. We got about by walking and taking an occasional taxi (cheap).

Hotel: Hostal San Lorenzo, calle Clavel 8, ES 28004, Madrid; Telephone: 915.213.057; Fax: 915.327.978; e-mail info@hotel-sanlorenzo.com.1 We stayed twice at this two-star hotel, in two different rooms. Room 105 was pleasant though cold at first, taking an hour or two to warm up. Comfortable adjacent twin beds, short bathtub. Room 109 was similar but on an airshaft rather than on street, and noisy from a ventilator if the window was open. I could make dialup connections to the internet with my laptop. Breakfast here was okay but a little expensive for what you get (toast or croissant, coffee, orange juice); we took breakfast elsewhere after a day or two. The hotel's a ten-minute walk from the important museums, the Puerta del Sol, and the Plaza Mayor. We would certainly stay there again. €75/day, higher at certain periods.

Restaurants: La Fuencisla, calle Augusta Figueroa, just east of calle Hortaleza. A small bar on the street; behind it the dining room, say eight tables, paintings crowding all the walls, a very traditional cuisine served to locals. A good idea to reserve: we didn't and were lucky to get a table on a Tuesday afternoon. Delicious *sopa castiliana, cocido*, good desserts, well chosen inexpensive house wine.

Restaurant Botin, calle Cuchilleros 17, tel. 913.664.217. The oldest restaurant in the (western) world, says the Guinness Book of Records, but well worth visiting. Dining rooms on three levels, from the tourist Siberia upstairs (but very pleasantly lit and spacious) to the grotto-like cellar. Garlic soup, green beans, roast beef, suckling pig, fresh pineapple, fig ice cream, and a bottle of wine: €72. Yes yes.

El Cenador, Calle Prado 4, tel. 914.291.561; 914.291.549. Exceedingly posh interior and service; a place to take your time. Delicious leek-cheese tart, two orders of bacalao, two splendid desserts, and a half bottle of house-chosen wine (a very good white), €68. I'd go back any time.

Restaurante La Trucha, calle M. F. Gonzalez. This is said to be outstanding for fish. I found it acceptable but no more; Lindsey liked it better. Dinner for two, €74.

Prado Museum Café is a good option for either a drink and pastry or a full lunch to break up a six-hour day in the museum. Not expensive, decent food.

Right next to the Hotel San Lorenzo is the Bar Vieja Casca, on the corner of Calle Clavel and Calle Infantas del Rey. Here I had some of the tastiest Serrano ham of the trip, and Manchego served drizzled with oil, and pleasant *manzanillas* and a fine *anís*; and here we took our breakfasts. The atmosphere is marvelous.

Los Galayos, calle Botoneros 5: roast peppers stuffed with bacalao, brandade, particularly good suckling pig, torrone ice creams, an excellent Faustino Rioja: €82.05.

Café la Internacional, plaza Vazquez de Mella 11: Manchego, *chorizitos, pan tumaca, tarta*, tea, water, wine: €36 for four.

ÁVILA: A manageably small city high in the mountains north of Madrid, quiet in the month of February, notable for its perfectly preserved walls, this proved to be well worth a day's visit even if you're not particularly interested in St. Teresa of Avila. You don't really need guidebooks to enjoy her museum, the walls, or the idiosyncratic cathedral. Try to be there at twilight and, I'm sure, off season, when the austerity and calm bring Italy's Pienza to mind.

Hotel Restaurant Las Cancelas, Calle Cruz Vieja, 6 (05001) Ávila; tel. 920.212.249; fax 920.212.230; e-mail: reservas@las cancelas. com. A very attractive bedroom in a very attractive two-star hotel just a couple of minutes from the cathedral and inside the city walls. Dialup internet hookup possible. I would certainly stay there again. Breakfast was reasonable, and the restaurant looked pleasant — though we didn't eat there, I'd try it next time. €63 excluding breakfast.

Restaurant El Rasto is one of those enormous Spanish dining rooms, nearly empty the cold Friday we were there (admittedly at an early hour). A fine meal here, quietly served by women (which is unusual) for €48, a bargain.

SALAMANCA: A university city full of life and youth, with perhaps the most beautiful public plaza in Europe, an amazing double cathedral, and enough unexpected pleasures to make a trip to the tourist office well worth while. This was our second visit and I could return for more.

Hotel Torre del Clavero, C/ Consuelo 21, Salamanca; tel. 923. 280.410; fax 923.217.708; e-mail: info@hoteltorredelclavero. com. Again, a very pleasant hotel, well centered a few minutes from the Plaza Mayor, with in-room ethernet high-speed internet connection. Two days: €175.

Restaurant: Bruin Café Erasmus. Amusing for being *typisch Nederlands*, except that there are no *pannekoeken* ; a very lively youth scene.

Restaurante Isidro, Pozo Amarillo, 17-19. A local hangout, says Rick Steves, with a nice bar and a long, well-lit dining room; very friendly service; and unmemorable but sound fare.

SEGOVIA: Famous for its castle, its cathedral tower, and its Roman acqueduct, this is a city that really offers little more to the tourist.

Hotel Infanta Isabel, Plaza Mayor 12; tel. 921.461.300. Very attractive lobby; very spacious but old-fashioned room with good bath; no internet connection possible. Restaurant looked attractive though we didn't try it. Good location at top of main pedestrian shopping street, heart of town, easy walk to castle and aqueduct, the two principal sights.

Restaurante Mesón Cándida, Plaza Azoguejo, 5: a very old, traditional, pleasant place, big comfortable dining room upstairs, amazingly cluttered with, among other things, currency from every country in the world — diners apparently leave banknotes as a Kilroy-was-here gesture. Excellent — what else? — roast suckling pig.

Judería, calle Judería Vieja, 5: here you can have strange Sephardic cuisine, though we noticed the omnipresent Serrano ham in its chrome-plated ham-vise on a serving table, and here Lindsey had couscous, and I had something called *markla hlua* that turned out to be a Venetian kind of combination of meat scraps, rice, raisins, and nuts. And here I had the best dessert of our trip, dates, filled with almond cream, and accompanied by a mandarin-orange ice cream.

TOLEDO: Even off-season this town is Tourist Central, and I think I know why: El Greco. You'll want a guidebook here; there are many places to visit, lots of paintings to see, and centuries of history, some of it bloody indeed. It's a tiring walking town but a car will be no help at all. We gave Toledo a full day and two nights, and that was just about the right amount of time.

Hotel Pintor el Greco, Alamillos Del Transito,13, tel. 925.28.51.9. Recommended by Rick Steves, this is a pleasant enough hotel but sited a bit off-center, near the city walls — an easy walk to some sights, farther from others. For two nights, €112, with no internet possible.

Restaurante La Perdiz, Calle de los Reyes Católicos 7: another Rick Steves recommendation, so we thought we'd test his judgment, and had a fine meal in a rather plain, non-touristy dining room: *migas del pastor* (sautéed breadcrumbs which are very tasty); fresh tuna in a warm salad; medallions of venison; and fine desserts: a fig "soup" and dates with almond ice cream.

CÓRDOBA: This city is an absolute must for its Mezquita, one of the most amazing buildings in the world, a place that has to be experienced because photographs hardly convey its mysterious beauty. Many guidebooks completely ignore its Alcázar and the castle gardens, and that's a pity; Lindsey thinks this one of the great gardens she has seen.

Hotel Boston, calle Málaga 2, tel. 957.474.176; fax. 957.478.523; http://www.hotel-boston.com. Pleasantly situated on a large plaza a ten-minute walk from the Mezquita and Alcázar, but difficult of access, with stairs to the elevator, which can only be summoned by desk clerk in the second-floor lobby, and without internet access. We had three single beds in a our room, private bath, for €58.

Restaurant: On a previous visit we learned that the thing to do here is simply to eat tapas, and this time we had very quick and tasty ones at Taberna Rafael, finding it completely by chance while walking from our hotel toward the Mezquita.

ANTEQUERA: No particular reason to visit this town, quite off the usual Andalusia Córdoba-Seville-Granada triangle; but the dolmens on the edge of town are moody and impressive; the cathedral has a magnificent carved-wood (and thankfully not gilded!) retablo; and the castle setting is pleasant to stroll.

Hotel: Here we simply went to the tourist office and took the cheapest one they mentioned; I don't recall the name or location. It was clean and convenient, with offstreet parking, and colder than all Billy-be-damned, with not a very good breakfast.

Restaurante El Escribano, *bacalao* orange and onion salad with wonderful lettuces, *migas*, fine potatoes with the cutlets, beautifully made *leche frita* ("fried cream"; really a delicate but firm custard): very good indeed, and in a beautiful setting up near the castle and cathedral.

ARCOS DE LA FRONTERA: a tourist center, one of the "white towns" in the Andalusia mountains. This must be unbearable in season; there's an enormous tour-bus parking lot on the outskirts. We liked the town principally for its fine views out over the surrounding countryside.

Restaurante El Convento, Marques Torresoto 7: salad, garlic soup, partridge in almonds, pigeon, meatballs, flan, mousse, *tocino*, wine & water, €80.38.

RONDA: another tourist-town, famous for the terrifying stone bridge linking its two halves. Guidebooks tout a walk around the old part of town, architecturally interesting.

Restaurante Asador Casa Santa Pola, Santo Domingo, 3: fried goat cheese, a hearty and substantial "grandmother soup," *berenjenas, lomo, solomillo, pollo*, three desserts, the requisite water and wine brought our tab to one of the highest on the trip: €128.93 for three people. But the dining room was handsome and comfortable, the service attentive, and the kitchen very competent.

TARIFA: One very rainy afternoon didn't really give us much of a chance to investigate this charming ancient town whose narrow, crooked streets keep suggesting you're somewhere else — a small town on the French Riviera? Sardinia? Perhaps, as one of the guidebooks suggests, North Africa? I'd go back in a minute — preferably on a dry day.

Hotel La Mirada, San Sebastián, 41; tel. 956.680.626; fax 956.681.162. Outside the walls, a twenty-minute walk from the beach, not quite so far from the center of the old city; no internet possible; clean and quiet; bad coffee — get your breakfast elsewhere! Double room with extra bed, €60.

Restaurante Morilla, calle Antonia Maura 13: chicken soup, two salads, spaghetti bolognese, wine, water, and two desserts, €45 for three people — a bargain. Not the best service, but crowded.

JEREZ DE LA FRONTERA: We went for the flamenco festival, but it's famous also of course for its sherries, and a tour of Tio Pepe's home is well worth its small ticket price.

Hotel Ávila, Calle Ávila 6 (I think), tel.   956.334.808, fax
956.334.807. Five-minute walk from the center of town; no internet access; not a very good breakfast (though this is unfair, as the
power failed before it was served, stranding a couple of people in
the elevator for a few minutes). Double room with extra twin bed,
€69.

Restaurante Domecq el Gallo Azul, calle Larga 2: tapas for
three at a table outside, including roast peppers, *bacalao croquetas*,
tuna, a couple of *finos*, a Fanta, and a final *anís*: €14.40. Another
bargain, and delicious!

Bodega Gonzales Byass, Manuel Maria Gonzalez 12, this is
the dining room at the end of the Tio Pepe tour, where our tapas
included fine ham and Manchego cheese and potato chips, a tenth
of *fino*, and a glass of sweet cream sherry for dessert, for €13.50

SEVILLA: the fourth-biggest city in Spain, about the size of San
Francisco, deserves at least a week, a good map, and one or two
good guidebooks. This was our second trip and I think I now have
the hang of the city center, whose shopping and restaurants are rewarding.   The Cathedral is my current favorite anywhere; the
Alcázar is impressive and worth the entry price (as is its garden);
and there are many other rewarding places to visit.

Hotel: We stayed in apartments on both our visits, the most
recent one rented over the internet. I complained about it at length
in these dispatches, but it was actually quite comfortable and very
nicely situated; we just had to get used to heating bath water on the
stove, and picking our way through construction debris in the street
— the latter no fault of the landlord.

Restaurants: Seville has a number of well-thought-of restaurants, but the most rewarding eating we've found is in the tapas
bars, where the food is tasty and inexpensive and deceptively filling.
The ones we've liked are:

Bodega Taberna Rafaél Deanes, where? : roasted peppers,
patatas ali oli (creamy garlic sauce), fried anchovies, ham, *bacalao*,
shellfish, water, wine, only one dessert: €28.28 for four persons.

Barbacoa Coloniales, calle Dormitorio 1: tapas *papas brava*,
salmorejo con jamón, eggs, *croquetas*, *solomillo*, pepper paté,

calabacines, pepper *ali oli*, three wines, two *finos*, two waters, €26.85 for five persons.

La Sacristia, calle Mateo Gago: a great many tapas of *bacalao*, fried anchovies, shrimp, potatoes *ali oli*, drinks for all: €5.10 for four or five of us.

Toboso, calle Cano y Cueto near the Plaza Refinadores: this is a fine little tapas bar with excellent tortilla (omelette) tapas and, I'm told, even better little *bocadillos* (sandwiches) of ham and *bacalao* and smoked salmon. Nearby is the bigger and busier Bar Modesto. There are many other fine tapas bars: Las Teresas, calle Santa Teresa 2, is one of my favorites.

The one real restaurant meal we had in Seville this time was at Enrique Becera, calle Gamazo virtually next door our apartment off the Plaza Nueva, where we had vegetables bound with eggs, green salad, roast lamb stuffed with spinach (me), merluzza and some other fish (them); and a tenth of Rioja Muga '01 (delicious!). Very expensive! As I say, your best bet in Seville is the tapas.

* * *
*

Two trips to The Netherlands
2005

Stavoren (p. 177)

Again to Amsterdam
August 31, 2005

ONE OF US, I won't specify which, determined that the bus to the airport left at 11:45, so we got to the bus stop at about 11:30. Two busses soon arrived, one with a few passengers, the other empty. Both drivers strolled away for a few minutes, for a smoke I suppose or a humanitarian mission to a facility inside the Sonoma County Airport, where we were catching our bus to SFO. When they re-emerged they informed us that they had no intention, neither of them, to go on to San Francisco.

So we drove, and Eric came with us, as he'd planned to take our car back home, and we pulled into SFO right behind the bus we should have taken — at 11:15, not 11:45. Then, on going through security, one of us, I won't specify who, had to unpack one of our backpacks completely, because the x-ray machine insisted there was a pair of folding scissors in it, though we both knew we'd never owned a pair of folding scissors. But there ultimately they were, in a first-aid kit meant to cope with blisters, an issue never far from our minds as we embark on another walking trip.

Oh well. My report on the flight is nothing but favorable. The Dutch national airline KLM has kept its old-fashioned, comfy attitude toward service. The bar is open and free; the meals were tolerable; the in-flight entertainment can't be beat — each seat has its own DVD player, with dozens of movies, documentaries, and features available — as well as scores of music recordings. I watched a British documentary on 5th- to 10th-century Islamic innovative mechanics, optics, and chemistry; and then I listened to the Mozart clarinet concerto, two Schumann string quartets, some bossa nova, and cuts by Teddy Wilson, Billie Holiday, and the Modern Jazz Quartet.

The plane left on time and arrived fifteen minutes early. There wasn't much leg room, of course, but one expects that. Six or eight passengers in our crowded coach section were coddled a little bit extra: they turned out to be a sailing team returning in triumph, as they'd just taken a prize in San Francisco. The pilot congratulated them on the public address system, and we all applauded them.

The baggage took almost no time to arrive. (Of course we checked only one piece, since much of the trip this time will be on foot, and we'll be carrying everything for that period on our backs.) We enjoyed re-acquainting ourselves with the big modern airport at Schiphol, whose crowds of travelers seem particularly cosmopolitan — though there are many Dutch, Dutch of all sizes and colors, businessmen with cigars in their pockets, nuns in their crisp grey suits, tattooed mothers tethered by green plastic leashes to two or three little kids pulling in various directions, pretty girls whose skin is peaches and cream, or café au lait, or nearly ebony, all chattering away in Dutch, whether to present friends or, as is increasingly the case, absent ones momentarily in touch thanks to Nokia and Motorola and Vodafone.

We're in a cheap hotel, the Seasons, on the Stadhouderskade, not far from the broad Amstel river, the river whose dam lies at the heart of the old city. There are cheap hotels there, too, near the Dam: we didn't take one, because I assumed they'd be noisy. And of course it turns out the Stadhouderskade is an arterial favored by braying emergency vehicles: it's going to be a noisy night.

But the beds, though narrow, are soft and clean; the bathroom is acceptable though lacking a tub; and there is wi-fi — though it isn't free, and I've yet to figure out how to send group e-mails on it. Perhaps that's insoluble: if so, this blog will be the only way for me to entertain myself with my Dispatches, at least for the time being. We'll see how it goes.

Parliamo italiano
Amsterdam, September 1

A LONG REST AND A SHORT WRESTLE with technology in our little hotel room, and we were ready for a walk and maybe some dinner. I recalled a pleasant place we'd found last time we were here, *een eind*, as the Dutch say — an unspecified but not terribly great distance — down the canal.

(Or would it be up? Somehow the half-ring of five concentric canals in this city seem to go neither up nor down, but sideways, because if you walk along any of them long enough you'll find you've been led imperceptibly to have reversed your direction...)

That wonderful Amsterdam light! It's been a rainy summer, though yesterday was clear and bright, and the warm still air had brought out dozens of lazy boaters, relaxing in sculls and rowboats, or lazing about on the decks and flat rooftops of their houseboats.

The surface of this particular canal, the Singelgracht, was dark in the late afternoon, dark green or sometimes almost brown but sparkling with those sudden flashing reflections of the sky in the vivacious wakes of the boats.

Above, the dark greens of the lacy leaves of the elms, whose black rough-textured trunks and surprising green foliage do so much to soften the urbanity of this city.

And away from the Singel, as we walked narrow streets toward Leidseplein, the light raked in low and luminous against the brick façades, the sparkling white enamels of woodwork, the impeccable glass windows. People were out sitting on stoops with a bottle of Pinot gris or a pitcher of lemonade. These neighborhoods always remind me of the best of New York, the friendly blocks in Greenwich Village; perhaps there's still a touch of Dutch in what was once Nieuw Amsterdam.

We happened on an Italian delicatessen and asked for a restaurant recommendation. Do you speak English, I asked the fellow who was sweeping the doorway, Not really, he answered. His Dutch was heavily accented, too, so we tried Italian, which relaxed us both considerably.

I've only been in this country six months, he explained, so I haven't really learned Dutch yet.

The Casa del Gusto had good selections of dry pasta, cans of Italian specialties, a promising case of sausages, hams, and cheeses. The woman behind that case said they'd been open only a month, specializing in small-farm products from Tuscany and Umbria.

They recommended an Italian restaurant, Biscia, in a nearby hotel — one of the best restaurants in Amsterdam, they said. It turned out to be Bice: we'd been misled by their soft Tuscan dialect. Bice is a chain of upscale restaurants, with many outlets in Italy and elsewhere — white linen, good crystal, upscale menu and wine list.

Parliamo italiano, I suggested to the waiter, let's speak Italian, my Dutch is pretty bad, and he happily agreed, and we had salads and pasta and a half bottle of Pinot grigio, the first of which was corked.

I recalled a previous evening in Amsterdam when we were offered two consecutive corked bottles. Maybe it's particularly a problem in this climate: whatever the reason, you want to be on guard. In any case the replacement came quickly and good-naturedly.

Back home we watched the news. Distant disaster always has a surreal component, and yesterday's news was no exception. A thousand pilgrims dead of their own fear and religious fervor. Another thousand or more, no doubt, drowned in a city insufficiently guarded against a constant threat.

Holland had its own tragedy fifty years ago when a freak North Sea storm breached sea-wall dikes and drowned, as I recall, well over a hundred thousand.

There's much sympathy here for the victims of Katrina, but some concern, I feel, as to whether Americans give sufficient attention to preparedness.

In the meantime we try to justify having a good time. *Quando si mangia bene la vita ha un altro sapore*, the card from Casa del Gusto advises us: When you eat well life has another savor. We try to keep that in mind.

Today the weather is cooler: perhaps we won't need thunderstorms to break yesterday's still heat. We'll loaf our way through the day, maybe with some familiar Rembrandts, maybe with some familiar pancakes. I'll let you know how it turns out.

Botanicals
Amsterdam, Sept. 2 (and very early in the morning it is!)

A LEISURELY MORNING WAITING for breakfast, included in the price of this slightly louche hotel but not served until the ridiculous hour of nine a.m. — for reasons that became clear later in the day.

A motley group in the breakfast room — Lindsey and I quite the oldest; one couple looking to be in their forties or fifties but yearning for youth; the others in late twenties or thirties. Nearly all the men in casual cotton trousers and tee shirts, the latter often emblazoned with slogans. Nearly all the women either dressed in the latest slob manner, folds of skin emerging here and there, often pinned or clipped with oddly positioned jewelry; or in a retro flower-child fashion, long gauzy skirts and translucent tops.

Tattoos, more often than not.

Juice, coffee, corn flakes, three cheeses, four sausages, hard-boiled egg, three kinds of bread, two kinds of roll.

And then a walk to the Botanical Garden, said to be the oldest in the world (though I find it hard to believe China didn't plant one before 1680). It was a short walk, over the broad Amstel River, then northwest a few blocks, crossing two or three canals.

We walked round the Garden before entering it — by mistake, of course, not design — and stopped to watch a huge drawbridge lift, stopping cars and bikes and trams and pedestrians, to let a barge go by. This happens several times a day, but it always seems like an event; and I'm sure it contributes to the resigned equanimity of the Dutch.

The Garden is worth much more comment than I'll give it here. It began as a collection of medicinal plants, carefully studied, propagated, and tended for scientific value. What a near loss it was to human knowledge when synthetic medication was invented — late in the 19th century, one of the many helpful signboards told us.

There's still a prominent section devoted to medicinals, and it was arresting to notice a cannabis plant, taller than I am — the first I've seen in the out-of-doors, I think, certainly the first of anything like that size.

There's a prominent half-circle of beds, say half a hundred-foot circle divided into three wedges, each with a number of con-centric beds. Here hundreds of plants are set out to demonstrate a new "molecular" classification system the botanists are erecting in place of the familiar old Linnaean system, taking DNA proximity, not the similarity of physical structures, as the basis of organization.

Along one side of the vast gardens there's a series of beds trac-ing the evolution — pardon me, revelation— of plant life, from the time of the trilobites — they can't quite get back to the primordial soup, apparently — through such landmarks as the carboniferous era down to fairly recent divergences into flowering plants, gymno-sperms, cots and dicots, and so on.

Any of these could have occupied us an entire day, but we gave it only the morning, ending up with the two enormous green-houses, each quite tall enough to house the tallest of palms, and big enough to make them seem not tall at all.

There are some old plants here. A fascinating huge-leafed Gunnera was planted in the 1880s and is thriving, and two south-ern hemisphere trees of some weird kind are three times that old.

There is also a very nice café, and there we took our cappuc-cino and the requisite *appeltaart*, Dutch Apple Pie to you, sweet and buttery and crunchy and flaky, its complex texture offering apples, raisins, currants, streusel, and flaky pastry, the whole thing a con-tinually developing revelation of vanilla, apple, wheat, grape. What a celebration of botanicals!

Since I'm on a culinary note, let me tell you about dinner at Le Hollandais, around the corner from us along the Amstel. Ten years old, neither horribly expensive nor cheap, with an extremely interesting wine list and a fairly extensive menu —

But we chose the daily special: a salad of mizuma and mâche and sauteed chantarelles and slices of house-made Toulouse-style sausage; then braised goose with potatoes Dutchess (ah there, humor on the menu) and onions; then chocolate ice cream in a chocolate shell — to which we added a second dessert because it sounded so special: something between a Bavarian cream and a pudding, with almonds and spices, very Dutch, completely new to us.

With all this (well, not with the desserts) glasses of a fine red Pyrenees wine whose name I have here somewhere. Price, 32 Euros each, another twelve for the wine.

Our friend Kees suggested the place, and we found it with no help from our desk clerk, partly because the whole damn hotel lacks a phone book of any kind, partly because she was busy helping another guest find the best hash and weed in town. And then I realized this hotel, and indeed a good many in its economic class, caters to soft-drug tourists, and that indeed that is a significant part of the Amsterdam tourist industry.

Certain parts of town look like the Haight Ashbury of the 1970s, in quite a studied manner. The only difference, really, is that there's nothing coy or play-hidden about it; it's all quite open. You smell marijuana smoke often on the street, and I smell it occasionally in the hall outside our room, though it's never penetrated into the room itself, which is thankfully clean and well ventilated.

Again this evening we watched a little CNN, sad and unbelieving at the events unwinding in New Orleans. I don't have to tell you how it looks from here. Our friend Tom said the Dutch just don't understand why the pumps, and the generators powering them, were housed below sea level in many cases. The Dutch learned better than that centuries ago.

Your country doesn't like to pay taxes, he pointed out, and it's been obvious for years that the infrastructure isn't maintained, that people don't spend money to guard against future disasters. It's very sad.

But tomorrow we'll drive with Petra up toward Hoorn and Enkhuizen, which we hardly know, to do a little research toward our walk; and then we'll spend the night, and Saturday night too, in Voorburg, on the edge of The Hague, among our extended but very close Dutch family. And we will be counting our blessings, and grateful for them!

Some words on Katrina
Saturday, September 03, 2005

UP THIS MORNING LATE, to log on to Tom's marvelous high speed connection wirelessly, and read the news, oh boy.

In *Le Figaro* two or three things quickly catch my eye. An account of *Les Américains consternés par la fragilité de leur puissance*, America in consternation at the fragility of her power.

Another account, *L'administration Bush aurait ignoré les prédictions des experts*, discusses the Bush administration's having ignored expert predictions of the New Orleans disaster.

Somewhere, I've already lost track of the URL, there was a fine round-up of the world press response to the crisis.

And in *Corriere della Sera* an editorial, *Il mercato non ci salverà*, suggests that optimism won't "correct" the market's disruption following this disaster, and a market recovery won't resolve the real crisis, because it extends far beyond the state of the dollar.

The financial fallout will be bad enough, as *L'économie américaine déstabilisée* points out. According to this article the grain market, for example, is collapsing, at least for the moment, because the barge traffic between wheat storage in the midwest and freighters in the Gulf of Mexico is interrupted.

And warehouses are affected. Do you drink coffee? According to *Le Figaro*, a quarter of the stock of coffee in the United States is rotting in a Procter & Gamble warehouse in New Orleans.

But this is only to discuss the economic fallout from Katrina. The real meaning of the disaster goes farther, much farther. I think the Katrina disaster will quickly prove to be much more influential on the course of social and political American history than was even 9/11. For one thing, it will be very hard indeed on the incumbent Administration. The President, poor man, is never terribly expressive of his emotions, and this was clearly not a moment to hide them. He was elected for two reasons: He's a the kind of guy you'd like to have a beer with, and he's the kind of guy you want to keep the steady course. What we needed in New Orleans was another kind of man, someone closer to Mister Rogers. No one has ever confused George W. Bush with Mister Rogers.

Second, the American penchant for gambling. We've been betting badly lately. In Iraq we bet on hidden WMDs, on quick military victory, on easy democratization of the Iraqis: we lost each bet in turn. And like so many compulsive gamblers when confronted by a loss we redoubled our investment, throwing good money — not to mention less replaceable capital in the form of friendships and credibility — after bad.

Similarly, we bet the levees wouldn't fail. Preventive maintenance is boring and expensive and frequently its payoff is a long time coming: we're an impatient nation. We bet the levees would hold, and we bet wrong.

Finally, worst of all it seems to me, a very ugly side of the American mentality has been revealed, the side that is callous, even contemptuous, of losers, of victims, of the poor and downtrodden. I know: it's axiomatic that Americans stick up for the little guy. But they stick up for him when he's still got some spunk: nobody loves you when you're down and out.

A few months ago a taxi-driver in Seville asked me about the American health system. Is it true, he wanted to know, that there are many people without any medical coverage?

When I explained the situation he shook his head sadly. A nation that doesn't provide for its poor is like a father who refuses to care for his children, he said — a phrase that's stuck in my mind ever since.

The citizens of New Orleans were told they must evacuate. Those with cars drove away. Others got out in rental cars, or other transportation.

But thousands were left for a number of reasons. They didn't have transportation. They didn't have money for transportation. They were too sick or frail or old to leave. They simply didn't understand the gravity of the situation. Or they were simply too skeptical of a government announcement to heed.

The whole world is looking at the faces and the bodies of these people, listening to their outcry. They are almost invariably poor. And like all the poor in our country they are for the most part sick, frail, old, children, and/or illiterate. They get their information from pictures, not the printed word. Their dietary advice comes from advertisements for sodas, potato chips, and fast-food restaurants. Their health advice is little beyond pharmaceutical advertisements.

America has turned her back on a large percentage of her children, and they have grown resentful. New Orleans is perhaps only the beginning of their outrage. It is an outrage that transcends race. It is an outrage that just might have a profound influence on the future of American politics. At least I hope so.

Elfring days
Rien, Sept. 6

WE TRIED TO PUT POLITICS and the news behind us and have fun and be sociable for three days, visiting the Dutch sector of our extended family, the Elfrings, who were host to our daughter Thérèse for a year nearly thirty years ago.

We've remained in touch ever since, and grown closer over the years. It's a wonderful family. Saturday and Sunday we were in den Haag, first with Tom and Judith, who spent a few weeks in our house five years ago. (Can it really be that long?)

Sunday we visited Joost and Tanja, who were in our house for a week in July. You don't spend time with Elfrings without bicycling, and Sunday we biked maybe eight or ten kilometers out into the country around den Haag.

Sunday night there was a party, where we met Judith's father, a fascinating man who has published significant books on cerebral neurology — it was fun to defend Mozart against his champion Bach, and to explore ideas of scientific materialism and the irrational.

We then went up to Friesland to visit Kees and Irma, who have settled in a marvelous 18th-century house there, and who took us on a leisurely cruise through nearby canals. But a report on Rien, and Friesland, must wait another time: conversation has once more trumped writing.

Zuider Zeepad
Stavoren, Sept. 8—

WE WALKED THE FIRST DAY TODAY — 15 kilometers, with a small bit of cheating. Actually two bits: we took one short cut, shaving maybe a couple of kilometers off the "official" route mapped in our guidebook; but, a bigger cheat, we left our backpacks behind in the hotel here.

Stavoren is the oldest town in Dutch Friesland. It got its charter in 1180; was completely destroyed in a rise of the old Zuider Zee in the 15th century, was rebuilt by 1680. It was the first port inside the Zuider Zee, and was an early member of the great Hanseatic League of port cities controlling shipping between the great grain, ore, and timber cities of Eastern Europe and England and the other western European nations.

It was this trade that first made the Netherlands rich, and it wasn't long before Holland — that tulip-and-cheese-producing peninsula from Amsterdam in the south to Enkhuizen in the north — looked enviously toward Friesland, on the north side of the

Zuider Zee, and sent an armed contingent to subjugate the country, back in the 14th century.

Holland failed that time, but when later the Twelve (I think it is) States of The Netherlands formed the present country, back in the 16th century, Friesland fell in with the scheme.

It remains culturally and linguistically a bit detached. The place-names here, on the signboards as you approach a town, are bilingual. Friesian is close to Middle English. Dutch is somewhere between a more recent English and some kind of German, I suppose. The two languages are not really mutually understandable.

Yesterday we took the train from Amsterdam to Enkhuizen, where we visited a fascinating museum devoted to the Zuider Zee, and then took the boat across to Stavoren.

"Zuider Zee" means, as you might guess, "South Sea." In the Hanseatic days what we now call the Baltic was the East Sea. The North Sea has kept its name. The West Sea was, I suppose, the English Channel, and the huge gulf driving into the present Netherlands was the South Sea.

Much of the Zuider Zee has of course been "poldered," diked off and drained for farmland. This was done here and there, in bits and patches, with some pretty big sections reclaimed by the 17th century. A huge section was reclaimed quite recently: Flevoland. And another dike was built between Flevoland and Enkhuizen.

This was to have been drained ten or twenty years ago, but environmentalists protested, and the project was cancelled — though I was startled to see that Mappy.com, the internet mapping site specializing in Europe, shows that section of the IJsselmeer, which is what what's left of the Zuider Zee is called these days, as dry land. It isn't.

Our current project is to walk the Zuider Zeepad, a long-distance walking tour tracing the shoreline of the old inland sea; and it seemed appropriate to begin by crossing it by boat. The Enkhuizen-Stavoren trip takes an hour and a quarter and costs about ten dollars, and it was very enjoyable — brisk weather but not cold, and many fine tall ships to watch, some of them two- and three-masters.

We checked into the Vrouwe van Stavoren, whose name refers to an old story about a merchant's widow who enchanted a boat that brought her huge quantities of grain, and then a golden ring, which was lost, and swallowed by a fish, which was then caught, and... Well, you get the idea.

Today's walk was along the beach for the first half, walking atop the grass-covered sea-dike, maybe eight or ten meters high, grazed by hundreds of swans and sheep, and skirting fine fields of grass and pastures for brown sheep and Frisian and Holstein cows — for you can be sure this is a cheese-producing country.

After five miles or so we turned inland for the second half of the walk, through villages and into an imposing forest. Here we took our short-cut, seeing no reason to walk back out to the coast only to reverse our course. We ended the walk on a broad sandy road two kilometers long through a majestic old forest of beeches and elms, with a few Scotch pines and larches.

Here we met company — folks on bicycles, or strolling, or pushing baby-strollers along the road. And then, since the hotels in Riis were full, we were obliged to take the bus back here to Stavoren for a second night. Well, why not: this way at least we didn't have to carry our packs.

Dinner tonight at the Crazy Whisky Guy, as Kees called him, a restaurant that offers four hundred different Scotch whiskys, and food that flatters them, all brought by a fine fellow in kilts. I had a pork tenderloin wrapped in bacon and *nagelkaas*, a favorite cheese of ours, a matured farmer's Gouda-style cheese studded with cloves; and it was not bad at all.

Tomorrow we'll take the bus from here to Riis, this time wearing our back-packs, and hit the road, again through the forest, toward Balk. It's a pleasure to be doing this again, to feel the familiar rhythm of left foot, right foot, to note the birds, the sheep, a dog chasing a rabbit, another vaulting a hedge in pursuit of a tennis-ball; to note the tiny wildflowers on the dunes, the spirited Arabians and docile Frisian horses in their pastures.

It all seems right— scaled right, smelling right, quiet, tranquil, comfortable. I suppose we don't deserve such comfort in a world that seems to be going to pieces.

In the midst of the final wood today there was a neoclassical temple built in 1814 to commemorate the peace ending the Napoleonic wars. From this very site, I was told by a fellow taking a break from his bicycling, the Nazis launched their V2s during the Battle of Britain, and later for the destruction of Antwerp.

I hope such days never return here, I told him and his wife, but I'm an American, and sometimes I think we're turning into the new Germany. Yes, his wife agreed, nodding, but smiling too, with her fine Dutch teeth, to show there was no personal animosity.

Riis to Harich to Balk
Balk, September 9—

THE SECOND DAY IS ALWAYS the hardest day on these walking trips. This is our fourth such trip, and the generalization holds. And this not only because we cheated yesterday and walked without packs. My seventeen pounds didn't really bother me that much today.

Instead it was the heat and the humidity and the invention they conspired to perfect, mosquitos. We walked about fifteen kilometers, starting in the town of Riis where yesterday's walk ended, getting there from Stavoren easily by bus. There was a little walking alongside paved road, on the flanking bicycle path, but soon enough we plunged into woods, and here there was no breeze at all, just the still occasionally damp air motionless under tall elms, oaks, and pines.

We walked on wide packed-dirt roads, on looser equestrian trails, occasionally on narrow footpaths. Often these roads cut straight through the forest, a kilometer or two at a time; but occasional footpaths curved or twisted their way. The forest floor was always interesting: puffballs, amanitas, shelf mushrooms and other fungi were everywhere; big bracken ferns; occasional wildflowers.

An efficiently laid-out path would have spent no more than eight or nine kilometers from Riis to Balk, but efficiency does not motivate the Zuider Zeepad. One very long detour took us to a three-hundred-year-old oak. Another, of perhaps three kilometers, brought us to the town of Harich, with its twelfth-century brick steeple.

We took plenty of rests en route, and dragged ourselves into Balk a good five hours after setting out from Riis — not very good time at all, considering we hadn't found any place to have lunch. We ate our apples and almonds in front of a house under construction near the old oak, and took a cup of tea at the one stop offering anything like that — a golf course clubhouse, closed to all but members in principle, but graciously offering us a cup of tea outside on the terrace.

Riis was little more than a couple of old-fashioned resort hotels offering little more than beds for those who like to take strolls in the woods — though apparently there are enough of them; a couple of tourbusses standing in the parking lots explained why it was that we couldn't get a room in either of them last night.

Harich seems to be an upscale residential suburb, with fine houses widely set behind their extensive lawns and gardens.

Balk is a more ordinary town, several blocks long flanking a small central canal leading off the river Luts. Tomorrow we'll walk to the nearby inland lake the Slotermeer, a major recreation area that explains the prosperity of Balk, the largest town hereabouts and a thriving retail and restaurant city — though apparently with only one hotel: most of the people coming here for vacations apparently bring their campers.

We dragged ourselves up the main street and sat down at the first place offering a beer. It turned out to be our hotel, so we quickly checked in, showered, washed out a few clothes, and hit the terrace for an old genever and a beer and an *uitsmijter*, that unique Dutch open-faced sandwich of meat (ham in this case), cheese (our beloved *nagelkaas*), and three fried eggs.

We were sitting at a sidewalk café on the main street, and the passing scene was lively. I thought of Nathaniel Hawthorne's story "Scenes from the Town Pump," describing a similar outlook. Here came a shaggy white little dog, who busied himself at various posts, looking longingly up toward the signatures of dogs taller than he.

Here was a side-by-side bicycle for two, with a pretty young nurse pedalling, her ancient companion, probably the resident of an old people's home, erect and stoic beside her.

Now a couple of boys, nine or ten years old, on their bicycles, navigating the busy narrow street with the competence that comes of being left to their own devices, and the confidence that follows such trust. One, the smaller, smiled at me as he passed, and called out *Hooi*!

It's always fun in Holland to collect greetings. The standard is *Dag*, the "g" aspirated roughly like a Spanish "j." (In fact I think that's where the sound came from, but I could be wrong.)

It's short for "good day," which is a little more formal, the sort of thing you'd say to an old lady, and often do, for it's rude hereabouts to meet someone without a greeting.

In the morning it's *"morgen,"* in the afternoon *"middag,"* in the evening *"Goede avond."* But in general it's *"dag,"* or variations on *"hooi"*: Ho, or Heia, or something that really sounds more like a harrumphing throat-clearing than anything else. But all of them are sociable, as are the Dutch, almost always.

Errant trousers
Lemmer, Sept. 10—

WHAT IS THE NAME, she asked in Dutch, Shere, I answered in English. How do you spell that, she asked in Dutch, Yes, I answered in Dutch, *nou, ess*, um, aitch...

Oh, she said in Dutch, what? *Na*, I said in Dutch, not Shere, the name is Elfring. Good so, she said in Dutch, and I silently congratulated myself. Elfring is a good Dutch name and any Dutch hotelperson will know how to spell it.

And how do you spell it, she asked in Dutch, Oh, I answered, well, a, ell, um, eff, um...

Oh, I said, remembering that we were not in just any province of The Netherlands, we were in Friesland, and Boksma is a common Fries name; no, the name is not Elfring, it is Boksma.

Good so, she said still in Dutch, that's fine, Boksma, and when will you be here, so we can show you the room.

All this because we've finally figured out the rules have changed; we can't count on finding rooms. Maybe it's because this is so heavily touristed, this part of the country; maybe because the weather is so good, or because it's final days of summer. Whatever the reason we've run into problems, so today we booked into this hotel Wildeman for tonight and tomorrow, resorting to the old one-way bus trick on this otherwise walking trip around the old Zuider Zee.

Yesterday's hotel was nice — a small hotel with crumby rooms, no tub, no telephone (and hence no e-mail), but a fine breakfast and a friendly staff. In fact the staff was the owner: he'd bought the place only a month or two ago, his first hotel, and he was so pleased with us that he gave us a bottle of Beerenburg to carry with us, and I was so pleased with him that I left my second pair of pants, the ones I wear in the evening, and I'll have to go back tomorrow to get them.

We set out this morning in a fine rain which soon grew heavier, forcing us for the first time to break out our thin plastic ponchos, which normally ride in their own envelope, taking about as much room as a thin wallet.

We walked down to the marina on the Slotermeer, a large inland lake pretty well invisible in the mist, and walked a couple of kilometers along the lake on top of a grass dike, sharing it with a flock of apprehensive sheep who kept edging away from us, seemingly leading us on to who knew what goal.

We then turned back inland, leaving the sheep behind to shift for themselves, and came to the pretty town of Wijcker, with a fine old church whose door stood open. Inside someone was playing the organ, somewhat tentatively, and I heard a man's voice singing along quietly, and saw a stout woman waiting alone on a pew in the otherwise empty church.

Aha, I thought, a mother waiting for her child to finish his organ lesson. But that was not it at all: she was sitting out the tryout
a visiting organist was giving the instrument.

Outside a young dutch couple drew up on their motorcycles, a
Suzuki and a Honda, hers and his, both of them in black leather
neatly setting off their blond hair and pink faces. And we hit the
road again, this time for Sloten.

This proved to be the smallest of the Eleven Frisian Cities, a
"city" of only seven hundred souls, but furnished with a fine historical museum, with sliding drawers filled with neatly displayed
prints, coins, maps, and portraits. Upstairs there was a cleverly arranged series of peepshows: when you bent to look into them they
lit up automatically, some revealing objects, others changing pro-
jections of some kind, many of the peep-slots between small speakers just reaching your ears, playing music and a recorded narrative
of the sights. I'll probably have more to say about this when I get to
a real keyboard: writing on this folding apparatus isn't a lot of fun.

We took a walk around the town, which is an island at the
crossroads of the water road from the Slotermeer to the IJsselmeer
and the land road from Germany to Friesland. At one corner a
beautifully restored flour windmill stood, and on its balcony a tenor
stood with a ghettoblaster for accompaniment singing from *Die
Schöne Müllerin* (naturally) and, ultimately, the Ave Maria aria
from *La Rondine* — touching, affecting, pleasing our handful of lis-
teners below.

Across the bridge the local fire department was practising the
deployment of an impossibly long firehose, unspiralling it, shooting
down a couple of plastic water bottles, then winding it back up
again into neat spirals.

We tried to find rooms at one of the two B&Bs in town, unsuccessfully, and then settled for this hotel in the next town, coming
here by bus. Tomorrow we'll walk back to Sloten, and then come
back here by bus again, me by way of Balk to pick up my errant
trousers. I hope it doesn't rain: today ended fine, clear, and warm,
but my shoes will take all night to finish drying.

Erasmus

Kampen, September 12 —

DO YOU HAVE THE KEY, she said, No, I said, I gave it to you, No you didn't, she said, where did you leave it, The last time I saw it I'd left it in the door, I said, There it is, she said, in your backpack.

Do you have your wallet, she said, Of course I do, I said, picking it up out of my backpack and slipping it into my pocket.

Your pants are unzipped, she said, No they aren't, I said, You're trying to make me think I'm losing my mind again, my pants are zipped. Well you're always complaining I don't tell you when they're unzipped, she said.

We were going out to eat. The hotel guy had recommended a place right down the street. I checked it in the listing I'd downloaded to the Palm from "Iens," a sort of Dutch version of Zagat. (Imagine an encircled "C" here, or maybe a small "tm".)

Outside of Marius, which is 1) in Amsterdam, 2) owned by a friend, 3) truly exceptional, d'Oude Vismark, here in Kampen, is the most enjoyable restaurant I've eaten in here in the Netherlands on this trip. Two reasons: The food and wine; The owner.

Half a dozen starters, a couple of soups, six or eight main courses; a sufficient list of mostly French wines. A fine room, partly recalling the traditional Dutch brown-and-mirrored restaurants, partly quite updated. A view looking out on the IJssel and its splendid lift-bridge crowned with four beautifully gilded pulley-wheels. ("Cheaper to maintain," our host explained.)

I can't describe my dinner, because I photographed it all, and I can't really look at the photographs until I have my computer. It's one of the disadvantages of living with only a pocket computer, this Palm, which does very nicely for many things, but certainly can't keep up with the hundreds of digital photos we seem to accumulate.

What I had was the "surprise" three-course dinner, which included beef bouillon, wonderful duck paté in a sort of eggnog sauce, beefsteak, and three or four little desserts.

Good as the food as, both in concept and in execution, the truly memorable aspect of the evening was the running conversation with our host-and-waiter, the co-owner Ron Wesseler. He seems to have had a full life, and to be content with narrowing his activities down to running this admirable restaurant, enjoying his granddaughter, and spending a couple of months a year in Goa.

Last night's restaurant, De Connoisseur, in Lemmer, featured a shrine-like corner with a large photograph of a striking-looking man who, the hostess explained, was simply a friend of the place, a man who'd died a number of years ago at the age of ninety-two, a former Minister of Finance who knew how to live.

Tonight's restaurant featured a blackboard, not really prominently hung at the end of the bar, on which Mr. Wesseler writes a maxim every few weeks. Tonight it read something like Live a pleasurable life: do something nice.

You must dance with life, he said at one point, when we were talking about the pleasure of living. Yes, I said, but your own countryman Erasmus, who is the most intelligent commentator on life I've ever read, said that if you invite a wise man to a dance, he will dance like a cow.

In that case, Mr. Wesseler said, I would not dance with him; I don't think I would like to dance with a cow.

On the main street in this fine old baroque town there's a life-size statue of a heavy-set cow rearing well up on her hind legs, almost as if she were dancing. She isn't, though: the statue recalls a typically funny-but-tragic moment in Dutch history when an obscenely rich man, having built an obscenely tall but quite beautiful tower just to show how rich he is, on noticing grass growing atop it, had a full-grown milk-cow hoisted to the roof to graze on it.

The poor thing died of suffocation in the sling, but ever since the plaza at the foot of the tower has been called Coeplein, Cow Plaza. And now there's the statue, quite near the tiles in a sidewalk commemorating all the finest minds and most successful movers and shakers of the Kampen citizenry over the years.

Mr. Wesseler brought my main course, a series of nicely carved slices of rare meat. This is a Brazilian, he said. I thought morosely of our Brazilian boy Julio, who was so diconsolate when he arrived to spend six months with us as an exchange student, and I served him a rare steak in *marchand du vin* sauce, and he manfully dealt with it, and told us only the next day that he was a vegetarian.

I don't like to eat Brazilians, I said, but I will do my best.

(Erasmus had gone on to say: Invite a wise man to a feast and he will spoil the company, either with troublesome discourse or morose silence. In that case, Mr. Wesseler said, I will not invite any wise man to dinner.)

The dinner went through a bottle of Soave and a bottle of Sauvignon blanc, since many of us had fish or sweetbreads, and a glass of surprising German red Rheingau, since I had my Brazilian, and ended triumphantly with Corenwijn, since it is one of the jewels of the Dutch nation, and then we went out into the beautiful sparkling night.

Do you have the key, she asked, as we approached the hotel, No, I said, I do not have the key. You said you had it when we left, she said. I did have it when we left, I said, but I don't have it now.

Perhaps it's in your jacket, Mac said. Where is your jacket? Yes, I said, There you are, I put it in my jacket pocket, I don't have my jacket, I left it in the restaurant. And back I went for it, and there it was on the floor behind my chair, and all is well.

Livestock
Groningen, September 13, 2005

FIRST, LET ME SAY THAT my preparations were not as good as they should have been: therefore this may be the last message for a while.

On the other hand, we're encouraged to hear from the two friends with whom we're travelling that we seem to be in good shape — physically, in any case. Today we walked about fifteen kilometers, half or so in a fine mist, which some others of us called a rain, and others a heavy mist.

It was another *grasdijk* day: walking atop a grassy dike scattered with, excuse me, sheepshit, from a few kilometers north of Kampen to the next town, Genemuiden.

At one point we noticed a sheep lying on her back, waggling her four feet toward a heaven evangelical in these parts but no kinder for that to quadrupeds. I hopped the fence to go up and do an errand of mercy, but I was confused by her rolled-back eyeballs. Was this ewe crazed, poisoned perhaps by unknown Dutch weed, or perhaps simply at the end of her probable lifetime? *Geen idee*, as the Dutch say, no idea. Marjorie shouted something I coudn't make out. I gave it up and walked along the top of the dike, motioning to the others to continue in that direction.

At a gate I turned back down to the road where they were and we continued. Soon a bicycle came our way bearing a young woman with a fine complexion, a neat dark coiffure, and a relaxed expression.

There's a sheep in trouble, I said, Do you know whose sheep it is? Yes, she said, I saw it, I go to help.

We switched to Engish. Is it your sheep, I asked. Yes. I saw through the window, and I saw people there, and waited to see if they would take care of it.

She cycled on to the gate, tossed her bike against the fence, loped up to the top of the dike, and did what I should have done: took hold of two handfuls of wool, pulled on the sheep, set it up on its feet.

We talked a bit more when she came back down to the road. It was her sheep; she'd seen us; when I failed to correct her damn ewe she cycled out. A poor example of intelligent design, I said, an animal that can't right itself when on its back, no better than a turtle.

Yes, she agreed, it isn't a good design; maybe they should have air bags.

We walked on, soon coming to a farmhouse from which a couple of pups came running to us, one a very young collie, the other a toy shepherd of some kind. They didn't make a sound; simply came running up to nuzzle and sniff — and follow us a little too far, until I picked up the toy shepherd and tossed it over the electric fence into the pasture it shared with a few sheep, a goat or two, and a small Shetland-type pony.

We walked on into Genemuiden, a town whose name I'll always have to look up, and had a ham-cheese *tosti* and a bowl of *mosterdsoep* and a beer, and then, since the mist had lifted and the sky was blue, we went on for another six kilometers. At the point of no return the rain began to fall, of course, or the mist began to congeal. But it was a fine walk, with swans, white sheep, Egyptian geese, brown sheep, lapwings, crows, cattle, and sheep.

Ultimately we came out onto a road next to a pasture full of mottled red-and-white cows. A man was about to drive his huge tractor into the garage, and I went up to ask what sort of cattle they were.

Geen idee, he said, no idea. Then he thought about it and said MRI, Maas Rooi Ijzen. That meant, I thought, Maas (River) Red Iron, and I began to doubt him. But it sounded authoritative, so why not stay with it.

We waited fifty minutes under some elms for the next bus and rode it into town, wondering what the hell the computer display was we were looking at.

Oh, the driver said when we reached our destination, the train station at Kampen, it isn't yet in action, on most of the other routes it is. It's a thing that tells you always where you are, and how many minutes to the next stop, and where it is.

A good thing, I said, I often want to know where I am.

But, I reflected later, a better thing would be a device that tells me where I am when I am not in the bus, and where the hell the bus is, and where I can catch it, and when.

But now we are in our hotel; the clothes are drying, and tomorrow since it will be raining pitchforks we take the train to either Groningen or Nijmegen, we haven't yet decided which, and switch from this Zuider Zeepad to the Pieterpad, which we already know, for the last few days of this walk.

I hope I'll be able to sort out the technology to keep you informed.

But I was not able to, apparently, as the next dispatch was sent long after...

Provence interlude
September 23, 2005—

LET'S SEE... WHERE DID I leave you? Friesland? Kampen? Groningen? It all seems so long ago. The walk continued sporadically, a day or two at a time, two or three days between. The best walking, in many ways, came last; two glorious days tramping across the heath and through the forests to the south of Groningen, the heath in full bloom, almost like the lavender fields of Provence.

Which, speaking of, came next. After a mad taxi-drive Nice airport to hotel we met Hans and Anneke at the hotel door — they had just arrived, after spending two hours driving around in Nice looking for it. Particularly annoying since I'd chosen it precisely because it seemed easy to find on entering the city.

Then a nice day driving up through Vence, stopping off at Fondation Maeght to look at a retrospective of European postwar modernism (always one of my least favorite periods, but interesting as a corrective to my prejudices). We stopped for the night at a little country hotel near Tourettes-sur-Loup, a pretty little place run by a young couple, and ate there as well, decently enough.

Next day, Friday, we drove on to Draguignan, avoiding it at the last minute, and into the edge of the Var, still one of my favorite regions. Here we negotiated the narrow winding roads among wild pine-and-oak forest, hugging hillsides, stopping off at Ampus, Tourtour, Chateaudouble, and finally Villecroze where we put up at a very fancy B&B in an old *bastide* brought up to date with paintings, flowers, paint, curtains. Out my window I see the swimming pool and two parasol pines.

The grounds contain a fine kitchen garden, a small vineyard, an herb garden. The place is owned by a childless couple in, I'd say, their forties, she a Parisienne, he a Trieste-born Italian who studied in France (agronomy, specializing in soils) and who speaks easily in French and English but whose Dutch is nonexistent, though he took a course or two in Waginingen. I asked him about the parasol pines, and he said that although everyone says they're the same tree as the maritime pine and the stone pine he believes they are not. *Science*, he said, dismissively, in the same tone he'd said *Berlusconi*.

An acceptable *boeuf daube* night before last in a nearby restaurant a few minutes' walk from our B&B. And, oh, I forgot, a strenuous scramble yesterday up a stony path among the pines outside Villecroze — a walk described as Easy by the bureau of tourism, which provided us with an English-language guide to the paths, which assured us we'd never lack for trail blazes — which petered out entirely when we were say a kilometer from the start, and left us in the midst of the *garrigue*, to find our own way should we choose to go on, which we wisely, I think, did not.

Yesterday a tour of the eastern edge of the center Var, a fabulous bit of country rumpled by pine-covered ridges and oak-strewn valleys, narrow ones for the most part with the clearest imaginable water rushing through. Two high points: the fish soup in La Provençale in Aups, better than ever, and the abbey at Le Thoronet, a bit too scrubbed and "restored" but magnificent in its volumes and rhythms, its austere stonework, the tranquility of its setting.

And the towns and villages: Salernes and its tiles; Entrecastaux with its surprising Le Notre garden; Carces; Aups itself with a busy market where I could finally replenish my sock drawer. These towns are well separated; although the intermediate-size supermarkets and do-it-yourself building supply centers are springing up on the outskirts, there seems little sprawl.

It's pig season, and there are solitary "hunters" standing in their army-surplus camouflage at the sides of roads, waiting for the dogs to chase a pig toward them to be shot. Of course there's not a pig left in the country dumb enough to fall for it, so the entire affair is mostly a ritual, like the one that makes our fish soup so much more pleasurable, scraping the garlic on the toast, spreading the *rouille*, scattering the gruyere...

I sit awaiting breakfast at a table outside, near the pool. It's a quiet morning. The air is soft and a little heavy: it may rain later, though the sky looks promising. The light is rosy here, bringing surprising things out of the intense greens surrounding us on all sides. And it smells wonderful: soil, cut grass, the foliage beginning to turn —

Oh! A couple of shots just rang out! Someone may have *sanglier* for dinner!

Dogs and Cats
Healdsburg, October 6, 2005

I AM NOT A DOG PERSON, no no no no, not in this country. We had a dog, of course, when I was a kid, sixty years ago and more; just about everyone did. A toy shepherd named Butch. But none since. I tend to agree with Emma, who doesn't like dogs because, she says, they pee and they slobber.

Cats, yes; we like cats just fine, and for thirty years or so we had at least one and usually two. The last two, Joe and Blanche, lived to be nearly twenty, and I miss them still.

And so when I walk into a hotel to check in and see a cat in the lobby I immediately feel things are breaking my way. The old Hotel Figueroa in Los Angeles; the Sylvia in Vancouver.

And when you duck into a bar or a café and find a cat sleeping in the window, or under a chair: you feel immediately there's tranquility here, and after all that's what you're looking for.

Dogs are another matter, but not in Europe. Every time we go to Europe we begin again the list of disadvantageous differences, disadvantageous to our own country I mean — the never-to-be-written-or-published book Why Can't We... — and one of the chapters will surely center on Man's Best Friend.

Kees and Irma, for example, have a wonderful border collie called "Yella," spelled Jelle I think, a Frisian name having nothing to do with his colors which are the regimental black and white of his breed. Perhaps that's "her" breed: sex never seemed to be an issue with this fine animal.

One night sleeping I developed a Charley horse, that excruciating sudden pain in the calf of your leg. I couldn't cry out, as I generally do, because I'd have awakened everyone in the house. Instead I whimpered, and immediately there came Jelle full of sympathy and concern, nosing me to be sure I'd recover. There was something immensely reassuring about this and I've had to revisit my attitude toward Albert Payson Terhune.

We had breakfast a couple or three weeks ago in Groningen, that fine regional capital in the north of The Netherlands. Curiously every chain café in the town center was out of milk at seven in the morning — they only serve fresh milk, it seems, in their cappuccinos — and we ended up at an upscale Café-Conditerei serving pastries and coffees to comfortable-looking people at small tables, nearly each with a newspaper, most of them conservative.

There were no fewer than three dogs in our part of the room, a smaller raised central room with perhaps eight tables. They were small fat shaggy dogs with short legs and tiny feet, and they moved rather sluggishly I thought if they moved at all. One did, ultimately, giving up its post under another table to come stand patiently at the feet of my own chair, foolishly thinking I was about to give up a piece of croissant.

(Or perhaps, given its shape, hoping for a sugar cube. I think this was one of the few places that hasn't given up sugar cubes in favor of those ridiculous little paper tubes of sugar, no doubt forced on the restaurant industry by the Dutch Society of Friends of the Horse in an almost completely successful effort to interfere with my passing out sugar cubes to horses on our perambulations through the Dutch countryside.)

These dogs were no harm to anyone, not even the waiters who brought things here and there through a space whose navigation was made difficult by its forest of tables and chairs and seated readers of newspapers. (I wonder how the room looks to those dogs, who see it from a vantage much closer the floor.)

They were really small slow sculptures, clean as a whistle (this is the Netherlands, after all), quiet, friendly and patient, never demanding. They were, in short, almost cats.

We had lunch last week in a café in Amsterdam — a bar-restaurant, really — at about four in the afternoon, an hour when I never really expect to find anything. Only one other table was occupied, by two English girls looking over a fashion magazine and not really eating much of anything.

We ordered off the lunch menu: a salad of some kind for L., a merguez sandwich for me. That turned out to be a sort of hamburger bun, toasted, with four grilled lamb sausages (very good, by the way), sliced tomatoes and cucumbers, and some onion. Delicious; and afterward I asked the waitress, now tending bar, the name of the fine sleeping cat perched on the ledge-overlook near the English girls.

Caspar, she said, and that's Gaston in the window, pointing to Caspar's match.

I know, I know, the health authorities in this country would shudder at the thought. I don't know why they don't in the Netherlands, whose health laws are sometimes even more insane than our own. But I retort that important studies have revealed that children who grow up with household pets are sixtyseven percent less likely to develop asthma. Don't ask for the source of this information: I can't provide it. But I know it's true. It stands to reason.

The canals, luminously black if that is possible,
dappled in ever-different patterns (p. 218)

Christmas in Amsterdam

Again in Amsterdam, again
Amsterdam, December 20, 2005

THE APPROACH TO SCHIPHOL was unfamiliar, partly because it was quite dark, partly because we approached it from the south; so the first thing to pop into my mind was how the airport has changed in the last thirty years.

The first time I landed here was in 1973, in the springtime, early in an afternoon, on a bright clear day, and I was struck by the many stands of poplars throwing shadows across the green green lawns and fields, and the dark water of the canals, and the many neat thatched-roof brick farmhouses. None of those is left, as far as I can tell.

But the approach was very beautiful. We dropped down through cotton-ball clouds completely covering the ground, expecting to see nothing, to be in a thick fog: but underneath the night landscape was brilliantly delineated by the thousands of lights — white headlights and red taillights tracing the roads and highways, an occasional flashing red light suggesting an incident (the Dutch word is more expressive: *calamiteit*); masses of golden lights denoting piers, docked ships, factories and warehouses about to spring into action, and surprising white rectangles: the huge greenhouses supplying the cut-flower industry.

The night flight was fine elsewhere. Since a belligerent passenger had to be ejected and therefore his checked luggage found and unloaded, we left Atlanta forty minutes late, and it was dark by the time we'd crossed into South Carolina. We flew up the coastline, surprisingly staying a mile or two inland the whole time, and watched the lights, spare in the tree-covered suburbs, brilliant in the frequent towns and cities. Then it was pitch dark, black as the inside of a cat as David G. used to say, until the amazing lights of

Dublin suddenly appeared below us, the swerve of shore and bend of bay unmistakable to any student, however rusty, of *Finnegans Wake*. And then the dark Irish sea, and the scattered lights of the British Midlands, and the sudden appearance of the Europoort as we entered Dutch airspace. We are in another cheap hotel just outside the old city, as usual: we sleep cheap, in order to eat well. The Hotel Prinsen has we think the smallest room we've ever rented, just big enough for a double bed, a desk the size of a sewing machine, two chairs (one with a broken seat), an armoire big enough to hang six coathangers in, and an in-room bathroom with shower, no tub. There is one light bulb in the room. There is a telephone and it has a dataport for e-mail, but there is no high-speed internet connection, so we will not be surfing the web, or uploading blogs and photos, unless I carry my laptop over to the Apple store and piggyback on its wireless — but that's a fair walk, and we're likely to have more interesting things to do.

Therefore I revert, I hope, to my old system of e-mailed travel dispatches to you — to you who may be reading this, and a hundred or so others. As usual I ask that you let me know if you want me to drop your name; and as usual, recently anyhow, I'm uncertain that even this method will work. There are times I think the Golden Age of internet and e-mail are behind us. And then, who knows, perhaps I'll get us all in trouble with the Administration! The day may come when we'll have to resort to simple family ciphers, like the Mozart family!

We are just across the Singelgracht from the Leidseplein, now alarmingly like the Rembrandtplein, awash in cheap restaurants, suspect "coffee shops" (as they call pot-smoking clubs here), and souvenir stands. Only a block or two away from the square, though, you find the older kinds of street: apartment houses, offices, streets full of antiques, little specialty shops: bookbinders, stationers, hairdressers, a fine Italian delicatessen that provided tonight's *finocchiona panini*. And, of course, we're close to the Museumplein, where the van Gogh and the Rijksmuseum are — currently undergoing extensive renovation, hence greatly reduced in accessibility.

But the trams and the pedestrian-streets encourage urban wandering, always delightful in this delightful city. We ducked into a little *pannekoekenhuis* today for lunch — a bacon pancake for Lindsey, bacon-and-apple for me, with a glass of milk, and tea afterward: just us, and the lady who presides, and one or two other customers who dropped in, regulars apparently. We talked about the crockery, nice pieces of old French manufacture — Deshoulliers, Delaunay, and a piece or two of Apilco; and even the latter is now not to be found except by great luck, and here they were being really used, as they were meant to be, in a curious *pannekoekenhuisje* filled with enthusiastic savage paintings of nude African women, and Christmas ornaments, and miniature bronze sculptures for sale, because the bourgeois Dutch still love their miniature bronze statues, and why not?

Paper Breughels
Amsterdam, December 21

NUDGING LINDSEY IN THE RIBS, cradling our three suitcases between my knees, I indicated the guy across the aisle in the crowded number 2 tram. A perfect Dutchman, he was sitting in a shapeless grey topcoat, not fat but well too large for the plastic seat, holding an envelope nearsightedly close to one eye, squinting up at it under his glasses, his forehead thereby lopsidedly furrowed, his fortyish face expressing combined attentiveness, disbelief, unrecognition, effort, and finally unconcern.

He looked familiar, and my cheaply printed placemat at Le Soleil a couple of hours later told me why. Pieter Breughel may have painted his crowded scenes of peasants and burghers over three hundred years ago, but they are vivacious and accurate, catching real people in real attitudes and gestures. In America we're used to seeing the results of generations of mixed breeding; in Europe, even in world capitals like Amsterdam, you often see the opposite, the pure stock resulting from generations of love affairs between neighbors. My friend on the tram was pure Nederlander, and could have stepped out of a Breughel.

Of course Amsterdam is an international city, so there was a young Japanese couple standing on the tram, their huge backpacks stowed behind them on the floor. He had bought his tickets from the nice man sitting in his wicket at the entrance — I wonder if he shouldn't have bought tickets for the backpacks as well — and was now inspecting a fold-out paper map of the city, no doubt looking to see where their hotel might be.

Not far from ours, I bet. As we were finishing our lunch *pannekoek* at Le Soleil, where the nice French china sits on the paper Breughels, in they stepped, much nicer-looking for having parked their packs somewhere. We nodded and smiled on their way out, but I don't think we registered on them as they had on us. No doubt we blend into the general confusion of exotic foreignness.

Even in December this part of town is lively with youth, much of it inexpensively arrived from distant parts. I suppose a certain number of them are attracted by the legal marijuana; one occasionally smells a whiff in the street. It's only one form of the Dutch penchant for *gezelligheid*. "Coziness" is the usual translation, but that word emphasizes physical snugness, and an equally important part of the word implies social and above all familiar mutual presence among friends.

You see it over and over in the paintings: Jan Steen, Frans Hals, even Vermeer. I am looking forward to my own *gezelligheid* with some of those paintings in the next few days! But we look forward also to conversations in the *bruincafes*, the old smoky wood-panelled bars where you sit at a nice big table nursing a gin-and-beer (serial, or alternative, not mixed!) and catching up on gossip and shared memories...

Even the buildings here are *gezellig*, companionable is the translation that comes to mind, standing in their complacent rows along canals or streets that may well once have been canals themselves, all built in the same era, whether one or two or three hundred years ago, and so all the same height (determined I suppose by how many steps one could reasonably expect anyone to deal with), and mostly the same style, individuating themselves as we people do with individual haircuts and neckties (I date myself), step-gables and pilasters; jackets and shirts, front doors and fanlights.

Our street, Vondelstraat, curves nonchalantly away from the Singelgracht just the country side of Leidseplein, a narrow street fronted by three- and four-storey buildings now housing inexpensive hotels and offices as well as residential apartments. Last night, returning from a walk, we were struck by its quiet domestic perfection. The street is the right width, in ratio to the height of the buildings facing it. The buildings make a fine ensemble, each differing from its neighbors enough to be identified, but agreeing in general to further civic ease and composure.

There is one eccentric building, and it is just across the street from our window. But it is a fine eccentricity. The materials are all the same, bourgeois brick, brilliantly clear glass, clean plaster; but the architecture appeals to delight as well as solidity. I don't know what the Dutch call this school — I'll have to ask — and it doesn't really exist in my country. I've seen it in Madrid, and there's a whole delightful neighborhood of it in Rome. It's somewhere about the time of Art Nouveau, between Victorian and early Modernism, neither of which it has anything remotely to do. It enjoys its forms and surfaces, decorating and emphasizing them with traceries of sgraffito in the plasterwork, and capping its modest exuberance with tiled turrets and lookouts and gables.

Eten bij Marius
Apeldoorn, December 23

THE TOWN IS REALLY DEAD, I observed to the night clerk. You noticed, she answered laconically in her nicotine baritone. She showed me the hotel booking-chart, only a few of the squares on this week's grid filled in. Normally, she said, turning to the January page, it's like this: every square filled in neatly in blue ink. She turned page after page: all of them crowded.

You can get a room in almost any hotel this week, and I bet you could do a little haggling for the price. Out of curiosity I asked at the much fancier Hotel Vondel down the street, whose wi-fi wireless internet connection I could use here in the Prinsen if I wanted to pay the Swiss firm that's taken over that utility an obscene amount of money. We have a very nice room for 99 Euros, the clerk said. Thanks, I said, I'll tell my friends, and turned to go. Or tell them it's ninety, he called after me.

Amsterdam, I've heard from many sources, has more hotels than any other European city. The city's full of casual travelers, whether to satisfy hungers discouraged elsewhere, or for business or commercial reasons, or (like us) drawn by its bracing combination of beauty and entertainment. And while we notice especially the foreign visitors, with backpacks or Gucci suitcases, of course there are plenty of Dutch visitors as well, who come into the city for shopping, or the concert or theater, or to eat.

We ate night before last at what I've decided is my favorite restaurant in the world. I think it is an epochal breakthrough, the model for what I hope will be a future norm. Marius is in an unlikely quarter, easily reached by cab or on foot from the huge Centraal Station, on a quiet street near the harbor. It's a modest storefront on the street, fifty meters or so from the Zoutkeetsgracht terminus of the number 3 tramline, which is how we travel.

Inside there are two large tables and two or three smaller ones. In the back, a small kitchen. I suppose you could seat thirty people here at the most. There is one woman waiting tables, one man washing dishes and doing prep, and one cook; and he is both one of the most accomplished chefs I have ever known and our dear friend Kees.

We are here in the Netherlands to attend his parents' fiftieth wedding anniversary. Our daughter Thérèse lived with the Elfrings for a year as an exchange student, thirty years ago, and it's no exaggeration to say that her family has become ours, her parents something like brother and sister to us, their children our niece and nephews. We have often traveled with Hans and Anneke: last February for a week in Spain; last September for a week in Provence; in previous years on bicycles in Holland, or by auto to Death Valley, or Lake Tahoe, or Glacier Park.

Kees is particularly close because he worked for two years, on separated occasions, at Chez Panisse, and knows our family and friends particularly well. Unlike his brothers and sister he did not follow an academic career from his adolescence: he was always interested in cooking. He trained at the Dutch national culinary school — the government wisely invested a lot in what it calls the HoReCa industry back in the 1970s and '80s, and the present result is a country with as high a level of hotel, restaurant, and café accommodation as we've found anywhere.

He went on to work "stages" in professional kitchens: in Brussels, in the Netherlands, at Chez Panisse. He then opened his own restaurant in a small town near his native city, Apeldoorn, in the center of the country. Het Pomphuis was a marvelous place with an extensive menu, and we mourned its demise a few years ago when it closed after nearly ten years, the victim, perhaps, of professional burnout — nothing is more demanding than the restaurant business.

Imbued with the spirit of Chez Panisse he decided, after taking a year off to travel — a bicycle tour across Australia was one project, mercifully cut short after a couple of hundred miles when a cheap automobile proved a better alternative — to open a greengrocer business in Amsterdam, bringing in the best primeurs he could find locally and on regular trips to Paris, shopping them to fine restaurants and shops in Amsterdam, and demonstrating their use in a small kitchen he set up in his warehouse.

"Marius," he called this business, since of the names of the old Pagnol trilogy both Cesar and Panisse had been taken by then, and his truck was emblazoned with a fine panel depicting the sort of produce he was selling. But he was ahead of his time, I think, and while he gained respect and admiration for the concept and the effort, commercial success remained problematic.

The thing is, Kees is a cook, born and trained. He belonged in a restaurant where he would have total control over every aspect, where he could converse with his clientele while turning out dishes whose artistry, intelligence, specificity, and ethos would not be compromised. Two or three years ago the restaurant became available, like magic, at exactly the right time.

His original concept for Marius was bold and imaginative: he would serve a "staff meal" early in the evening, say at six o'clock, sitting down himself with his dishwasher and waiter and twelve or fifteen diners who would have a simple two-course meal (as I recall it) with a simple dessert and a glass or so of simple wine: the cost would be twenty euros. Then, at 8:30, he would serve a more complex meal, one similar to what Chez Panisse does downstairs, with three courses before cheese or dessert: this would cost 35 euros — I work from memory here, and the numbers could be wrong — and wine would be extra, still pitched fairly inexpensively, but chosen from an interesting list of wines of "terroir," wines with character and authority, listed with an eye to the dishes they would ultimately accompany.

In the last year the first component of the format has been dropped. What we had for dinner on Wednesday, Dec. 21, was typical of what is now offered. We began with olives, salami, and bread, with an aperitif — white wine with a few drops of Punt e Mes for me.

Then dinner proper began with a "slow-cooked" tuna, poached you might almost say very slowly in olive oil with chopped garlic and basil, until the result is neither cooked tuna nor tartare, the flavor of the carefully chosen oil rounds out and completes that of the tuna, and the texture remains firm and flaky. With this, a section of leek, a quarter of fennel, and a wedge of Chioggia beet, similarly prepared in an anchovy sauce.

Next came another fish course — after all, we were sitting near the shore of the greatest inland sea in Europe. This one was monkfish, but just the cheeks, served with spinach and morels in a classic beurre blanc, with only a trace of lemon. What you tasted was the fish itself, again with texture an important part of the dish, every component of which carried the first course forward while offering a gentle contrast.

And then strips of wild duck breast, with potato dice crisped in goose fat — a fine winter dish. With these, a nice cool flinty but floral Jurançon white, then a modest, fruity Montalcino red.

Kees was able to sit with us and with others from time to time, letting both diners and kitchen rest between courses. We sat down about eight o'clock, and left in time to catch the last tram back at about midnight. The dining room was full of enthusiasts — a musician specializing in early music; the proprietor of a fine delicatessen and two of his staff; a couple of wine writers and their wives; various others. Everyone was involved, engaged, rewarded: to eat this meal, in these surroundings, among these people, was like hearing a fine performance of jazz or chamber music, discussing things with the musicians between sections of the program, sharing a common intelligence, enthusiasm, delight.

What we need now of course is for every neighborhood of every city to develop its own restaurant on this model, and for the chefs involved — the waiters and dishwashers too! — to be honored and rewarded by their communities. Such a world of restaurants could easily coexist with fast-food outlets and chain white-tablecloth places; every kind of business can and should have its clientele, every kind of membership its club, its retreat.

Haarlem Afternoon
Amsterdam, December 24

WALKING THROUGH THE RED-LIGHT district toward the train station we stopped to admire a curious storefront. A guy in work clothes carrying a bundle of what might have been clothes stopped when he saw us. It's the oldest shop in the red-light district, he said; it used to be some kind of store, but turned into a smoke shop quite a while ago. The cops have shut it down, that's why it's all locked up and boarded over. They must have been selling the wrong kind of drugs.

The guy seemed a little disreputable but friendly enough, and his English was very good, so I fell in with him as he walked on toward the station. I was born here, he explained, I know this area well. I live around that corner, in a basement, but I have to find another place, I have emphysema, it's very hard for me to find a place in Amsterdam, I can't climb stairs.

Yeah, I agreed, I've heard it's very expensive in Amsterdam, maybe you should try Venlo, or Roermond. (I was kidding: those provincial cities are far from here, on the German border, east and well south.)

Venlo, he scoffed. Not likely.

Amsterdam's huge, magisterial, brick railroad station hove into view as we rounded a corner. Ah, there it is, I said; isn't it beautiful. Well, the guy said, yes, maybe, but you know before it was built Amsterdam was open to the harbor; now the sea is all blocked off, and people get stressed and upset. People have to be open to the water. Excuse me, I've got to rush now, I have to get down to Schiphol, I have a hearing there. A guy insulted me and I had to hit him and they arrested me and now they want to put me in jail. Nice talking to you.

I hope they don't put you in jail, I said. Me too, he said.

But if they do, I said, have fun in there. Don't worry, he said, I'll do that, I always have fun. And he hurried on, in a deliberate sort of way.

We'd been shopping at the Nieuwmarkt, near the Mint: Lindsey wanted to buy some organic apples, as she's making dessert for tomorrow's Christmas dinner at Hans and Anneke's — the couple whose anniversary brought us here for the week. As we entered the market square I heard voices singing: a very nice group of carolers were singing at the other end of the organic market. Lindsey found her apples, and I stood gazing at a display of all sorts of organic grains — kamut, spelt, two or three wheats, oats, that sort of thing.

Do you see anything you could cook at your restaurant, someone said, and I turned to find the woman who'd asked about the movie *Sideways* a few nights ago, when we ate at Marius. We talked a little while, and I found myself asking how I could find an apartment for a month in Amsterdam. The city has insinuated itself.

At the train station we stopped to admire a *draaigorgel*, a "draw-organ," so called I suppose because it's mounted on a cart you pull down the street. We've seen a number of these over the years, in one Dutch city or another. I suppose they're run by electricity, generated by a small gas engine — whatever the power source, it's pretty quiet.

The organs play from punched cards, thick ones made of fiberboard that are hinged together accordion-style into very long chains that fold up like a book. You can apparently find everything from arrangements of opera arias to Christian hymns, Strauss waltzes and polkas to Mozart sonatas. We heard *Jerusalem Jerusalem*, a rousing solemn hymn that I didn't recognize right away, but Lindsey immediately began singing along, and I joined in as best I could given that I woke up with laryngitis this morning.

These organs are beautifully decorated, with painted panels before which stand figurines variously beating time with a baton, or striking bells from time to time, or even playing tambourines — though all that was apparently too frivolous for *Jerusalem Jerusalem*, as the figures remained still, and so did we.

Then we went on. We were off for the afternoon to Haarlem, because Richard wanted to see the Frans Hals Museum, and I wanted to see the Great St. Bavo Church. At the tourist office we discovered that the church closed at four, while the museum was open until five: so we had a quick coffee and *appeltaart*, then stepped into the church.

Perhaps you've seen reproductions of one or another of Pieter Sanraedam's magnificent paintings of the interior of this church — small paintings that seem as big as a billboard, accurately suggesting the immense scale and the odd tranquility and rationality of what I think is one of the greatest peaks of architecture, rivaling the Mosque in Córdoba, the abbey at Tournus.

Sanraedam is buried in the floor here, and we stood reverently (well, at least I was reverent) on his stone; and then we looked at Frans Hals's grave, out of reach behind the choir screen, and then we walked about quietly drinking in the light and space. A friendly staff-person approached, and I was afraid he would ask me to remove my hat, which I had irreverently left on because it was in fact really quite cold: but he only wanted to tell the girls to enjoy the church, and to be careful not to sprain their necks looking up at the distant ceiling, we want you to be healthy.

There is no way to convey the size of this place. I could mention that it's 38 meters from floor to ceiling, or 48 from ground to ridge, or 80 to the top of the spire, but those are just numbers. I remember once walking all the way around the *Matsonia* as she lay in drydock: this church is, I'm sure, much bigger — and made of stone. Good thing it doesn't have to float.

On, then, to the Frans Hals Museum, down several blocks of pedestrian shopping streets, with hardware, cheese, toys, CDs, clothing, shoes, books, antiques, wine, hairdressers, a violinmaker, cigars and a dozen other things all vying for attention, the street crowded with people pushing bicycles or baby-strollers, walking arm in arm, carrying bags or bottles, and generally enjoying this Christmas Eve in a thoroughly decadent and delightful way.

The Hals Museum is in a former orphanage, of course — every large old building in this country seems to have been an orphanage, or an old ladie's home, or a leper colony, or some such institution of public charity. (Some, I know, were workhouses and prisons, but they don't boast about those.) Here we found an exhibition of paintings by — Sanraedam! And not only paintings, but the preparatory drawings for some of them too, fascinating drawings showing his careful perspective analysis of the architecture, then the improvements he made to reality to make the finished paintings more suggestive of what the eye takes in when actually within the church.

The Hals *schutterportretten*, of course, those great group portraits of high-society leaders of the civic militia, steely-eyed above their faintly ridiculous starched white ruffs. To the left of the doorway to them, one of Breughel's crowded paintings depicting Dutch proverbs: fire in one hand, water in the other; a man so virtuous he could tie the devil to a post; a woman who puts the blue shroud over her husband's head... with, thank heaven, a trot in four languages, so you can figure out what all these curious people are doing, some of them in quite a vulgar manner.

Lindsey discovered her camera was missing, so we called the desk at St. Bavo. Yes, someone had found it and turned it in. For perhaps the thirtieth time we'd lost something irreplaceable — all those photos taken at yesterday's party! — and found it again, and I was glad I'd given a euro to the draw-organ guy.

Christmas without glasses
Amsterdam, December 25

IT WAS A GLORIOUS SUNNY Christmas day in Apeldoorn, where we spent the day visiting the royal palace museum at Het Loo, walking in the park, visiting, and having a delicious Christmas dinner with Hans and Anneke. The park and garden at Het Loo are among my favorite places, and I had the delightful experience of seeing them as never before, because I left my glasses on the train.

Another fiasco, and this one unreversed, unlike our usual problems with lost and misplaced objects. It didn't help that it was largely my own fault. Richard and I were working on our laptops side by side on the train to Apeldoorn, and I'd put my glasses on the little table in our booth, beyond my Mac. When we arrived at Apeldoorn I got up, put on my scarf, put on my topcoat, put on my hat, handed Lindsey her beet bag with the apples in it she had bought for dessert, picked up my laptop which I'd slid into its shirt, and walked to the door at the end of the carriage.

Lindsey, Marta, and Richard followed me. I looked out the door and noticed the station wasn't quite crisp. Damn. I forgot to put my glasses on. They had already got off the train, and I went back to get my glasses — but they were nowhere in sight. I looked on the table, under the table, under the seats, on the seats, and reflected that the train was about to leave the station for its onward journey to Deventer and Enschede, and I didn't want to risk yet another disaster. So I got off without them.

Oh well. I'm nearsighted, but it's not that bad. I could see the trees in the park, for example, and the sky beyond them; I just can't really read road signs without my glasses, or billboards, or things like that. It could be worse: I have a spare pair — but they're in the car, and the car's parked at a hotel in San Mateo, at least I hope it is.

So we had a cup of coffee at Hans and Anneke's, after regaling them with the stories off all the mixups and mistakes of the last forty-eight hours, well anyway a few of them. Choosing the wrong car Friday night, so that when our train split we went to Schiphol instead of Amsterdam. Leaving a camera behind at St. Bavo Church in Harlem. Failing to keep up with Marta this morning, so that the tram left before the rest of us could join her. That sort of thing.

The palace at Het Loo was the summer palace, a sort of modest Dutch Versailles. It has historic importance, having been built in the 17th century by William and Mary, who furnished it with a magnificent formal garden and a surrounding English park. It was greatly modified by Ludwig Napoleon, put in charge by his relative early in the 19th century: Ludwig wanted something simpler, and ordered the garden transformed into a picturesque English-style park, and the ceiling murals whitewashed and plastered over.

Fortunately his improvements were reversible. The ceiling-boards were not painted over but simply detached and turned round, thereby preserving the murals under coats of dust. Queen Wilhelmina, who spent the last twelve or fourteen years of her long life here after the savage years of World War II, commissioned trompe-l'œil paintings of the lost plaster reliefs, basing them on etchings and paintings of the palace from its early days.

These documents also suggested the possibility of retrieving the formal garden, so in 1985 the government somewhat reluctantly voted the funds to do that. When a few feet of sand and topsoil were removed in a test area the original garden's outlines came to light, ditches, fountain footprints, curbings and all — even the dead roots of some of the larger perennials. Ludwig's gardeners had apparently simply trucked tons of sand in and covered it over, perhaps hoping for this distant day of restoration.

What you see now, then, is a museum of the original concept of the palace and gardens, with interiors decorated and furnished in period styles tracing the centuries of royal residence. The palace is no longer so used, though the present queen's aunt (I think it is), the Princess Margriet (I think her name is), does live in a smaller residence on the grounds for ten months of the year, leaving May and June for more extended visits to the grounds by us commoners.

My memory goes back to Wilhelmina, who was held up to us kids as an example of wartime inspiration and encouragement in the early 1940s. I did not know, however, that she was a skillful and enthusiastic painter. There's a quite good landscape of hers on an easel in one of the drawing rooms upstairs in the palace, and the museum of carriages and automobiles, in the royal stables, boasts her painting-wagon, drawn by a horse into the park when she wanted to do some plein-aire painting — a gypsy-wagonlike affair, fitted out with an easel, a comfortable chair, and boxes and drawers for supplies.

We stopped in the café in the former ballroom, handsomely paneled in painted leather murals, and had a bowl of Dutch pea soup and a glass of red wine; then went out into the park for an hour's stroll. I'm always affected by this park, which begins in a formal setting of lawns and allées of beeches, then gives way to mixed lawn and forest: oaks, beeches, birches, elms, and occasional conifers. The leaves are all raked up off the greenswards, protecting the lawns from decay and nourishing the trees under which they're stacked in thick beds.

The low silvery luminous Dutch light rakes in between and under the bare branches, and the paths, most of them brick and six feet wide or so, curve invitingly among these groves, sometimes following a channeled stream artfully leading from a spring through the gentlest possible descent to power the fountains in the formal garden. (I don't know where the water goes from there. Perhaps finally out to sea. There's not much shortage of water in this country.)

Table talk was lively, for this occasion introduced for the first time two couples among our dearest friends to one another. Politics and religion both came up, and the usual proscription was not only ignored but flouted. Herring and akvavit, salad and pumpkin soup, sauerkraut and sausages (in the Dutch style, with mashed potatoes and a few pieces of pineapple contributing their surprising flavors and textures); Lindsey's apple crisp; a bottle of good Soave; more talk, conversation, discussion, reservations, agreement — a lovely way to spend the day.

We managed to get back on the train without going to the wrong station, or getting separated, or losing anything. At the Amsterdam station I saw a couple of railroad employees standing on the platform in their snappy black uniforms. I'd had the foresight to ask my phrasebook how to ask about a Lost and Found: *Waar is het bureau voor gevonden voorwerpen?* (I'll find out later why a complicated word like *voorwerpen* is needed to say "things.")

You've lost something, he asked by reply, in perfect English. Yes, my glasses. Oh, what a disaster, he said. It's not that simple. By law a lost item must be held at the next station after it's found, to wait for a phone call. If no one calls it goes to the central office in Utrecht.

I'm not going to Enschede, I said; I'm not going to Deventer; I'm not even going back to Apeldoorn this time, and I'm certainly not going to Utrecht.

Well then you've lost your glasses. The law forbids any other handling of objects found in the train, even supposing it is found.

Well, I said, it's not a very rational system, but I can't think of a better one. I hope at least the glasses will be given to someone who can make use of them.

Oh no, he said, we certainly aren't allowed to do that. They'll just be ... (gesture of throwing away).

Outside the station a street-musician hauled his accordion up into the tram behind us. He sat behind me. After a few minutes a long disquisition I couldn't quite understand came through the loudspeaker, reciting a litany of streets whose names were familiar but had little to do with the trajectory we were supposed to taking. I asked the accordionist if our tram were indeed going to Leidseplein. Yes, he said, I'm going there myself, it's just taking a long way round because of something in the roads. Are you an actor?

Oh ho, I thought to myself, I'm apparently much more interesting without my glasses. No, I'm not an actor. Are you a musician?

Yes, he said, I play accordion, and guitar, and saxophone. I'm glad you do, I said, I always think musicians in the streets make city life a lot more interesting and pleasant. I'm glad to hear you say that, he said. I don't play accordion so good, but someone stole my saxophone.

I suppose accordions don't get stolen, I said. No, he answered, that's why I have one, but I don't play it that well. Still I get by. I've been doing this for twenty years. It's a good life, I have fun, and I manage to get by.

And we all got off the tram at Leidseplein and went our various ways.

When, if, should it be the case
Amsterdam, December 26

LYING AWAKE THINKING of too many things. Why? Because the pre-departure anxiety is setting in. When? five o'clock in the morning. What? Leftover thoughts from the beginning of this trip; unrecorded impressions from it; projects to be confronted when the trip is over:

The last few days have been filled with three recurring themes: language, food, friendship. The conversation friendship entails has often been at the table, or anticipating the table; and of course it always brings the mind back to language. Last night at the table after a question from Anneke had been discussed I observed that the Dutch, when speaking English, often say "when" where we would more likely say "if."

But isn't that what you say, she asks, I think I hear you say when at such times.

Well sometimes we do, you're right, but other times we say if, they mean different things.

Yes, Hans joins in, And you never really know when, or if, to say which one, so I use a construction, If. It. Should. Be. The. Case. And he smiled with the corners of his eyes, an expression no one can ever resist, but his nose also twitched the tiniest amount, showing those who know him well that he may be misrepresenting the case just the tiniest amount.

I think it's the problem of the translating dictionary. You know, the small ones we buy, often at the last minute, looking for a simple way to make an instant identification of an unknown word, in order to have instant comprehension of what is very likely to be a complex subject. And, given any language's fondness for synonyms and near-synonyms, but also for representing often quite dissimilar ideas with identical combinations of letters, these dictionaries, which instead of really defining an entry simply line up four or five words herded into place by a few commas, result in two problems: first, the user is lulled into a false sense of security thinking he's been enlightened; second, he's also quite likely misled by being given a number of possibilities, some contradictory, the result of ambiguity, and plurality of meaning, and the use of figurative language.

Which reminds me: I saw the word *calamiteit* the day we arrived. I think it was on a bilingual placard in the train, telling us how to sound the alarm in case of incident. (I think by "incident" it meant "accident.") The English side used the word "incident" to translate what the Dutch indicated was *calamiteit*.

I looked up *calamiteit* in my pocket Dutch-English dictionary, by no means an inconsequential edition, but it wasn't there at all. What a calamity! What does it mean, in the scheme of things?

It means all those things, Anneke said, it means incident, and accident, and calamity. Well, Richard said reasonably enough, but those are very different things, an incident is simply something that happens, a calamity, my God, that could be a disaster.

Yes, Anneke said, for example if there's a storm and a dike fails, that's a *calamiteit*.

I should say it is, Richard put in; that's exactly the way we use the word. A real calamity.

Anneke was a schoolteacher in her early life, and has a school-teacher's fondness for precision, correctness, and clarity. Her Dutch is very clear, and must have contributed to our daughter Thérèse's legendary success with the language when she was an exchange student for a year, living with Hans and Anneke's family. The story goes that Thérèse did not speak for weeks after her arrival, refusing even to try to speak Dutch, and then came downstairs Christmas morning speaking it fluently. She wanted to have it right, apparently.

I make hardly any attempt at correctness, but I do like to chase words down. There is no Dutch word for boredom, Richard announced the other day. Come on, Richard, there must be a word for boredom, everyone gets bored from time to time.

No, really, they have no word for it, the woman at the hotel desk told me so.

I looked up the word on my Palm's dictionary. Yes they do have a word for boring, I said, it's *vervelend*. Ah, Richard said, she mentioned that word, she said it didn't really mean boring, that there isn't any word for boring or boredom.

We were walking toward the Nieuwmarkt, not far from the Waterlooplein, up a residential street on, you guessed it, a canal. Ahead of us two *meisjes*, young women in their early twenties I'd say, were having a conversation, one on her front steps a step or two up from the sidewalk, leaning against the iron railing, the other on street level, leaning against her bicycle.

Pardon, juffrouwen, I said, *spreken U engels?*

Jazeker, of course we speak English, one of them answered, hesitating over the choice but quickly deciding to answer me in Dutch.

Maar sprekt je het goed?

Jazeker, ik sprek het heel goed. Of course I do. (The Dutch have a healthy sense of the propriety of simply indicating their own level of competence, and what sounds like boasting in English is simply stating the facts in Dutch.)

Then tell me, I said, is it true that there is no word for boredom in Dutch? (The girls looked at each other significantly: this guy, their look said, is a real loony.) I mean, I pressed, what do you say when you say something's boring? (They looked as if that were quickly becoming their condition.)

Het is vervelend, she answered quickly. But does that really mean boring, Richard wanted to know. Is that really the same thing? Well no, the girl said, no, it's not really the same.

We walked on. The problem is, of course, some words stand for ideas or feelings or things that a group of people have in common, and the longer the group uses those words for those things, the more the group has those ideas or feelings or whatever, and the law of divergence requires that as different societies continue this process, the generalized specificity of whatever the idea or feeling is differs more pointedly perhaps, certainly more subtly, from the similar word's meaning in another language.

I've been fascinated by the idea that the Dutch are thinking of changing their spelling again. They did that at least once before, in the 1930s I think it was, when they dropped a certain number of double vowels, and changed some spellings boldly in an attempt to regularize the orthography. The Dutch word for gift is *cadeau*, for example, a French word, I suppose it came into use during Ludwig Napoleon's reign, when the country was in fact a part of the French Empire. It was spelled the French way, *cadeau*, until that spelling reform, when it was brutally turned into the ugly *kado*. (Many Dutch continue with the older form: after all aesthetics is an important consideration, especially when a gift is concerned.)

I've asked a number of people, friends and strangers, what they think of this proposed spelling reform, and they've all rejected the idea, sometimes quite vehemently. Letters to the editor, though, where I first found out about this, are divided: presumably in the interest of equal time.

Some of the proposed reform is in the *cadeau-kado* mold. The word for "success," for example, is another French word, though without the accent grave: *succes*. The new spelling would be *sukses*, which looks all wrong. An even more shocking proposal is that proper nouns be spelled with lower-case initial letters, as proper adjectives already are. And Anneke says there's been a big push to clear up the question of — what do you call it? the line inside the word, between the letters?

Hyphen, I said. Hyphen, she exclaimed. Hyphen! What a strange word!

It's Greek, I think, I said. You're right, it is a strange word. And we have trouble with them too; I drop them all the time and

Lindsey wants me to put them back in, and then sometimes when I'm not supposed to have one I do put it in. They're troublesome.

Another word I've been puzzling over is *table d'hôte*. But I've run out of room; I'll deal with that later. I just have time to run this past the spell-checker.

(It eliminated six or seven hyphens.)

Rational/Irrational
In flight, December 27

THE ENTIRE TRIP HAS BEEN IRRATIONAL, I suppose. Irresponsible, even: to fly twelve thousand miles for a week! Think what that's done to our ecological footprint this year! And yet there was a responsibility of a kind, I insist; the significant moments in our lives deserve and indeed require our observation and participation, and the anniversary was significant — for Hans and Anneke, and for ourselves, as we anticipate our own in not much more than a year. So I do not apologize for irresponsibility.

Irrationality is another matter: and I blame the irrationality of the last week on an irrationally chosen agent, the Amsterdam canals. I first learned about them a long time ago, from my friend Jonathan Cott. I was about to make my first trip to Europe by spending a week in Amsterdam. I was going on a press junket — in those days I was an art critic on a daily newspaper, and press junkets were not yet considered unethical — to report the opening of the then-new Vincent van Gogh Museum.

Jon sketched a series of five concentric half-circles on some scratch-paper. Amsterdam is a series of five canals, he explained, and they always get you in trouble, because they curve invitingly as you go out walking, and if you're not careful you'll wind up walking the opposite direction than you intend

The Dutch dug their canals so, over the years, for a perfectly rational reason. They began by damming the Amstel river, hence the name, diverting the flow through a single canal, logically named the Singel. Over the years the dam was enlarged, and further diversionary canals were needed — named, every tourbook will tell you, in alphabetical order and in rising order of social class: the Herengracht or Gentlemen's Canal; the Prinsengracht, the Kaisersgracht. Hmmm. That makes only four. A final concentric canal was by now so huge in circumference no further diversions would seem necessary, so it was called, irrationally I submit, the Singelgracht. Another trap for the unwary!

The center of this system of horseshoes is, of course, the Dam itself, and beyond it, holding off what used to be the Zuider Zee and is now simply a harbor filled with artificial islands on which skyscrapers are beginning to rise, is the railroad station, blocking the calming influence of the sea, as my irrationally violent friend from the red-light district told me the other day, from the increasingly unnatural city-dwellers.

I called them "horseshoes," but the five canals in this set do not curve. Their banks are straight lines of rationally even lengths, and where they change direction, not really terribly abruptly, they do so at bridges accommodating the series of spoke-like main streets radiating from the Dam. Our street is the Leidsestraat, and we've often walked its length over the last thirty years and then some, and we never cross one of these bridges without looking up and down its canal in both directions to admire the view.

It is really quite beautiful, and by that word I mean inspiring, calming, appealing. Overhead the sky, usually silvery and luminous under some kind of high cloud cover, but not that rarely a fine sky blue; underneath, the water, luminously black if that is possible, dappled in ever-different patterns according to winds or boat-traffic.

Containing this scene, this animated visual activity which is in fact a sort of very slow vibration of complex but naturally rational visual force, are of course the banks and the canal houses. Some canals, the Singelgracht for example, are bordered by parks or broad boulevards; and some are shaded by rows of stately Dutch elms, bringing Nature back to the city with their black rough trunks and deliriously green foliage in summer, their delicately interwoven naked branches and twigs in winter.

These canal-houses were built centuries ago, when the canals themselves were laid out. The Netherlands is prosperous now and was prosperous then, and the city needed fine residences: but the rational Dutch provided for shops and warehouses on the ground floors of most of these buildings, dedicating the first floor off the street (the *piano nobile*) to ceremonial residential life, when significant events were to be marked, and the upper storeys to sleeping quarters, and lofts for the servants and, no doubt, further storage.

Some of the houses remind you of New York brownstones. Others are brick, or limestone. They're distinguished, as I mentioned a while back, by their gables, though a great many of them are quite plain in that respect. The tension between an urge to display wealth and taste, on the one hand, and to refrain from either Godless or uppity ostentation, on the other, is a constant feature of the Dutch mentality. These gables are only one witness to that: others are the variety of front gardens in towns and villages — some have clusters of severely trained topiaries; others are strewn about with statues, birdhouses, and toy windmills.

The famous Dutch windows, so clean they would be invisible if the glass didn't reflect the outside with a hard, brilliant retort, bear further witness. There are few curtains, though there are occasionally draperies, perhaps to keep away the cold. Some windows are littered with goofy collections of silly little toys: rubber duckies, statuettes of characters out of Disney, or science-fantasy movies, Rubik cubes. Others feature collections of sculpture: often small bronze statues of men on bicycles, or ballerinas, or tradesmen.

Others still may have only a glass vase of flowers, or more often a symmetrical pair of them, or a symmetrical pair of pairs of them, for the Dutch love symmetry as much as they do number, it's a part of the public reinforcement of rationality as it applies to the distribution of things in space — a recurring necessity in a small country, much of it below sea level, methodically juggling constant population increase with respect for nature and an urge to modest domesticity.

There's still traffic on these canals, though I suspect the five inner ones are banned to heavy or noisy traffic. In this weather — dry for the most part but cold — there's not a lot of traffic. Those white pedal-boats the tourists love to rent are tied up in a listless flock. You'll see a canal-tour boat now and then, but nothing like the high-season traffic. On some canals there are houseboats, with smoke curling out of their chimneys these days, and the perennial table-and-chair patio, indispensable to the Dutch who love to take their meals outside if it's humanly possible, looks pretty bleak.

Then there are the parked cars, many more than thirty years old, and still apparently spending most of their time at rest, diagonal and parallel and stopped just short of the canal. I walk in the street, often; there isn't really room for four friends side by side on what passes for the sidewalk — really simply a lane of the street protected by bollards and, occasionally, chains. We walk facing traffic, but we don't see any to speak of. Nor do we see that many people for that matter, though we did stop to chat with a man painting the iron chain in front of his house, with that curious Dutch enamel that dries to an incredibly hard glasslike luster. Dark blue, he said, and I suppose it was, but to my eye another in an amazing range of blacks.

Another thing: the axis of symmetry in this set of concentric canals is oriented northwest-southeast. This is even further disorienting. Nothing is ever simply north or south, east or west. And the light is so low and even, especially this month, that you can't get your bearings by the sun. Nor are there many landmarks to help out, for the tallest monuments — steeples on three or four great churches, the Mint tower, perhaps the pinnacles on the Rijksmuseum — aren't tall enough to emerge above the nearer rooftops. At lunch yesterday, at Elf, so named because it is on the eleventh floor of its building (*elf* being the Dutch word for eleven), I was surprised, looking out at the view, to find that Amsterdam is almost uniformly four storeys high or so, with only a very few architectural details sticking up out of the even plane of rooftops.

Architectural detail: that's what animates the view down these canals so. It's to a great extent a question of *grain*. The façades of these houses are grooved, engraved, relieved; they are decorated with pilasters, statuary, trompe-l'œil, dates and other inscriptions. Even as sober a house as the one John Adams lived in for a year during the 1780s, when he was ambassador from the new United

States — what an interesting time that must have been! — is animated by brick, plaster, pilaster, mullions — and, of course, a modestly self-congratulatory brass plaque commemorating his sojourn.

It's the constant bounce among all this grain, and the dappled waters, and very often the remarkable clouds; the bricks and bollards of the streets, the garlands of chain, that contributes to the mesmerizing vibratory property of the townscape; and that vibration balances the serenity, the tranquility of the human contribution. It's as if you're really the only person on the scene: the few strangers we meet are so remarkable we can only think of them as familiars, and we find ourselves speaking to them as if we knew them.

Closing the dispatch book
Healdsburg, a week later

AND SO WE'RE HOME AGAIN, after a final *uitsmijter* in an ordinary bar-café in the Marriott Hotel, and a trudge back to our hotel the Prinsen, shuffling through new-fallen snow and chuckling at the windshields, on half of which someone had scraped the word BRASIL through the snow, and getting up next morning at six to take the tram and the train to the airport, and then spending six hours at the Atlanta airport because San Francisco was all backed up because of the storm.

And we've unpacked, and sat stuck in the house two or three days because the river was up over the road, and six days in the Netherlands seem an awful long time ago, until I look back over my notes, to find:

> *A'dam details home mentally ill; hotels tech (iens, metro...)*

Yes, that strange and beautiful building across from our hotel room was a mental hospital. Richard and Marta found that out the day we went to Hans and Anneke's anniversary party: that night the hospital had a party of its own, with musicians in many of the rooms, and apparently even outside, and everyone staff patients visitors and all seemed to be having a good time; What's going on, Richard asked someone, Christmas party came the answer, and the other details.

I may not have mentioned (though perhaps I have, in which case forgive me) that the Dutch have four days of Christmas: St. Nicholas's Day on December 2, I think it is, when gifts are exchanged; Christmas Day on the 25th, when one visits one's parents; Second Christmas Day on the 26th, when one has a nice quiet day at home; January 6, Epiphany, when one celebrates the end of Christmas. This is all part of that Dutch fondness for *gezelligheid*, for comfort and company and snug domesticity — "values" more bourgeois than Calvinist, perhaps; but values it's hard to argue with.

*   *   *

I didn't write much about Hans and Anneke's celebration, because, well, one doesn't write publicly about the closely-held narrative of one's friends. (I already felt I'd overstepped propriety a bit a few pages back, in writing about Kees's restaurant Marius.) But our friendship with this family has given us some insight into what seems to me a characteristically Netherlandish approach to weddings, anniversaries, birthdays, Christmas: and over and again I come away from these insights, and the experiences suggesting them, with real respect for the "values," the attitudes and even the institutions, that underlie them.

I am not religious myself, and certainly not monotheistic; but I don't begrudge others their rituals. *Heer, dank U voor het lekkere eten* (Lord, thank you for the delicious eats) doesn't seem a bad beginning to a comfortable meal, once past the first word. And a longish but not quite too long disquisition on Generosity and Gratitude at an anniversary was certainly something to think about.

The speaker, in fact a minister, suggested that a good marriage is a gift; we ought to be grateful for it, and recognize the generosity of the source of the marriage — after all, no one forced any power to grant it. But one ought also to recognize that with the gift came a responsibility to make the best of it, to tend it — even to improve what Nature, as I prefer to think of it, has given. I thought, of course, about our own marriage, and those of a number of close friends and relations; and I looked around at the guests — over a hundred people, nearly all at least as old as we are (excluding the children and grandchildren of the anniversary couple). A surprising number had celebrated their own golden anniversary, or soon would; though a number of course were widows or widowers, and the event had its bittersweet quality when one saw one of those wiping away a tear or two.

* * *

That party was in Apeldoorn, as I've said, a hundred kilometers or so east of Amsterdam, and we stayed there one night at the Kaiserskroon Hotel, where the party was given. Quite a contrast with the Prinsen! Spa, pool, gym, restaurant, bar; busboys and waitresses; easy chairs and couches... and a bed nearly as big as our room at the Prinsen, and a room nearly as big as our floor at the Prinsen. You begin to think in terms of area, of square feet, when you spend much time in Amsterdam, where real estate, being confined, is precious. (One friend recently bought a house in a tiny town in Friesland. Why Friesland? Because a house there cost the same as a single garage in Amsterdam.)

But the Kaiserskroon, like the Prinsen, like all hotels I've stayed in in the Netherlands in the last few months, has no free highspeed internet connection! In the States we've come to expect that as a given at the cheap motels we stay in, the Comfort Inns and Econolodges. In Apeldoorn as in Amsterdam you are invited to sign on to a Swiss provider that costs as much for a day as ISPs charge here for a month. I think I know why: Internet connectability has become such a popular request that the providers have realized there's money to be made here: why give it away free, or at a minimal charge?

And to compound the irritation, the Amsterdam internet parlors don't allow you to bring in your own laptop, as I've done in Italy and Spain and here in the States. So we get our e-mail in the

Netherlands the old slow way, connecting to the telephone; and we have to forgo web-surfing.

That's too bad, because the Netherlands has two or three first-rate restaurant-listing websites. I use one a lot: *iens*, named for its proprietor Iens Surname; you can find it on the Internet: Google it. The reviews are not wholly reliable, coming from a Zagat-like sample of contributors; but as usual reading between the lines helps sort things out, and the hard information — hours, phone number, address — are indispensable.

I use iens rather than Simple Bites, whose reviews are more reliable, because you can put iens on your Palm, and I'd never go anywhere without the Palm — in a pinch it sends and receives e-mail, it keeps my journal, our address book and calendar, the Oxford English Dictionary and a fairly adequate Dutch-English dictionary.

And a wonderful thing called *metro*, which tells you how to get from A to B via tram or metro in any of 329 cities, from Aachen to Zwickau, and including Tampa, Tashkent, Tbilisi, and Timisaora. One of these days I'll have to install the BART database, to see how well it works here: the Amsterdam one is first-rate, giving tram options for all sorts of places — it's how we decide how to get to Marius, for example, from our hotel near Leidseplein.

With all this equipment in your belt-pack you can look up a restaurant in the next town, phone it and make a reservation while you're walking out in the heath or dunes or forest, and we've done this from time to time on our rambles across the Netherlands — though this six-day jaunt scarcely left time (or weather, come to that) for rambling. The country's flat enough that cell phones and wi-fi work very well indeed. On longer trips, when we cross a border, we simply change phone chips in our little phone, so our calls are never international; you can get a chip with ten minutes of calls for ten euros or so, and recharge it as necessary. On this trip I spent twenty euros, I think, for the phone, and didn't come close to exhausting its credit, which will be there for me next time we're in the country.

*   *   *

AND WE WILL BE in the Netherlands again within a year, no doubt; walking, no doubt; we're drawn to it by a mysterious attraction. As I apologized in advance to Richard at the beginning of our Amsterdam visit: I am tediously enthusiastic about the country. After all these years there are still corners we don't know at all. And the literature continues to turn up, in the library, in used-book stores, among the latest publications. Of them I would particularly recommend:

• James Boswell: *Boswell in Holland.* Edited by Frederick Pottle as part of the Yale edition of The Private Papers of James Boswell, this volume appeared in 1952. In it the 23-year-old Boswell is in Utrecht, sent there by his despairing father to study law; and in addition Dutch, French, Latin, and love, all of which he records with charming detail.

• Simon Schama: *The Embarrassment of Riches.* This study of what the Dutch call The Golden Century — the 17th century,when a country of farmers, fishermen, sailors, merchants, and clerics somehow made the first modern Republic — truly a sort of Venice of the north, founded on trade, exploration, and expert seamanship, enabling them to war successfully with Spain and then England. Schama explores the Dutch temperament across this century, across the complex social classes (never quite rigid in this country), disclosing the national qualities that still inform an enlightened populace.

• Geert Mak: *Amsterdam.* Alas I read a library copy of this book, and took few notes — because Mak, a popular Dutch journalist, writes so effortlessly and charmingly that you just keep reading and before you know it it's finished. Mak focusses on the city, but writes about its entire history, from its founding in the 13th century up to the great social changes of the 1970s. We plan to spend a month in Amsterdam one of these years, and this book will be an indispensable guide, not only to the geography but also and especially to the temperament. Amsterdammers have lived through incredibly hard times, and probably have hard times still to face — don't we all? But they have responded with a unique kind of tenacity, combining fierce defense with pragmatic tolerance. Mak discusses this, and the great Dutch preoccupation with societal provisions (prisons, almshouses, public housing), and the preoccupations with comfort and collecting, turning up fascinating individuals along the way, drunks, bigots, heroes, and ordinary people with extraordinary detail.

• Sacheverell Sitwell: *The Netherlands.* Sitwell concentrates on art, costume, and social life, describing maritime Netherlands (he does not visit Groningen, Drenthe, Overijssel, Gelderland apart from Het Loo, or Limburg and North Brabant) as he found it just after World War II. I know I've used the word "charm" a bit too often, but it's needed again here.

And I must include a book that meant a great deal to me when I was ten or twelve, and which continues to fascinate me, and which undoubtedly began my extravagant love for things Netherlandish:

• Hendrik Willem van Loon: *Van Loon's Lives.* Stuck in the little town of Veere, in the remote maritime province of Walcheren, during World War II, the author invites a series of great historical figures to dinner, writing a little biography of each of them to introduce them to his cook and houseman, then describing the evening that follows. Rossini cooks dinner for Chopin who serenades Emily Dickenson one night; Torquemada and Robespierre squabble another; Leonardo, Mozart, Peter the Great, St. Francis, Thomas Jefferson — all appear; only one guest refuses. The jacket squib calls the book a Handbook of Intellectual Liberalism, and that's not a bad description. It's also a testament to the Dutch intellectual and moral tradition, for van Loon wisely chooses Erasmus as his advisor in all these proceedings. It's a wonderful book, witty and discursive, with comments on food, art, music, governance, and history of course, and charmingly — there it is again! — illustrated by the author. (But I must say that I am struck, re-reading it now, by van Loon's casual denigration of Latin and Catholic viewpoints when they differ with his own.)

And with that, finally, you'll be happy to know, I end these Amsterdam dispatches, and 2005. We'll stay home for a few weeks, and then go back to Portland. Maybe I'll write you from there.

𝓛

sin Lindsey nada

*This book was set in a computer version of the Garamond typeface,
with titles in Papyrus, on a Macintosh computer, by the author; and
printed by the online publisher Lulu*

all photographs by the author

first edition

2007

www.ingramcontent.com/pod-product-compliance
Lightning Source LLC
Chambersburg PA
CBHW032048080426
42733CB00006B/204